LOVE

OR

CHILDREN

LOVE

OR

CHILDREN

When You Can't Have Both

SUE FAGALDE LICK & "ANONYMOUS"

Best of the Childless by Marriage blog

BLUE HYDRANGEA PRODUCTIONS
South Beach, Oregon

All information offered herein is the opinion of the author and the anonymous commenters at the Childless by Marriage blog. We claim no professional, medical, or sociological expertise beyond that open to any civilian researcher. We respect the privacy of our anonymous commenters and have pledged not to make their identities known for any reason.

ISBN: 978-17336852-1-4

Library of Congress Control Number: 2020916787

Classifications: Childlessness—Sue Fagalde Lick—second marriages—Catholicism—marriage without children—infertility—birth control—stepchildren—old age without children

Cover and interior design: Erin Seaward-Hiatt
Cover silhouette illustration © Oleksandr Berkan, courtesy 123rf.com

Blue Hydrangea Productions
P.O. Box 755
South Beach, OR 97366
(541) 961-4561
suelick.bluehdrangea@gmail.com

ALSO BY SUE FAGALDE LICK

Nonfiction

Childless by Marriage
Unleashed in Oregon
Shoes Full of Sand
Stories Grandma Never Told
The Iberian Americans

Poetry

The Widow at the Piano: Poems by a Distracted Catholic
Gravel Road Ahead—Poems about Alzheimer's

Novels

Up Beaver Creek
Azorean Dreams

Visit https://www.suelick.com/books

*Dedicated to all those anonymous women and men
who wanted to have children and never got the chance*

CONTENTS

INTRODUCTION

Childless by marriage. It's a phrase I had never heard before I wrote a book by that title, but it fits. Simply put, you do not have children because the person you married is unable or unwilling to make babies with you. It's not necessarily that you didn't want children or that you were physically unable to have them, although those may be factors, too. But with this partner, you will never be a parent.

Within the childless by marriage spectrum come many variations. The partner may be unable to produce sperm or eggs. He/she may have physical or mental health problems. He—and it's he more often she—already has children from a previous relationship and does not want any more. Maybe he said he wanted kids, but then he changed his mind. Maybe the couple can't afford to have a baby. Maybe they just keep putting it off until the woman is no longer fertile. Maybe . . . there are so many possibilities.

My story, briefly: I was married twice. Husband number one didn't want children, although he didn't tell me that until a few years in. It was always wait till he finishes college, wait till he gets a good job, wait till we buy a house. Then there came a time when I thought I might be pregnant. His tune changed to: If you have a baby, I'm leaving. What? Surely he'd change his mind. I wasn't pregnant, but the marriage didn't work out anyway.

Husband number two, Fred, a wonderful older man who already had three children, had had a vasectomy. He didn't want any more kids.

Somehow I still thought I would become a mom. But it didn't happen. My youngest stepson spent his junior high and high school years with us, but mostly it was just the two of us and our dogs. In 1996, Fred retired, I left my editor job at the Saratoga News, and we moved from San Jose to the Oregon Coast, where we lived our dream life. I wrote and played music, Fred volunteered at the aquarium and worked at a local winery. We traveled all over the world. But that all came to an end when he was diagnosed with Alzheimer's disease in 2004. He died in a nursing home seven years later at age 73.

My dog Annie and I continue to live in our house in the woods a block from the Pacific Ocean. We both wish we had some young people around, but our closest neighbors are also childless. We're dog people.

I was already working on my *Childless by Marriage* book when I started the blog in August 2007. I saw a need to start the conversation and found readers aching to talk about childlessness. After 13 years and more than 700 posts, we've still got a lot to say. Most of our lives have changed dramatically in that time. But this is still the only place I know where the focus is on being childless by marriage.

It felt like time to put together a new book that would capture the essence of the Childless by Marriage blog. Choosing from all those posts and thousands of comments is not easy. By far, the most discussion has centered on deciding whether to stay with a mate who says no to children or leave and hope to find someone else who is willing to create a family with them. This is risky, of course, because no one knows if we'll find someone else that we love as much as the person we already have. Or if we'll find anyone at all. It's a discussion that never ends and a question I can't answer for anyone.

Readers also write about the grief they feel over losing the chance to have children. They commiserate over the frustrating things people say to them—oh, you'll change your mind, why don't you just adopt, you'll never know real love if you don't have children—and the way they feel left out when their friends and relatives obsess about their kids. They share the difficulties of loving step-children. They worry about old age without children and wonder who will want their photos and keepsakes when they die. They wonder if "fur babies" are enough. Is a career enough? Should they feel guilty if they don't feel bad about not having children?

For some readers, children are still a possibility, while for others, it's too late, and they're trying to accept that it's never going to happen. It's hard. I was well past menopause before I could say the words "I'm never going to have children."

Readers of the Childless by Marriage blog cheer each other on and say here what they dare not say out loud to the people in their lives. Sometimes I just sit back and let them talk to each other, glad we're all here and understand what it's like.

The comments tell stories of women and men who are hurting and searching for answers. The wanted to have children, but they are in situations where it may not happen. In many cases, their spouses have decided they don't want to have children. Sometimes the spouse is reluctant, and then a physical problem ends the discussion in sorrow.

The most difficult comments come from people who are grieving so hard they feel as if they can't go on. I wish I had the magic words to make the pain go away. I advise them to talk to friends, get counseling, or treat themselves to a spa day, a nature walk, or whatever makes them happy. I urge them to remember the good things in their lives. But I know the pain will keep coming back. Even now in my Medicare years, I watch a baby born on a TV show and burst into tears. I watch my friends with their grown children and grandchildren and curse to myself because I will never have that. I keep writing this blog because I get it. In a world where one out of five women reach menopause without having children, so many people fail to understand what it's like. Here, we do understand.

I have tried to pick the best of the posts and the comments, maintaining the readers' anonymity. All of these are real people in real situations. Similar posts have been combined, and the comments have been edited for spelling, grammar and length, but otherwise remain as written. I wish there was room for them all, but this book would be about 2,000 pages long. You can find the rest of the comments at https://www.childlessbymarriage.com, which continues with new posts every Wednesday. You are welcome to add your own comments to all of the previous, including those published here.

1

WHEN YOUR PARTNER WILL NOT GIVE YOU CHILDREN

IN YOUR SEARCH FOR A MATE, you think you have found THE ONE. After years of bad dates, maybe even bad marriages, this man or woman is a keeper. And then, one day, after you've given him or her your heart, they drop the bomb. They can't or don't want to have children with you. He tells you he's had a vasectomy. She tells you of reproductive problems that will keep her from getting pregnant. He tells you he's not ready for children. She shares that she never felt the urge to be a mother. He says the kids from his first marriage are more than enough. You realize that if you stay with this person, you might never have children. Now what do you do?

Let's talk about that revelation. How do we find out that our partner isn't likely to have kids with us?

My first husband, Jim, seemed like he would be a great father. I watched him play with other people's kids and assumed that he would welcome our own. In our Catholic marriage prep class, we both signed a form saying we would welcome children and raise them in the faith. But once we were married, he kept wanting to put off pregnancy. The years were passing by. My friends and relatives were having babies, and I wanted one, too.

When I started taking care of the neighbors' baby, I saw a different side of Jim. He couldn't stand its crying, its smells, or its needs. Then, when I thought, despite rigorous use of birth control, that I might be pregnant, he announced that if I was pregnant, he was leaving.

Would he really have done that? I'll never know. It turned out I wasn't pregnant. Soon after that, our marriage fell apart for other reasons. I do know that he did not have children with his next two wives either.

Our divorce had nothing to do with having children, but under the rules of the Catholic Church, I was able to obtain an annulment on the grounds that he refused to have children. The diocesan tribunal in San Francisco ruled it an invalid marriage.

Three years later, along came Fred, cute, funny, loving, responsible, and gainfully employed, all the stuff a girl wants in a husband. The first time we made love, I rushed to put in my diaphragm, but it proved unnecessary. He had had a vasectomy after his youngest child was born. After we got engaged, we talked about reversing the vasectomy or adopting a child, but finally he told me that he really didn't want to have any more children. I was upset, but we went on to get married. Did I think he'd change his mind? Probably. I tend heavily toward denial. But in our 25 years of marriage, the only babies in our family were the ones his daughter had.

Looking back, I'm glad Fred was honest about not wanting more children. Over the years, I found that he liked children, but didn't want to be responsible for them. Like Jim, he wasn't keen on babies. To be honest, he wasn't even that good with puppies. All that noise and mess. I grieved the loss of the children I might have had, and, to Fred's credit, he felt tremendously guilty.

It's not always that one person is the bad guy. I can see Fred's side. He was 15 years older than I was, and he had spent years raising the three kids he already had. He had thought he was done with that part of life until I came along. If there's any blame to be laid, it's on me. Fred loved me enough that I believe he would have gone along with the process if I had insisted that I couldn't be happy without being a mother. Instead, I made a non-decision and the years passed until it was too late.

How about you? How did you find out children might not be in your future? Did they tell you straight out, did something happen, or did you guess? Did you believe them? If you cannot be happy without children, have you made that clear to your partner?

Professor: Before my husband and I got married, there was a pretty clear sense that he'd be open to talking about having children together someday, but as he still had four kids under 8 years old from a previous marriage, that wouldn't happen any time soon. We were married two-or-so years after we began dating. About a month into the marriage, I asked him if we could start talking about babies now that we'd tied the knot. We were walking the running track at a Bally's gym at the time, and he nearly fell flat on his face with a panic attack. I squashed the conversation. Three years later, while we were lying in bed in our new farm home, I asked him about it again. The same panic attack had him shaking and sweating in violent opposition to the idea. I'll never forget his words to me that night: "I just don't want to get pressured into this!" I realized then that I didn't want him to be pressured into it either. I wanted him to want it. I pray every night that his heart will change, but I know that it is very likely that it won't. I'm only 29 years old. I have lots of years of hoping left. But he's 44, and the love of my life. I truly don't believe that his reaction to my hopes will ever change.

Maria: "Fred loved me enough that I believe he would have gone along with the process if I had insisted that I couldn't be happy without being a mother. Instead, I made a non-decision and the years passed until it was too late"

I was combing your blog, and any blogs I could find, to sift through my own issues of whether or not to have a child. I am also married to someone who is not particularly interested in being a parent, but adores me and would support my decision to be a parent. This particular quote sent waves through me. I realize I have not been taking responsibility for my own future and was waiting for my spouse to suddenly become as excited as I would be about the prospect of being a parent. So, that said, I have made the decision to give it a try. I appreciate your blog, and your open sharing of such a painful and emotionally confusing topic. Thank you, thank you.

HE SAYS NO KIDS; WHAT DO YOU DO?

I have told you that my two husbands didn't want children. I should have mentioned that some of the guys I dated in-between would have been happy to father my children, but they weren't the kind of men I wanted to spend the rest of my life with.

Has your partner told you he or she doesn't want to have kids with you? Or is it just implied by their actions and reactions? How do you respond? Do you say, okay, I love you enough that I can accept your decision? Do you say, uh-oh, that's a deal breaker? Do you accidentally-on-purpose stop using birth control? Do you tell everybody in the world what a rat he is but stay with him anyway? Are you afraid to bring it up?

This is a tough situation, but the one thing I learned is that moping in silence or complaining to everyone but the person who could help solve the problem doesn't fix anything. So what do you do?

It's not always a question of wanting different things. What if your partner would like children but is physically unable to have them? Do you love him or her enough to stay with them anyway?

lizardgoat: I am 36 and my husband is 56. WHAT? Right there, you might stop reading. How stupid could she be? Married at 29 and thought we'd have time. Then financial troubles followed by crises. Now, he really doesn't want to (who could blame him at his age?), even though he agreed to a child before we got married. I've had an especially hard time since I turned 36. I slashed my wrists on Saturday. I knew I was angry, but I hadn't realized just how much until I found myself doing it. Don't worry, I'm medicated and doctored-up. I just feel so stupid. In every way. I am glad I found this blog. It helps, but is there anyone who has lost hope? How do you cope? I am just so sad.

Anonymous: I just had this conversation/fight with my husband. However, the roles are reversed. I am the one questioning whether I want kids, and he definitely wants them. I love kids, my friends' kids, our neighbors' kids, any kid. I am very good with kids and I would be a good mother. However, knowing I would be a good mother is different from wanting them. I just don't know if I do. My husband and I have been married for five years and together for a total of 10 years. I always thought the desire to have kids would come. I fully expected it to. I'm 30 now and that was the time frame we agreed to when we got married. At 25, I thought 30 would be a great time to have a baby. It was all so logical, married long enough, had our fun, careers in order, home purchased, etc.

While everything is where it should be (home, career), I'm still not ready. I don't have that "I need to be a mom" gene. Where it is? I WANT to have it, but I don't. So I'm asking him for more time, another year to be just us and then I'll bite the bullet and have a baby. The fight tonight came down to what if I never want kids. It's a valid question. I want another year, and "I'll bite the bullet." Those were my words. Because I don't want to be with anyone but my husband, I love him so much. And I really want to want to have kids for his sake and ours. I cannot accept losing him, so I'll do it, if that's the ultimatum. But he won't give me the ultimatum. He wants me to want a child for myself, for my happiness. So he wants me to decide what to do. He'll be unhappy in our marriage but he'll stay in our unhappy marriage. And if I have the baby now, when I'm clearly not ready, what if I'm the unhappy one? I know you're thinking *poor kid* (if we have a kid), but I honestly have faith in myself to love this child. It's not their fault I'm so messed up. I'm sure within the next year I'll be pregnant. And I will love my child.

Betsyb: Hi, I am 42, my husband is 41. We've been married for just over five years. I have two grown-up children aged 22 and 18 from a previous awful relationship. Until recently, my husband and I had an incredible marriage. We never argued, always respected each other and loved each other very very deeply. Two months ago, he left me!! He does not want to be 60 and never have become a father. I understand how he feels, but he refuses to acknowledge how I feel. I was a teenage mum and have spent my entire adult life looking after kids, and he wants me to go right back to the beginning and start again. He can't see what my problem is. He just says I don't love him enough. If I did, I would make the sacrifice for him. He says that I have "rejected" him. Now I am completely devastated, I can't eat, sleep and can hardly get up in the morning, which is a problem because I run my own business with other people relying on me. I really thought this man would "never leave me," "couldn't live without me" and we would grow old together. I even came off birth control and was prepared to take the chance for him, but nothing has happened. I've just been dumped anyway. I need to know if I will ever see an end to this pain.

SFL: Oh BetsyB, I am so sorry this happened to you. I can totally see both sides and there's pain no matter how you look at it. It seems like your husband waited too long to realize he had to be a dad. At 42, your odds of pregnancy aren't great. It's going to hurt for a long time, I think, but it will get easier with time. Meanwhile, I would encourage you to get into counseling to help you deal with the grief and figure out how to go on. Let the other people in your life know how you're feeling and let them help you. You're in my prayers.

Melanie: No man is worth sacrificing motherhood for. One day they will be gone, but your children and grandchildren are your legacy.

Anonymous: Hi, my wife is leaving me because I don't want a second child and it's killing me. I feel I am being punished for that decision. She says she always wanted two, but she never talked to me about it, so now I face becoming a part-time dad and I don't know what to do.

SFL: Anonymous, that's awful. My gut reaction is to say suck it up and have another child. But I worry that this disagreement has poisoned your relationship so that it will never be the same. Are there other issues? If it's just the baby thing, consider which would be worse, having another child or ending up alone? I'm sorry this is happening to you. I pray you can find a way to work it out.

HE KEEPS PUTTING OFF HAVING CHILDREN

Yesterday I received this comment from "Amber" in response to a post titled "Will I Regret Not Having Children?"[1] It represents so many of the comments received here at Childless by Marriage that I thought I would share it with everyone. It gets right to the heart of the problem. What do you think she should do? How long is too long to wait?

I am so glad I found this blog today. A lot of others are in the same sort of limbo I am currently in, and it gives me comfort to know that I am not alone. I have been feeling like I need to talk about this subject for a while now, but really don't have anyone to talk to. I am about to turn 30 (husband will be 31), have been with my husband for almost 13 years, and I feel more and more depressed lately about not having the two children I have always wanted. Through the years, there has always been some sort of goal to reach, whether it be finishing college, having reliable income, owning our own home, etc. We have now reached that point and yet again there is a stipulation. Now I am expected to wait 1-2 more years so that I am established in my job and we can enjoy having the extra income my new job has provided. I feel like I am the one that has gone through college and is making this money. If the bills are paid, what is the problem . . . ?

We are now financially stable and have traveled around. We aren't too old or young. I feel like the time is right. Any time I bring up the subject of having a baby, my husband shuts down and/or gets irritated. He says I am obsessed with everyone else and that's why I am so focused on children. (like it's not an original thought that I have always wanted to be a mother.) Honestly he makes me feel like I am crazy for wanting a family sometimes. I want to talk to him about it again, but I don't feel like I have the energy for the argument that I know it will cause just in bringing it up. I have thought about divorcing, but we are perfect in every area but this one, and I love him with all my being. Lately I find myself resenting him and growing more and more depressed at my upcoming 30th birthday (and then I get angry at myself for feeling that way, because I feel so selfish).

As you can tell, I am just a tornado of emotions. I help him and support him in reaching all of his goals and aspirations as a musician. I just don't understand how/why he cannot meet me halfway or try to understand my feelings of wanting a family. The fact that my younger sister is "fertile Myrtle" and social media is flooded with everyone's new families doesn't help when I start feeling sad like this either. I just don't know when to throw in the towel. When do you finally reach that point of enough is enough, before you run out of time and miss that window?

Well, readers, what do you say?

MJ: Amber, you are living my exact situation right now. I turned 33 this year, and after three years of marriage and 16 years together, the time is right. We have the job, the money and the home to have a family. The last of my close friends is pregnant, so I am feeling the pressure and know time is running out. My husband recently told me he's having second thoughts about children. Deep down, I knew the change in lifestyle would be difficult for him, to give up his leisure activities. For this, I feel angry and resentful because he knows how important this is for me—I've even had names picked out for years. There have been no surprises. I am scared to bring it up again because I don't want to hear the answer if it's no, so I've left it alone. I have made the decision to stay because of our history. I'm not prepared to give all that up for the chance of a family down the road with someone else. To me, I look at this as a form of infertility in a weird way. I wouldn't leave him if he was unable to have children. I am living on hope right now—some days are awful and some days I find myself at peace.

The fact of the matter is that you cannot compromise on this. However, I feel you deserve an explanation for why he is skirting the topic, and if he is having second thoughts, he has a responsibility to tell you. This conversation needs to happen in a pressure-free environment without judgment or anger. Prepare yourself for whatever his answer may be. Once you hear it, you can decide if this is a lifestyle you can live with or not.

Amber: I have actually suggested counseling. He is not so agreeable. I would go by myself, but am not sure what good that would do without both parties present. He just does not believe that it is that "big of a deal" yet. I do know that he has hesitancies about being a parent because he thinks it will hold him back from traveling for vacations and playing music. As Maria said, he does feel the same age as when we met and does talk about other people and the families that they have started at a younger age, how they can't "enjoy life because they're tied down," etc. I'm going to try to discuss this again tonight once we have wound down from the day. I am hoping that after dinner and drinks we can have an adult discussion and put it all out on the table. It is very difficult to get him to open up on this subject.

Roxanna: I am so relieved to have found this site as I thought I was going crazy constantly going over and over in my head the sadness I feel over not having children. For years I have masked my feelings and smiled, pretending everything was okay. My husband and I have been married for nine years. He has three children from two prior marriages. The two youngest, 12 and 14 years old, have lived with us for over six years.

My husband won't entertain the idea of having any more children and has even told me he forbids me from bringing it up. As I watch him interact with his children, as the years have passed, I have become resentful of him to the point that I don't even know how to engage in a conversation with him about how utterly sad I feel every single day. I am 34 years old, my husband turns 43 tomorrow. I love him, but I don't think I love him enough to understand why he makes me go through this!!!

SFL: Welcome, Roxanna. I feel for you. As soon as a man says "I forbid you" to do something, my hackles go up. He's not the boss of you. You have to be able to talk about it before you and your marriage explode. I hope you can find a way through his brick wall. Meanwhile, we're here for you.

mrspolyglot: All I'll say is this: My husband promised before we married that we'd do whatever it took to have children. After we got married, he reneged on that. He wouldn't hear of fertility treatment, and he told me I was on my own when it came to adoption.

He has two kids via adoption from his first marriage and a grandchild.

One time, I got upset and he told me that I should have insisted on fertility treatment if I was that bothered. (Conveniently, he forgot that he had told me he'd leave me if I insisted on it.)

I'm pushing 60 now, and I love my husband, but I resent what he did every single day. My advice: if you're still young enough, speak to your husband now. If you don't, you'll always regret it.

WHY WOULDN'T HE/SHE WANT TO HAVE CHILDREN?

Here at Childless by Marriage, one reader after another reports the same problem: One partner wants kids and the other does not. Period. End of discussion. If infertility is an issue, there are ways to work around it, such as in vitro, surrogates, donors, or adoption, but no. They don't want to talk about it. I always encourage readers to keep the conversation going, but I had a tight-lipped first husband who wouldn't discuss it either, so I understand if you keep running into a dead end.

Why are some people so sure they don't want children? Let's look at possible reasons:

1. They hate children: Kids are needy, whiny and sticky.

2. Money: Raising children is too darned expensive.

3. Conflicts with existing kids: They already have children from a previous relationship. Between child support, dealing with the ex and taking care of these kids, they can't imagine bringing more children into their lives.

4. Fear: of pain, conflicts, cost, life changes, and passing on physical or emotional problems.

5. Age: They don't want to be the oldest parent on the soccer field.

6. Career: Having kids will totally screw it up.

7. Freedom: They want to do whatever they please whenever they please.

8. Marriage: Will having children ruin their relationship? Will the wife focus all her attention on the kids? Will they fight over how to raise them? Will they never have sex again?

9. Inadequacy: They'd be a lousy father or mother.

10. Responsibility: Don't want it.

11. Overpopulation: The world has too many people already.

12. Messed up world: Why subject a child to wars, terrorism, climate change and a culture gone to hell?

Do any of these sound familiar? Can you add anything to the list? Do you think it's possible to change their minds? I look forward to reading your comments.

Candy: My husband had his one and knew he never wanted to do that again. Just again this week, I was told "be glad you don't have kids because they . . . Blah blah blah . . ." It's so dang easy for someone with kids to say that, and I find it highly rude and insensitive. I equate that to telling someone in a wheelchair to be glad they can't walk because their feet would get tired if they had to stand on them all day. Grrrrrrrr . . . .

Erica: I agree with you Candy, and the wheelchair thing is a pretty good analogy. Sometimes I get comments like that when I tell someone about a trip or a vacation. Recently I mentioned that I was in Las Vegas the previous weekend and I got a "life is good without kids, huh?" As if I decided to forgo the family I always wanted and potentially die alone so I can be in Vegas for three days. Sure, I love traveling and do it as much as possible but of course I would give it up if I could have children instead. Traveling and vacations are just my consolation prize.

Dean: I'm afraid that I was the one in the couple (actually, we broke up) that didn't want a new child. Certainly my reasons were 2, 3, 4, 5 and 6. No special order, but 2 and 5 ranked high. I can't figure myself having a 20-year-old son in my early 60s.

"HONEY, I CHANGED MY MIND"

In Carolyn Hax's July 20 advice column[2], a reader asks what a lot of folks ask here. She and her husband originally agreed not to have children. Now she's having second thoughts. She has a whole script worked out to discuss this with her guy, hoping maybe he has changed his mind, too, but what if he says he still doesn't want kids?

Hax asks the reader if she can accept it if her husband sticks to his no-kids decision. She offers comments from other readers who have experienced this situation. And one of them mentions this blog. Whoever you are, thank you. Tell your friends.

So, people do change their minds. They think they're okay with not having children, but then everyone around them is having babies, they are aware that they're running out of time, or they realize they agreed to a childless marriage just to keep the relationship going. Maybe they thought stepchildren would fill the space where their own children would be, but they don't. Am I ringing any bells for people?

Maybe you're not the one changing your mind. Maybe it's your partner, who suddenly says he wants kids or that he (or she) has decided he does not want them. He/she cites money, freedom, jobs, age, bla bla bla.

Where once you thought you agreed on this huge decision, you don't anymore. You had an agreement. You knew what you wanted and were living your life counting on that agreement staying the same. Now what do you do? Do you leave? Do you urge your partner to leave? Do you get counseling to help you accept the unacceptable? This is the heart of the whole childless by marriage dilemma.

As longtime readers know, this is what happened to me. I stayed. I didn't have children. I cried where my husband couldn't see me. I wrote a book about it. He didn't change his mind. Now I'm a childless widow living with my dog. It's not as tragic as it sounds. I have a good life, but I still wish I had found a way to become a mother and grandmother and great-grandmother.

I want to share some comments that you might have missed:

On July 20, Anonymous said:

In my fourth year of marriage, during marriage counseling, my husband told me he never wanted me to have children because of my autoimmune disease. I divorced him because we had agreed on children, and we had picked out names. One unsuccessful relationship after another led to me missing my window. I never did get to have a child. But I have a stepson who lost his mother at a young age. We love each other so much. Jumping in as a parent of a teenager is very hard. But to hear him wish me my first happy Mother's Day was priceless, absolutely priceless. My ex has been married twice after me, and he plans on having children. Sometimes I hate him for what he did to me. But now I have my wonderful stepson whom I never would have met if it wasn't for my ex. My husband now is pretty awesome, too. I love my boys like crazy. So, happy ending!

Yesterday, another Anonymous commented:

I feel like I am the only woman in the world who started out not wanting children, grew to change my mind, and had my husband on several occasions scream at me that I can't change my mind. He expects me to be around and support all of his friends' families and every time, I die a little more inside. I am scared for my future, aging, lonely, and just sad I married someone like this.

Yet another Anonymous wrote:

I was lucky enough to fall in love in my mid-twenties with a man who, like me, was somewhat leaning against having children. I was pretty sure I didn't want children, having had, since childhood, a feeling that motherhood probably wasn't for me. But after we married, I wanted to wait a few years before making a final decision to see if my feelings, or his, would change. They didn't. What happened next was a series of vivid dreams in which I would inexplicably find myself six or seven months pregnant, too late to change my mind, horrified and terrified, and trying desperately to convince myself that having a baby would be okay while knowing it would not. At least twice, I woke up clutching my belly. Husband and self are now in our sixties, happily married and childless. I know that by not having children, we gave up some wonderful things. And I know my sisters will have the support of their children as they age, and I won't have that special kind of support. But I remain convinced that I made the right decision for me, and my husband feels the same way. My childhood was happy, my mother is warm and wonderful, and I really can't explain why I knew I didn't want to become a mother while my sisters wanted to be, and are, great mothers. I do know that especially after those dreams, anyone who might have tried to persuade me to have a baby would not have been successful. To the list of reasons why some people don't want children, I'd have to add "Unexplainable but extremely strong gut-level knowledge that having children would be a huge mistake."

Everybody's different. I thank you all for your comments. Keep them coming. This is one of the few places we can discuss this stuff without judgment, and I appreciate every one of you.

HE FORGOT TO MENTION HIS VASECTOMY?

I received this comment from Anonymous:

I am in my mid-30s and my husband is mid-50s. We have been married eight years. Before we decided to get married, we agreed to have at least one child together (he has two adult children). We have never prevented pregnancy. I thought something was wrong with me! Why couldn't I get pregnant when everyone else around me was popping out babies left and right?

Just before our second anniversary, he casually referred to the vasectomy he had over 15 years before, after the birth of his last child. What? All the time we had talked about and planned to have a baby, he had not once mentioned a vasectomy. We even had baby names and schools picked out for our future child!

To say that I was (am) devastated is a true understatement. Six years have passed since then, and I still have not come to terms or in any way accepted this "forced" childlessness. My heart hurts so much sometimes that I don't feel like I have the strength to take a shower or brush my teeth. The only thing I ever really wanted to "achieve" in life was being a mom! I know that adoption or IVF are out there, but I sure don't have the money.

I try to tell myself that having a good relationship with my husband and no kids is better than having a poor relationship with him and lots of kids. This doesn't heal or even soothe my ache; I just hope if I repeat it enough, I will start to believe it someday. I wish I knew what to say to all of us suffering from childlessness. My hat is off to you, Sue, for trying to help.

"Oh, by the way, I had a vasectomy 15 years ago?!!" I think this kind of deception goes way beyond "little white lies." What do you think?

aliwade1: Why is she still with him? I would rather be alone than with a man like that. Not only he did not mention the vasectomy, but she thought they were planning a pregnancy. How cruel of him. My hubby told me within weeks that he had a vasectomy after the birth of his second child. We looked into a reversal together, but life and my health got in the way. At least he was honest. We were able to investigate all options together and now we can both be sad that we did not get the chance to be parents together. We get on with life, and now we are grandparents (both of his kids are parents themselves now).

dawnsey: Sue, I am this Anonymous. What I didn't feel like sharing previously was that I had been married before. Due to another set of circumstances, my ex and I never had children either. I was heartbroken then about not having a baby. After my divorce, not only did I hurt from being childless, but I carried around a lot of shame for not being able to keep a husband. We were separated for almost a year before a divorce was even filed. During that time, I thought we would work out any and all problems and get back together. That was when I got the idea that a great relationship with my husband with no kids was better than a poor one with lots of kids. I had prayed that he would get back with me, then vowed to never ask him for children if he did want me back. We never got back together.

A few years later, when my (now) husband told me of his vasectomy, I felt all of the old pain of being childless again. Yet this time, I felt like any hope or goodness I had left inside of me was violently ripped away. I felt nothing for days. I couldn't even cry. Looking back, I believe I was in some kind of emotional shock. When I was finally able to feel again, man, I felt it all. Anger. Bitterness. Hopelessness. Fear. Shame. At some point, I decided I did not want to be an angry, bitter person. That was when I started applying the "good relationship/no kids" thought again.

I feel like he and I have an okay relationship now, though I do not open up and cry on his shoulder when I have my sad days. As a matter of fact, I have only told one other person (until now) the real reason I don't have children. I only told my mom to get her to stop nagging me about when I am going to start having kids. Like 10 grandkids from my other siblings aren't enough! Yeah, my family get-togethers emotionally suck!

Sue, upon reading my original post, I realized that I didn't actually say "thank you." From the depths of my heart, "THANK YOU" for starting this blog. Just being able to tell my story, without those who actually know me knowing my story, has helped relieve some pressure I've been holding inside. I actually came across your blog because my mom told me a couple days ago that I need to start getting some help with all my emotional baggage. She says that despite my best efforts, I am becoming bitter. I was too fearful to talk to someone face-to-face like a counselor. That is when I hit Google and found you. Again, thank you.

(It just dawned on me that I have never even talked about this face-to-face with my mom; it's always been over the phone. Hmmm . . .)

Candy: My husband was upfront about his vasectomy. But he said he could have it reversed, then changed his mind after we got married. Then he said we could adopt, then changed his mind. Then he said I could get artificial insemination, then changed his mind . . . .

Now this weekend I see on Facebook yet another classmate has become a grandparent. I have since stopped following her. Not the least bit interested in all the baby pictures.

I have good days and not so good days. Today is a not so good day.

Thanks for letting me share here. There is no one on the planet that I share this crap with.

I apologize for my negativity tonight.

Annie: The worst happened to me as well. I found out four months ago my husband had a vasectomy 10 years ago—less than six months before we met. We have been "ACTIVELY" trying to conceive for the last three years. Also picking baby names, me testing every month like a fool, and him telling me every month, "Don't worry, honey, we will try again next month." I am devastated. I have moved out. I honestly will never be able to forgive him for the pain. I am 33 years old. Do you know what that means?? To divorce and find someone else, etc., can take easily up to three years. I am devastated. He says the lie got too big, and that he actually wants children but that I was not approachable to tell the truth. Really?? For 10 years?? What to do??

Tom: I can completely understand the anger and frustration a woman might feel when she finds out her husband has lied about a vasectomy, but I'm shocked no one is commenting about what women do to trap men.

When women lie about birth control and give birth to a child that his father did not want to have, there usually is so much resentment and anger that the child will grow up unloved or raised by a single mom because the dad left. Perhaps you can't see why this isn't worse but it is.

In the former example, no innocent child has to suffer, but since it's a man that lied, we find that worse than when a woman does.

I sure hope laws will make it so that when a woman wants to get pregnant, a man has to sign papers up front stating that he agreed to be a father. Otherwise, the woman should be fully responsible for the child, especially financially so as to not hold a guy hostage and demand him to pay even though he did NOT want to be a father.

SFL: Tom, you are absolutely right. When I was young and fertile, people encouraged me to do that very thing, to have an oops baby and force my ex-husband to be a father. It would be easy to do. But I refused because it's just not right. You don't do that sort of thing to someone you love. But I'm sure it happens, and anyone who does that deserves the consequences. Thank you for adding this important comment to the conversation.

Tom: I wish there were more women like you. Most women however find a guy and even though the guy clearly states he does NOT want to be a father they go ahead and get pregnant against his will, thinking the guy will change once the baby is here. This, I think, is the biggest problem women have, thinking they can change a man.

Of course, after the men leave, the women cry that the guy is a deadbeat dad and what not.

A tip here for women; if you want kids, find a man with the same dream and if after a year of trying go see a doctor or leave and find another guy. Don't get pregnant to trap a man, because he will either leave or you will be stuck with a hostage, and why would you want that?

Mike Hunt: I don't understand how women here can claim that their husband "forced" them to be childless. If the doctor says there is nothing wrong with the woman's reproductive system, and they want a kid, then they should just leave and find another guy who can knock them up. Or buy sperm from a sperm bank if they want to keep their husband around.

HE HAD A VASECTOMY; NOW WHAT?

I keep receiving comments lately from women whose male partners have had vasectomies–surgery to prevent them from producing sperm. A vasectomy is intended to be permanent birth control. But people don't always see it as permanent. The guy can just have surgery to reverse it. Right?

It's not that simple, my friends. Here's why.

1. If a man has had a vasectomy, at some point he was sure enough that he didn't want any children—or any more—that he was willing to have surgery to make it permanent. That's pretty darned sure. Maybe, as in my husband Fred's situation, he had no idea that his first marriage would end and along would come a younger wife still wanting babies. In our case, we talked about having the surgery reversed, but Fred finally admitted he really didn't want to start over with another baby. If I had had older kids, it would have been okay with him, but he found the whole baby and toddler thing exhausting and didn't want to do it again when he was pushing 50. Your man may be younger and more interested in having children, but never forget that at some point, he was sure he didn't want to get anyone pregnant.

2. Reversal doesn't always work. The surgery to reverse the vasectomy is much more complicated than the original vasectomy surgery, and it's not always successful. There may be blockages or the man may have developed antibodies to his own sperm. The longer it has been since the vasectomy, the worse the odds. If it has been less than three years, chances of getting pregnant are better than 50 percent, but after 10 years, only about 30 percent result in pregnancy.

3. It costs a lot of money, estimated $5,000-$15,000, and most insurance companies consider it an elective procedure which they don't cover.

I hate to bring more grief to people who are already suffering over the possibility of not having children, but we need to face reality. When you hook up with a man who has had a vasectomy, he is infertile and he may or may not be willing or able to change that. But that doesn't mean it's impossible. People do have the surgery and father children. Talk to your doctor if you're thinking about it.

You can find more information about vasectomy reversals at these websites.

http://www.vasectomy.com/vasectomy-reversal/faq/vasectomy-reversal-success-rates-will-it-work[3]

http://www.webmd.com/infertility-and-reproduction/vasectomy-reversal-vasovasostomy[4]

https://www.vasectomy.com/vasectomy/faq/is-a-vasectomy-reversible[5]

Anonymous: Thank you for this post and all of the information. Sue, did you feel second best, that he gave his first wife children, and no matter how much it meant to you, he just couldn't give you children? (I know you had written that if you had fought harder, he would have tried for a baby with you.) I know that while my boyfriend had thought of getting a vasectomy reversal, he doesn't want to, and I'm usually fine with that, as long as he will want to adopt with me. I think those of us wanting babies should consider what would happen if you did get pregnant but had a miscarriage, or there was something severely wrong with your baby? Would you feel like the time, energy, money, and spirit were wasted? Or was just having a shot worth it?

SFL: No, Anonymous, I didn't feel second best. Fred always made me feel like Number 1. I knew he loved me, and I realized too late that I should have fought harder. Here's something else to consider. Fred and his first wife adopted their first two children because they could not conceive. The doctors never figured out why. After 17 years, she became pregnant and their younger son was born. So it's entirely possible that Fred might not have been able to make me pregnant even without the vasectomy.

And yes, there is always the chance that something will go wrong with the baby.

YOU'VE GOT TO ASK THE HARD QUESTIONS

Two days ago, Richa wrote:

I am going through the worst pain of my life. On the second day of my marriage, my husband told me that he already has two kids so he would not want kids from me. It came to me as a shock. He just announced his decision and never thought about what I wanted. Today, after four years of marriage, I keep fighting for kids, but he just turns a deaf ear. I have started having menopause, and he never ever discusses anything about my pain of being infertile. Many times I talk about adoption, but he doesn't even want to do anything about it. I loved him, but I hate him for this. I am really not a risk taker and because of insecurities that life offers, I continue to live with him. But it is really difficult to forgive him for all this.

On the second day of their marriage???

As someone far removed from the situation, I'm thinking I'd be screaming, "Annulment!" But then I try to put myself in her situation on that day. She loves this man. For months or maybe years, she has been planning this wedding and this life together. Now, with the wedding dress not yet put away, the gifts not yet all opened, the ring still new and shiny on her finger, her new husband drops this bomb. She feels stuck. Heartbroken. Disbelieving. Surely he doesn't mean it. He'll change his mind.

He didn't.

Why didn't he say something sooner? Did he just realize he wasn't comfortable with the idea of becoming a father? Was he afraid he'd lose her if he told her the truth? Is he just a jerk?

What would you do if you were that woman? From the comments I have received here at Childless by Marriage, I know that some of you ARE that woman or that man who found out after the wedding that you did not feel the same way about having children.

There are certain questions that need to be asked before a relationship goes too far. Maybe I'm influenced by the finale of "The Bachelor"[6] TV show that happened on Monday. I hope I'm not spoiling anything, but Nick chose Vanessa. Unlike the usual "bachelorettes" who swoon into their engagement as if it were the happy ending of a fairy tale, Vanessa still has lots of questions and concerns and is not ready to plan a wedding until she gets some answers.

I'm with Vanessa. Love is great, but you've got to get some things straight before you make a long-term commitment. The following is a list of things you really need to talk about. If your partner refuses, see that as a giant red flag.

How do you feel about having children with me? Do you want them? How soon? How many? What if we have fertility problems? Would you be willing to try in vitro fertilization or other techniques? Would you be willing to adopt children?

1. Where do you want to live? Would you be willing to relocate? Are there places you would never want to live? Would you be willing to change jobs so we can live where I want or need to be?

2. What are your goals in life? What do you dream of doing? Do you have a secret desire to be a singer, mountain climber, or astronaut? What would you regret never having a chance to do?

3. Are you religious? What church do you belong to? Would you be open to changing churches or expect me to convert?

4. Republican or Democrat?

5. Have you ever been arrested?

6. Do problems with alcohol, drugs, mental illness or domestic violence run in your family?

7. Do certain diseases run in your family?

8. How will we handle money? Who will be in charge of the checkbook?

9. Dog or cat?

It's funny. We learn our sweethearts' favorite foods, favorite music, and favorite football teams, but we don't always know about the things that really matter. If I don't eat sweet potatoes or okra, so what? But if I won't set foot in the church that means everything to you, that's a problem. Likewise if I say no to the children you have always wanted. Sometimes we don't ask because we're afraid the answers will destroy the relationship. They might, but better now than when it's too late.

So ask the hard questions. Sometimes people will give you the answers you want to hear instead of the honest truth. But push for real answers. It will save a lot of heartache later.

What do you think? Let's talk about it.

Matt: "So ask the hard questions. Sometimes people will give you the answers you want to hear instead of the honest truth. But push for real answers. It will save a lot of heartache later."

This. This so much. We hear about people changing their minds over time. It's totally probable. But it's not likely that this is what actually happens. People generally do know what they really want deep down. Ask any child and you'll get an honest answer. But years of opinions, education, upbringing, hard experiences . . . often put a thick veil over their heart's desires. Often, an "honest" answer has much to do with a lifetime of conditioning and little to do with how we actually feel.

I've been there. In the first few years, my partner was willing to have a child with me, but she pretty much left the final decision with me. I was dealing with my own insecurities at the time, and I was unaware of what I was going through. So, I said no each time the topic came up. As I got older, I realized I declined having kids not because I didn't want them, but because I was scared. By then, it was too late. I don't resent her for not pushing hard enough. She couldn't look inside my head at the time. And me, I probably still would've said no as adamantly. Do I feel regret and grief? Yes. Would I leave her? No. Once you've been together for many years, you've built a relationship with someone you know now through and through and which supports a large part of your life and identity. If things otherwise work out swimmingly, are you really willing to sacrifice it all? Especially if you are older, the clock is ticking and the pressure really is on to get to know someone well enough before you have kids with them. This isn't as easy as it was when you were in your early 20s.

When it comes to hard questions: ask them early on, push as hard as you need to feel confident, and revisit them regularly. Don't ask once casually while dating and then revisit the issue the day after marriage. Ask every few months or so.

I think this is something we should impart on young people besides the ideal of romantic love which is so omnipresent and pervasive in our culture.

Jenny: Agreed. Don't just ask about having birth children. Check what their Plan B would be in case of infertility. Turns out mine and hubby's were different. He was okay with IVF, but not adoption. IVF didn't work; his plan after that is lots of holidays.

After 25 years of big holidays and weekend trips, I'm really not that into them anymore. Just got back from one and I'm having to come up with creative responses to all the "Wow, your photos made me so jealous. Was it fabulous? How lucky are you?" comments. Yeah, it was okay. Just okay, but it's not what I really want to be doing—is what I want to say.

Crystal: This reader's story is quite shocking to me. But only because he announced that he would never have a child with her on Day 2 of the marriage. I think there are many of us who are/were in the exact same situation but the one who didn't want children kept quiet about it for a lot longer. That is what happened to me anyway. As far as asking the hard questions goes, to be fair, I myself DID ask those hard questions. His answer was, yes, I want to have children, someday, when I'm old. So I thought, great, I want kids too, we'll just wait a few years. The problem is he was lying. He never wanted to raise children. He just liked the idea of having kids around to take care of him when he is an old man.

So back to the reader. I think he has done this woman a huge favor by actually admitting he doesn't want children. The problem is that he did it in the most crooked way possible, right after the legal documents were signed and the vows spoken. As Christians, we are taught to always forgive, be understanding, and to love our spouses unconditionally. But we cannot do that if we were deceived by the spouse before the marriage. So when he said, I will love you for better or for worse, he was lying. He only wanted the better, for him. In this case, it is clear, the marriage is based on deceit, which makes it invalid according to some church doctrines. I do think this woman loves her husband, and I also think that she did ask him questions before the wedding about having kids. He may have nodded in agreement, or just simply said nothing, which she may have taken as an agreement to wanting children. This is also lying. It's called a lie by omission.

In my own experience, the type of person who manipulates the situation by omitting pertinent information like this is not trustworthy. This man will rob her of her property, her time and her joy in life if she still wants a child of her own. I'm sorry to be so critical, but I'm one of the women who chose to leave. I think the reason there are so few of us reading this blog is because the women like me are few and far between and also have moved on with our lives and no longer wish to dwell on being married without children.

BEWARE OF UNREASONABLE BABY EXPECTATIONS

He's 36, and he wants to have children, preferably several. But *she's 46*, past the age when most women can get pregnant without heavy medical intervention, and she has almost finished raising the daughter she had with her first husband.

He's going through a divorce that nearly destroyed him emotionally and financially. His two half-grown kids are breaking his heart. And now his girl-friend is badgering him to get married and have children. She won't stop talking about it when he barely has the energy to get through his day as it is.

Before they got married, he said he didn't want to have any children. She said kids were never a priority for her either. But then a couple years into their marriage, she saw all her friends having babies and started wanting one, too. When she mentioned her new desire to her husband, he told her he still had no desire to have children. Now she is certain she must become a mother or die of grief. It's all his fault for denying her this essential part of life. But he told her all along that fatherhood was not on his bucket list.

Dear friends, I read stories like this almost every day in blog comments and in private emails readers send to me. Most of the writers are heartbroken and struggling to figure out what to do. Should they leave their partner in the hope of finding someone eager to make babies or stay and risk ending up alone and regretful in old age? I sympathize. I really do. When I married Fred, I was 33, and he was 48. He had three children from his first marriage and he'd had a vasectomy. Even after he told me he didn't want any more kids, I fantasized that somehow I'd get pregnant anyway. Of course I didn't.

Like the readers described above, I had unreasonable expectations. I married an older man who had already done the baby thing. He had barely finished his divorce before our wedding day. His kids were in all kinds of trouble.

His financial security had just been demolished. Finding and falling in love with each other was like a gift from God. To demand children on top of that was asking too much. If I really wanted kids, I should have found a man my own age who was aching to be a dad. I chose Fred.

Readers, I know how much it hurts not having the babies you always wanted. I still cry over it. It kills me to see families with their children and grandchildren and realize I'm alone. Add active hormones and people having babies all around you, and it can be brutally hard walking around with an empty womb. It's difficult to see clearly when you're in the thick of it. But sometimes you have to be realistic. If you really love someone, consider their side of the situation. Instead of browbeating them, love them and do your best to understand.

Say the serenity prayer. It helps: God, please grant me the serenity to accept the things I cannot change, the courage to change the things I can, and the wisdom to know the difference.

Anonymous: I'm trying so hard to be realistic right now. My husband said we could have a baby and abruptly changed his mind. I planned for a baby for almost a year, even buying things to make a nursery. Now, I can't even bear to go into the room that was set aside for our child. I've been in therapy, cried, drank—you name it, I've done it. I pray and pray, but the hurt only worsens by the day. I love my husband dearly and would never leave him, but I can't understand how he could do this to me and to us.

Anonymous: Anonymous, have your baby anyway. Men are clueless.

Anonymous: Oh my gosh, never force a child on another human being. If you want a kid that badly, divorce your husband and find someone else to have a child with. Never "oops" someone into a life they don't want. That's disgusting.

HOW DO YOU DEFEND YOUR NO-TO-KIDS PARTNER?

Your family is ganging up on you about why you don't have children. "What's the hang-up?" "Don't you want to have a family?" "Is there something wrong with you?" "Everybody else has them." "We can't wait to become grandparents." Etc.

What do you say? Do you tell them honestly that you don't have children and may never have children because your spouse or partner doesn't want them?

Do you explain that your mate already has all the children he (or she) needs or that he thinks kids will cramp his style? Or that he believes only a fool would bring children into a world that is going to hell in a handbasket? Do you tell them further that you really do want children and you sit alone in your car and cry about it, but you're stuck because of your partner?

Is your first response, "Well, sure, I'm going to be honest. I'm going to defend myself. It's not MY fault." Wait. Tread carefully here. This is your partner, the person you love, the person to whom you have committed your life. How do you think your family is going to react? Will they just say, "Okay. We understand." I doubt it. They're going to hate your partner. And they're going to think you're a fool for staying with this person who in every other way is your soul mate. From now on, the relationship between your partner and your family will be tainted. Depending on how your loved ones relate to people, they may jump all over your partner or just quietly seethe and talk trash about him to each other and to you. You will be stuck in the middle.

Has anybody experienced this? Show of hands. That's what I thought. My family was pretty quiet about Fred. They knew he'd been married before, they knew he was older, and I must have told them he'd had a vasectomy. I didn't have to say he didn't want any more kids. That was irrelevant. In their eyes, he *couldn't* have them.

But what if there's nothing wrong with his sperm or your eggs? To your knowledge, you could get pregnant right now—Excuse us for a half hour. Okay, done. The baby will be ready in nine months—how do you defend the two of you as a unit when the world starts ganging up, demanding answers, demanding action, demanding a baby, especially if that's what you want, too?

I wish I had the answers to these questions. I don't. I spent more than 30 years evading the nosy questions. I said, "God had other plans." "It just didn't happen." "We have Fred's three kids."

I generally believe in honesty, but what happens when that honesty turns your family—or your friends—against your partner and against your decision to stay with that person? You and your partner need to be a team if the relationship is going to last.

Is it possible to get to a place where you can calmly say, holding your loved one's hand for emphasis, "We have agreed not to have any children, and I hope you will support our decision"? Or maybe, "We already have [Insert names of stepchildren]. I hope you will love them as much as we do."

It gets a little easier as the years pass and the ability to bear children falls into the past tense. You can say, "We never had any children. Tell me about yours." Let them think what they will, place the blame wherever they want, but don't give them time to dwell on it. If you need to elaborate, perhaps just say, "We have had a wonderful life together, just the two of us."

Time for you to chime in. Have you been put in the position of defending your partner for his/her failure to make you a parent? How have you responded? How have people reacted? Can you support your partner when everyone else seems to be against him/her? What do you suggest childless-by-marriage people say when their loved ones insist on answers?

lifeANZ: We started saying together that if it happens it happens. We realized not pointing the blame and not divulging our personal lives has been the best solution. Now when I do occasionally have someone that does push, I tend to be blunt about the fact that I had a miscarriage and that tends to shut them up pretty quickly.

Anon S: To my parents (especially my mother, who talks behind my back), I say nothing because my parents would prefer to speculate instead of asking a caring but direct question. My brother once told me that Mom is afraid to ask me why I don't have children because "she didn't want to ask and then have you cry."

My parents also gave my recovering alcoholic husband gifts of alcohol on Christmas, so . . .

To my close friends (or people I believe I will become close to), I'm honest. I tell them that our marriage was very difficult in the beginning and we waited . . . Then our marriage became wonderful, but the "ship has pretty much sailed." I'm matter-of-fact about how the cookie crumbled. I suppose if someone didn't care for my husband, they could easily "blame" him. But it's the truth. I don't harbor or show any resentment towards my husband, so I don't expect others to either.

To random people I meet who ask me, "How old are YOUR children?" I say, "Oh, that never happened for us." I let them speculate, which I am fine with. (vs. having my own parents speculate. lol.) Most people are far too kind to pry.

If someone is a judgmental jerk, I lead them to believe that it's a tragic medical thing in the hopes they feel a little bit bad for being so nosy (forgive me, Lord). If the person or social situation is making me uncomfortable, I usually revert to, "Oh. No children for us . . . we have dogs." I don't like to make dogs the default, but when I get nervous this very easily shifts the conversation and gets me off the hook.

I find that the older I get, the less people ask. It's those newly married couples who struggle. That's who I feel for.

SFL: Thank you for sharing this. The varying responses make sense, and I love how you let the "judgmental jerks" think you're a victim of a medical tragedy. It's none of their business anyway.

WOULD YOU MARRY SOMEONE WHO IS INFERTILE?

We often talk here about couples in which one partner is not willing to have children. Sometimes they discuss it before they get married. Other times it comes as a rude surprise to the partner who wants kids. But what about situations where one partner, for whatever reason, physically cannot produce sperm or eggs? What if you knew that going in? Would you sacrifice children for love?

I've been doing a little reading about marriages in which a partner is infertile. Many of the listings that come up are religious discussions. As you might expect, the Catholics dominate. The main thought is that for a marriage to be valid, the couple must have a sexual union. If the couple is infertile, that does *not* invalidate the marriage; they're still married.

Some folks are using the same arguments in their debate about gay marriage. After all, a same-sex couple cannot procreate without outside help. But they do have a sexual union. I'm not going to debate whether or not gay marriage is a good thing. I think if people love each other, they should be allowed to be together. But it does underscore the question I am asking today: Would you marry someone who is unable to provide the necessary sperm or egg to conceive a child? Or is that a deal breaker?

In my case, I knew Fred had had a vasectomy. I also knew it had taken 17 years for him and his first wife to get pregnant and that his two older children were adopted because it didn't appear that they were able to have children. But in my usual unrealistic way, I figured we could overcome all that and pop out some babies while I was still in my fertile 30s. What if I had known that there was absolutely no chance? What if instead of saying he didn't *want* more children, he'd said, "I *can't*." Would I have married him? I think I would have. I really loved him. But I'd have been forced to consciously choose a life without the children I always thought I'd have. (Yes, we could have had the adoption talk and I would have learned that no, he didn't want to do that, so the result would have been the same, but that's a whole other discussion.)

What if I were the one with the fertility problem? Would I expect a man to give up children for me? Would I be constantly afraid that no man would have me if I couldn't give him sons and daughters? How and when would I tell the guys I dated? Would I feel guilty about depriving them of kids?

When couples disagree, that's hard, but infertility is a whole other thing, full of sadness. It's not a rare thing either. The U.S. Centers for Disease Control and Prevention web site[7] lists statistics for infertility. The percentage of women ages 15-44 with "impaired fecundity" is 10.9 percent or 6.7 million. Stop and think about that. One in 10. On the male side in the same age group, 13.9 percent were surgically sterile (usually vasectomy), 4.2 percent sterile for other reasons and another 5.2 percent considered subfertile, meaning conception was possible but not likely. That's a lot of guys, nearly a quarter of them.

How do you feel about that? Would you marry someone you knew was infertile?

Professor: What a looming question!! My hubby had the "VasClip"[8] vasectomy near the end of his first marriage after four kids. When we got together, I was hopeful because he'd said that the clips were "reversible," which was easier on his conscience. I, on the other hand, have been anovulatory all my life—no idea why, but I've never been able to ovulate. When I began to want kids, I learned about the pill Clomid, which has cured anovulation in *some* (far from *all*) cases. When I looked into the VasClips, I learned that not only was the "reversibility" not a guarantee, but the clips had been taken off the market due to an enormous failure rate. That got me thinking . . . what if the problem is with me and not with him? The more stories I'd read about women getting pregnant (against their wishes) by men with VasClips, the more I wondered if God's plan was cut-and-dry that I would not have children, and that it was actually a blessing to be married to a man who didn't want them. With so many complications in the way, I'm not sure I'd want to force the issue by demanding a reversal and injecting myself with hormones. Though I really, really do wish I could conceive.

Anonymous: I am in that situation now—after a lot of reproductive assistance, we've exhausted the possibility that I will ever have children. My husband has three grown children from a previous marriage and also has had a vasectomy. We tried using donor sperm with no luck; it's most likely because of my age. I simply missed the baby boat, which is heart-breaking and there's nothing to be done about it. I have not figured out a way to cope with it—it will be a life-long regret.

Your late husband's situation is interesting. Would it have made a difference to you if Fred was not the biological father of that third child?

SFL: It sure gets complicated, doesn't it? Professor, you don't know whether the problem is your lack of ovulation or your husband's clip job. A failure might have worked to your benefit, but then there's the egg problem. You could go through all the hormones and surgery, and it still might not work. It's so hard.

Anonymous, it is heartbreaking. We don't get another chance once that boat has sailed. You ask a very good question. What if Fred had told me all of his children were adopted, which would mean he might not be able to give me any children? I think I would have married him anyway. At least I would have known the situation right at the beginning.

Catherine: I read this with great interest as I can't have children. I had to have a hysterectomy. I do fear that I am not good enough for someone who wants children—that I would not be worthy of love over having a child. Who would really love me despite this? I do have a long-term friendship with someone but haven't done anything about being more because I know he wants to have children and I can't have them. I just figure that is not in the cards for us or, if it is, can I ever let him love me despite this?

I do see a counselor, and it's great but I still wonder what is out there for me? Someone with kids who lost a wife or is divorced? Maybe, maybe not.

I struggle a great deal seeing my coworkers doing all the things one thinks they will do—get married and have kids, but I am worried I will never let anyone really love me—and why would they since I can't have kids? Clearly, this is an issue for me, and I do talk with my counselor a great deal about it, but it is still a downer most of the time.

But, I tell myself it's all for some reason and I hope someday soon I'll know what the reason is and that much good comes from it. Some days are easier than others of course, but there are days that I do wonder if I will ever know that reason. I sure hope I know it soon.

Karam: I think marriage is based on love, and love doesn't see fertility or infertility. But actually it all depends upon the couple. For some it doesn't matter and for others it does.

Savannah: I was a month past my 18 birthday when I married my husband, who was barely 19. His parents fought us tooth and nail through the entire engagement telling us how "young we were." And yet, after being married for six years, we finally learned the hubs had a zero sperm count. When we mentioned it to his mom, she said, "Oh yeah, it's because of that steroid drug you took for your kidney infection when you were 17." That was the FIRST time this came up! I've always wondered why they didn't try to use that in their campaign to stall our marriage. Really, it's probably because their religion believes in no sex before marriage and they didn't want us "fooling around" if we knew we wouldn't have a pregnancy scare. But six years after we were married, this finally came up! Even if she had told us when we were young, I still would have married him. I love him that much.

SFL: Savannah, you nailed it in your last sentence: "I love him that much." That's what it takes to overcome the no-kids situation. I can't believe his parents didn't say anything all that time. That's just not right. Thank you for sharing this.

Anonymous: I feel your pain, Catherine. I did feel this way at some point. But I believe the way you feel will pass. I am infertile and was born this way (with no womb) and yes, at first I thought, "How will anybody want me?" But people will fall in love with you regardless, like my husband did with me. The important thing for me was to become satisfied and happy about who I was. Okay, so I couldn't become a biological mum, but I could adopt. So this became my way of having kids and I accepted this as my role in parenthood. I hope your work with your counselor is helping you accept that you are a wonderful and whole person in spite of your infertility, and that it helps you realize that there will undoubtedly be somebody you will meet whom you will love and who will love you in return, irrespective of infertility.

superorduffer: Hi Anonymous, I am a male, infertile since childhood with zero sperm count and Indian. I used to be depressed, as I know I will not marry because I used to think that no girl can understand this. (I had talked about this matter to my previous girlfriends, and after listening to this they dumped me. I never lie to any girl whom I want to marry). But after reading all the comments, I feel that love does exist, and I will now look for a woman who is infertile so that we can adopt kids and will again believe in marriage.

Anonymous: As a guy, I see no problem marrying an infertile woman who is qualified as my right life partner. To me, it's not obvious that as married couple we have to raise our own biological child or even any child at all. We have a lot of positive things to do together whenever possible in order to fulfill our lives and make them successful. I personally don't feel any obviousness in children or future generations. However, all people don't feel and perceive in the same way.

DARE WE ASK FOR MORE THAN ONE CHILD?

My mother used to tell me that shortly after I was born, Grandpa Fagalde said, "Well, when are you going to have your boy?" Exhausted from giving birth, she wasn't thrilled about the idea at that moment, but a year and a half later, she had my brother. Like most of the families on our block, our parents had two children, a boy and a girl. A full set. We fit perfectly in our three-bedroom baby boom houses in the suburbs of San Jose.

Fast forward to 2020 and the Childless by Marriage community. So many people here are hoping, praying and pleading to have a baby, just one, but I suspect we really want a full set, too, which means more than one.

If we only had one, he or she would be an "only child." Although lone children can thrive, happy to receive all of their parents' attention, they will go through life without the companionship of another person who has exactly the same family history and who will be around for major family events. They might also provide nieces and nephews for you to cherish. God knows I would hate to have gone through the recent loss of my father without my brother. We were a team throughout that ordeal, and he has handled the brunt of the estate management.

In so many situations we read about here, a person would be lucky to have a single child. The partner is already reluctant, or the body is not cooperating. If one sperm and one egg actually get together, and if the pregnancy lasts the whole nine months, and if the baby is born healthy . . . dare we ask for more than one? Should we just pray for twins?

Sure, having more than one child is double the cost and double the effort. My mother always said she sometimes thought she'd lose her mind those first few years with the two of us in diapers and into everything while Dad was at work all day. But it was good for us. We always had someone to play with when other kids weren't around. We fought a lot, but we were united against the world. Now that our parents are gone, we still have each other. I have always wished I had a sister, too, but Mom and Dad didn't cooperate.

As Catholics, if they were following the rules, my parents would have had more children, but honestly most Catholic couples use birth control of some kind. As a working class family living off my father's income as an electrician, they would have struggled to take care of a larger family. Two was enough for them.

Many of our readers have married someone who already has children from a previous relationship. So did I. Two of my friends in that situation had one more child together. For medical reasons, they could not have more. Others had more than one. I'm not going to say the children from the second marriage blended perfectly with the kids from the first. They did not turn into the Brady Bunch[9]. They got along, but it was always clear they came from different tribes.

Back to the original question. While we're asking to have one child, dare we ask for two—or more? Or would negotiations completely shut down if you went that far? Are any of you "only children?" Do you wish you had a brother or sister?

Driving down the road, I often follow cars with stencils on the back window representing their families. Have you seen them? There's the mom, the dad, the multiple children and the dog. How many people would we like on our back-window stencil?

I look forward to your comments.

Interesting reading:

"The Rise of the Only Child," Washington Post, June 19, 2019[10]

"The Truth about Only Children," The Guardian, May 31, 2018[11]

"The Case Against Having Only One Child," Elizabeth Gehrman[12]

"Thirteen Things Everyone Should Know About Only Children," Greatist.com[13]

Yari: One factor people often consider is money. A decent person might see that they can only afford one child, and so they have only one. If a parent knows they will struggle with two, maybe even to the point where the food budget will be too tight, they might choose to stick with just one child.

When it comes to children, there is no guarantee. No guarantee that one is better than two, or that three is better than two. No guarantee that they will take care of you when you age (as many people often assume). No guarantee that they will be who you want them to be.

So, have as many (or as few) children as you want, and do your best! That's all we can do, IMHO.

SilverShil0h: I would be fine having one child. I'd support them finding and nurturing friendships. Hopefully I could impart the benefits of being alone and with others. I have siblings. We are in the 50-60s range and have grown vastly apart. There are no guarantees that a sibling guarantees a friend for life.

mdoe37: I am an only child born 10 years into the marriage. Yes, there are benefits. BUT I grew up quite over-protected because I was an only. I was also the only grandchild on one side (virtually ignored by the other). I have no close relatives, cousins, etc. My mother only had one because she felt she couldn't handle more than one. Thus, she was not interested in my having friends over, sleepovers, etc. However, because she was a helicopter parent, I couldn't go to other kids' houses, as she felt their parents didn't supervise closely enough. My mother had little interest in providing any sort of extra-curriculars and they were discouraged. So yes, I was very much more at ease discussing finances and investing at 12 than talking with kids my age.

It was sad and lonely. I was not prepared to date because I wasn't allowed the boy/girl social time. Got into a rather early marriage (fail) as a result. I simply didn't have good social skills or boundaries.

Now, I'm in my 50s spending part of my time dealing with my elderly mother. There are no relatives left, none to help, and my parents' friends are all gone. So, I'm still the dog and pony show for every holiday, birthday, need, appointment driver, etc. I planned on flying after my divorce . . . I'm stalled out. I'm working part-time in a dead-end job so that I can be available for needs.

My advice: If you feel you want to have one child, so be it. But please, please make sure there are adequate resources, family, friends, etc. Have a plan other than your only child in your later years. It isn't fair to expect one person (I am divorced and childless) to put everything on hold (when I really need to start retirement savings) to care for you. Be prepared to be flexible in allowing other drivers, housekeepers, etc.

Make sure that one child has a village. It really isn't fair otherwise.

Jenny: This is a fab topic and piece of writing, Sue. I am an only child, but I consider myself to be very lucky. I was brought up in a mid-sized village in northern England in the 1970s and 80s. I had an older cousin and one almost exactly the same age as me. We lived just streets away from each other, and from age about 5 or 6 were allowed to wander to and from each other's houses, to our grandma's house, and to play in the streets with the other kids. No need for pre-arranged playdates. I do not remember ever being lonely, and I know my parents were proud of everything I did and loved me. I could see it in their eyes. As a teenager, we had a great youth club that got me into sports that I still play today and others into music.

Basically I had the village around me, in terms of people and state-provided extracurricular activities. My parents still live in the village, and my cousins are a great support and source of company for them. I should add, it hasn't all been plain sailing, lots of family fall-outs over the years (I don't want readers to think lots of families are like the Waltons[14] and it is just theirs that is lacking!).

One of the reasons my hubby and I stopped fertility treatment was that we didn't really want to end up with just one child. He said, "I hate spoilt kids." (a bit of an underlying assumption that only kids are spoilt). Turns out he regards any support with extra-curricular activities as spoiling a child. I'd have wanted kids to try lots of different activities, to find what they are good at and to build their confidence. I'm okay that we didn't have kids together.

You are right, Sue. There was a vision of more than one child for us, probably the standard two. And all the comments made by your readers about parents pushing forward for that one child late in life are very valid considerations. It is really going to help the child if there are cousins and other extended family, either nearby or who will keep in touch and visit. And a community, where people of all ages get out and mix.

Anonymous: When I was little in the 70s, every family had MORE than two siblings and only children were rare. But a counselor friend once told me that since there are so many only children nowadays, they don't experience the same loneliness as only children used to. It is easier from the parents' perspective to have just one though. But you are correct, siblings generally cannot imagine not having each other, so in a way the second one is a gift to the first.

I think it's okay to want more than one. It's certainly not selfish. However, let's say if I had one, I just would not express [my desire for another] to a childless individual or couple.

I'm glad that you and your brother have each other.

Loribeth61: I always thought I'd have two children, maybe three. As the clock ticked down, I knew I'd be happy to settle for one, but that was not to be.

I know a lot of parents who have just one child get almost as much flack for that as we do for not having any. Sometimes it's a choice, sometimes it's just how things worked out, sometimes the parents went through a lot of infertility and losses to get that one child. It's really nobody's business!

ARE MARRIAGES HAPPIER WITHOUT CHILDREN?

Check out these headlines:

"Childfree Life: Kids Really Do Ruin Marriages, Study Finds"
—*Huffington Post*[15]

"Sorry, Parents: Childless Couples Say They're Happier Together"
—*Jezebel*[16]

"Happier Relationships for Couples without Children"
—the *Telegraph*[17]

Recent headlines shout that couples without kids have happier marriages. Down in the fine print, they back off a little, but the writers maintain that non-parenting couples pay more attention to each other and have more time and money to date, travel and generally continue the honeymoon indefinitely.

Well, that's true. I never had children of my own, but I did have a live-in stepson, so I got at least a taste of it. Whatever you do, 24/7, when you're responsible for a child, you have to consider that child's needs. She needs new shoes, so you keep wearing your old ones. He's got the flu, so you stay home from work to take care of him. You have less privacy and more expenses, and you can't just go off to the beach, a restaurant, a show, or Maui, or even have sex without thinking about the child. Can he go with us? Do we need to get a babysitter? He's got soccer practice, or his science project is due tomorrow, so we can't do what we want to do. Spontaneity goes out the window.

That's how it is with kids. And it does put a strain on marriages. You have wonderful loving moments when you thank God for your family, but you also argue over money, responsibilities, discipline, and priorities, and you don't have much privacy. You pay less attention to your spouse because you're focused on the children. These are some of the things that made my husband and perhaps many of your partners and spouses decide they didn't want to have any more children. Their first marriage failed, and the kids were at least part of the problem. They don't want the same thing to happen to this marriage.

Sound familiar to any of you? Of course you tell them it will be different this time, but their previous experiences with children tell them otherwise.

The articles in the Huffington Post, Jezebel and the Telegraph don't tell us whether the couples are childless by choice or by circumstance. I'm guessing it's by choice. But even if it isn't, I suppose we can take some comfort in knowing that even if we wanted children and grieve their loss, even if we see a great gaping hole in our lives, our marriages *might* end up being happier than those of our friends with kids.

In a book titled *Marriage Confidential: Love in the Post-Romantic Age*,[18] author Pamela Haag says marriages alter irrevocably with the arrival of children. Instead of focusing on each other, the mother and father turn all their attention to the children.

They become sexless partners in the business of raising children. One of my favorite lines is: "As far as erotic charge goes, one day you're sleeping with a lover-husband, and the next you might as well be in bed with a toaster." In this age of two-income families and "helicopter parenting," Haag suggests, there is no time or energy left for each other, or for a social life outside the family. The romance goes away.

I don't know. What do you think? Are childless couples happier?

Anonymous: Kids are a conscious choice. They did not ask to be born. It is true that priorities change, but it doesn't stay that way forever. Kids eventually grow up and leave the nest. I can honestly say that seeing your child's eyes light up when you walk into a room is definitely more fulfilling than being on an endless honeymoon.

Professor: I have to disagree with the comment that seeing your child's eyes light up when you walk into a room is more fulfilling than an endless honeymoon. My stepkids and I adore one another, and they certainly light up when I walk into the room. But their fawning over me will never be more fulfilling than sneaking away and soaking in private moments with my hubby. Kids grow, and our relationship with them changes. Our oldest is now 14, and the "crush" she had on me when I came into her life at 7 years old has morphed into more of a loving, adult friendship. My relationship with my husband, however, has never lost its honeymoon-ness. I believe it was Andrew Carnegie who said that it is imperative that a child understands that his parents love each other more than they love their children. Since we eloped many years ago, my husband and I have honeymooned in every home we've ever owned. And that will never change. Should one of us end up in a nursing home, that room will also be our honeymoon suite. This is the gift of our lives. And kids aren't always a conscious choice (even "the act" might not have been done by choice), just as being childless isn't always a conscious choice. I agree, Sue, that you can—indeed, must—choose to keep your marriage alive if kids do become a part of that marriage. Because if priorities change—if the child becomes more important than the spouse—even for a short time (if you can call 18 years a short time), the chances of them getting back to where they once were could be a failing prospect, and 18 years of hurt feelings could be impossible to overthrow.

Anonymous: It's a difficult one to unpick. My husband in particular prefers spontaneity and a slower pace of life. He also enjoys the extra money, meals out and the ability to get deals on low-cost holidays at non-peak times. I feel life is too slow. I can think of things to do to shake things up, but he isn't keen. Overall, I think my marriage is better for not having children, as we disagreed on so many aspects of child-rearing when we discussed it. However, the research reported in the Telegraph also found that although they were less happy with their relationships/partners, mothers were the group that were happiest with life overall. And I'd agree that my life is less happy for not having children.

2

STAY OR GO: WHAT SHOULD I DO?

THAT'S THE QUESTION THAT ARISES in the majority of comments here at Childless by Marriage. So many people, mostly anonymous, write that their partner says he (or she) does not want to have children. In some cases, they both agreed on not having kids in the beginning, but now the writer has changed her mind and is frustrated because her partner has not. In other cases, the partner has just announced that he isn't interested in having kids. Not now, not ever, and he doesn't want to discuss it.

The heartbroken writer says: Now we have to break up. They may have been together for five, ten or twenty years, but it's over because their partner does not want to be a parent.

Yesterday, Anonymous wrote: "My girlfriend of eight years has just told me she does not want children. She won't even discuss it. I'm gutted and know I can't stay with her. It is incredibly painful. She loves children and is great with them. Instead of even giving a reason, she just says she is 'at peace' with her decision."

But do they have to break up? Should you really throw away a relationship that is good in every other way over this issue? God knows it's a huge issue. Having children or not changes the whole course of your life, and if you have always wanted to be a mother or father, shouldn't you pursue that?

Maybe. But how do you know whether you will find someone else in time to procreate or that you will ever love another person as much as the partner you have now? You don't. So hold on. Don't be too quick to jump ship or to broadcast to the world that your partner is a rat. Take a breath. Talk about it. I know they don't always want to talk. Give them a little time. Find a way to approach the subject without accusations and threats. Maybe say, "I love you so much, and I want to understand . . ." Maybe you could each write a letter explaining your feelings. Maybe you could try counseling. Maybe there's a good reason or an obstacle that you can help them get over. Or not. Just don't give up too quickly. If you really love someone, you have to accept them as they are. If up until now, this person was The One, maybe he still is.

If the relationship is new and you really haven't established any strong ties, then adios. Tell them it's a deal breaker and move on. But if you have given everything to this relationship, maybe it's meant to be.

Ultimately, you need to ask yourself these questions:

1. Am I happy with my life as it is right now? If nothing changes, can I remain happy with this person?

2. Do I love this person enough to choose him or her over the children I might have had?

3. Will I be devastated if I never have children?

4. Am I willing to risk ending up childless and alone—or becoming a single parent?

Here are some articles to read that might offer some answers or raise more questions.

"The High Failure Rate of Second and Third Marriages," *Psychology Today.* **Sobering facts to ponder before you dump your partner.**[19]

"8 Tough Truths to Consider When Your Partner Doesn't Want Kids," *Huffington Post.*[20] **This writer really does give you some answers or at least a path to finding them. Read this and do some soul-searching.**

"I left the husband I loved because he refused to have children (and had IVF twins alone)"[21] **There's another way to go, as this** *Daily Mail* **piece describes. Would you be willing to have children on your own if you don't find the ideal partner?**

SHOULD SHE LEAVE HER CHILDLESS MARRIAGE?

Heavy Heart wrote:

I would like to hear advice from the ladies who remained childless past their child-bearing age. I am going to be 36 years old very soon, married to a man who has a 10-year-old son. When we first started our serious relationship five years ago, we agreed on having our own child. Fast forward five years. Now married for three years, bio mom drama subsided, financials are more stable. My husband says his life is finally "good." Can we now start planning for our child? My husband has been avoiding the conversation as much as he can. Excuses, excuses, and excuses. I am very close to asking him "YES or NO" and if NO is the final answer, leaving him, but I can't get to that final answer and I don't want to hear that final answer. He says he is on the fence because of the financial burden of having two children because he has to take care of his first son before having his second. He knows it's "unfair" if he says no, and he knows that I will probably leave him so he is avoiding the conversation altogether.

In responding to Heavy Heart, something suddenly clicked in my head. If they had the kind of relationship meant to last forever, she wouldn't think about leaving. I know that for me, leaving Fred was not an option. He was my person, period.

So I ask you: Is the marriage already too shaky to last if one of the partners is thinking about leaving for any reason, especially if they're giving their spouse an ultimatum: *Say yes, I stay; say no, and I'm gone?* And what about the husband in this case? People do change their minds, but they had a deal. Does he not love her enough to stick with that deal?

Heavy Heart, if you're reading this, I hope it's okay that I'm sharing your comment more widely. You are not alone in this situation. I hear variations of the same story all the time. Here are just a few of the many comments on this subject.

YariGarciaWrites: People need to really really realize this: When someone says they don't want children, and you do, don't go on a second date. There is a high chance they won't just "change their minds later." Honesty now helps avoid heartache and problems in the future.

Lucy: In my case, we did talk about it while dating. He promised me a house full of kids. Then we got married, and he changed his tune (just one of the many things he lied about before marriage). It's not always as simple as telling someone that they should have asked.

Tony: I say a deal is a deal. He agreed, time is right, and he needs to keep up his end. It's not fair that bio-mom had kids and you haven't. I say leave him with all deliberate speed if he says no. Frankly, I'd have pulled the plug when he started getting flaky about it. If you don't leave him, you'll resent him. And resentment will turn into hatred. Then what?

Anonymous: My boyfriend and I have been dating for going on five years, and he has said repeatedly that he does not want any more kids. He has two kids from previous relationships and basically refuses to even talk about what will happen if we have an accidental pregnancy. I do understand where he is coming from. He lost his daughter in a long, horrendous custody battle after his divorce, and although we see his son on a regular basis, he simply doesn't want any more children. I very much want to be a mom at some point, and though I'm only 25 (he is 33), I know I want a child of my own, too. I love his kids, but it's heartbreaking and makes me incredibly envious and even a smidge resentful. I have nightmares about being pregnant and him leaving me because of it. I'm terrified of the possibility of becoming pregnant because I love him more than anything and don't want to lose him, but what if I do get pregnant even while on birth control? I want to know he won't leave me in that circumstance, but he won't give me any reassurance on the issue. Any advice would be appreciated!

Anonymous: In this situation, I'd say to start looking for a new man who can fulfill your dream of being a wife and mother. Don't sell your life short to a man who doesn't care enough about your wants and desires to help fulfill them and be happy and proud to do so. Would you be "happy and proud" to give up the dream of being a mom just so he can be happy? Does he (and his kids) give you enough joy in life that you desire nothing else than to be with him/them? It's a hard choice, I know, but at age 25, you've got time to find a new relationship that can be better matched to you. Another angle is to ask why he doesn't want kids. For most men it's about money/child support. So if it's just about the money, work on "your" finances, find a better job, etc. and then afford the baby with or without him.

Anonymous: Leave him and find someone who shares your desire for children. You are too young to give up on your desire for children just to be with a man who is too selfish to give you a child. Trust me, you will REGRET spending all of your childbearing years with a man who won't give you a child. I have been with my husband for 14 years. I am 38, and my resentment about not having another child grows stronger by the day.

Don't give this selfish man all of your childbearing years. You will deeply regret it in the end.

Christian: I knew by age 14 that I did not want children. Never ever. Ever!

By that age, I had seen way too much mess already: Family feuds over custody battles. Family fortunes battled over and lost in court. Alcohol and gambling addictions. Family drama over nothing. That was 40 years ago.

Great women divorced me because I could neither believe my own strong convictions to not procreate nor resist their charms to agree to marriage. In my life, women always took the initiative and proposed to me. I never proposed first. Not wanting children in my then socioeconomic environment was unheard of. Perhaps I was hoping for these great women to overturn my inner convictions. To no avail. Like me, they ended up childfree anyway. And they stayed single, too, afterward. I guess I ruined it for them. For good.

I've still had a great life, perhaps because I stuck to my own true convictions. I live with a single-parent older girlfriend and four cats now. Perhaps, we should really, really listen to our inner voices, our gut instincts.

Heavy heart: Sue, you are right on that the marriage is shaky if I am thinking this already. The back story to this is, I never told anyone, not even my husband, but sensing that he might be changing his mind, I tried for two years to forget about having my own children. I read books and blogs to come to terms with the "childless forever" idea. After two years of trying to train my brain, no. I still wanted to have my own.

Tired childless stepmom brain started to think, "If my husband says No, then I don't want to continue to live this very painful life of a childless stepmom."

Thank you all so much for sharing your stories and advice. I talked to my husband, a 30-minute conversation. In a nutshell, he is not 100 percent agreeing, but it's "not fair to me, and it is important to me." He agreed to start trying for a baby next month. I am waiting to see if he follows up. I wanted to argue my case until he is 100 percent and wanted him to be actually "excited about it," but I decided to pick a battle and let this one go. I am happy for now that he actually agreed, but again, I will see for sure next month.

Thank you again, everybody, for sharing your story and advice. I am very grateful.

THEY STAYED IN A CHILDLESS MARRIAGE

Last week, I asked the question "Did They Go or Stay?" Several readers responded. In general, they stayed. Are they happy?

Kat: "Stayed in a very happy relationship. Found out last year that I couldn't have had kids anyway and needed surgery. Phew, glad I stayed."

Tamara: "I knew that he was special and that I would never find someone that I loved as much as I love him. I still wish we had a child, but in the end I know that an unknown child could not give me the feeling of love nor could it complete me as much as my marriage does."

M2L: "I have stayed, for now, and have watched my 'childbearing years' disappear. It is hard not to be resentful of a man who is now enjoying a grandchild. We shall see how it all works out!"

Jay: "I stayed, believing that God wouldn't bless my leaving. We'd both wanted children before we got married. A few years in, he changed his mind. My yearning has been powerful. I've forgiven him—over and over, as I continue to grieve unchosen childlessness. Now it's too late for me to have children. His lack of concern for my lost dream compounds the pain. I often wish I had left, as the refusal to have children was only one part of the unhealthiness in our marriage. Still continuing to evaluate whether to stay in this marriage."

Candy: I surely thought a lot about leaving, and I mean a lot. I couldn't imagine not having children, but when I really thought hard about it, I didn't want to walk away from my marriage vows. I really meant them when I said them, and to walk away just because I didn't get what I wanted just didn't seem right. I personally know women who are my age, never married and never had children, so in my thinking, I've got a pretty great life with a husband who loves me still after 31 years of marriage.

Erica: I struggled with this throughout my late 20s and 30s, and I think it came down to this: If I was going to leave, I had to be ready to be alone. I had to feel like, even if I didn't meet someone else to have children with, I was still going to be in a better situation out of the relationship than in it. It never seemed like I could really confidently say that, so I stayed.

I think most of us will not leave a marriage that is otherwise good. When I divorced my first husband, it was not because of his refusal to have children. I still believed we could work that out eventually. No, I had found out he was cheating on me and had been for most of the six years we were married. That's what I found intolerable.

The men I dated between marriages were all willing to father my children, but none of them would have been good husbands. Then I met Fred, and he was so wonderful I was willing to spend my life with him, no matter what. I wanted children but not at the sacrifice of a good relationship. And I did get a sort of "motherhood lite" with the stepchildren and step-grandchildren.

Which is more important, finding the right partner or having children? That seems to be the essential question. We shouldn't have to choose, but if we do, which way would you go?

THEY LEFT TO TRY AGAIN

Sifting through the hundreds of responses on the Go or Stay question, I find so many readers who are still trying to figure out what to do. But some have decided to move on. How did it turn out?

Anon C: I am 30 and have just broken up with my partner of five years. We love each other completely. We are really close, best of friends, and have been having a great time together. But the one big deal breaker has been kids. I am very regretful, but I know this is the right decision. Having kids is a deal breaker for me, and we would not have been able to be happy together if one of us had given in to the other.

Ali: I divorced my first husband because he did not want children. We had been married for five years (together for eight) and I was 31—this was 2002. I met my second husband after only a few months. Moved in with him after six weeks, and we have now been married for over 10 years. He is a dairy farmer and my best friend. The only sad thing is that we did not get the chance to try for a baby. He has two kids from his first marriage (who are both now parents themselves) and had a vasectomy many years before meeting me. At least I gave myself the chance to find the lifestyle I really wanted . . . I am so glad that I found the strength to leave my first husband.

AnimalLover: I was finally able to summon the strength to leave my alcoholic, drug-using ex-husband. He was emotionally abusive, deceitful, and would have made a terrible father. My life is 100 percent better since leaving him, but the dating scene has been rough. I am almost 31, and have found that there are few good men out there left to date. It's interesting, though, that the men I have dated since my divorce have ALL said they do not want more kids. I have finally met a wonderful and kind man that I am very much in love with, and he is everything that I have always hoped to find (and dreamed of while I was with my ex-husband), but he also doesn't want more children. I've been through enough toxic men to know what a good one looks like, and I REALLY don't want to let him go over something that I'm so ambivalent about. I'm also not sure that I have good enough reasons for even wanting to have kids in the first place—it's the traditional way of life, I'm afraid to be alone when I'm old, fear of regret, etc.

Wayne: I'm 45 and my girlfriend is 26. We have been together for almost five years. I met my partner not long after I split up from a 10-year marriage. When we met, I knew there was an age gap, but we were just having fun. Then the fun turned into love and meeting families. Next thing, she moved in, and holidays we had a ball. We really do get on.

I have a child from a relationship when I was 18 and my child has a child now. Yes, I'm a granddad. I said I never wanted kids as I felt I was too old and loved my life as it was with the holidays, meals out whenever we wanted, and a nice house and clothes. She told me that she loves me and that's more important than kids. Now almost four years in, she gave me two choices: to give her a child and marriage or there is no point in us going on. Yesterday when we were walking the dog, she asked me again, and I said I did not want kids and that's it. "I told you this years ago." She said, "I was hoping you would have changed your mind."

After long thought, I decided to pack my bags and go live with my mother for a while. I always knew in the back of my head this would happen. It's so sad. We really do get on so well in every way, but I feel I'm holding her back from what she wants.

Anonymous 87: I have been with my husband for 12 years, together for 10 years and married for two. I am 28, and I love him more than words can express. My first battle I had to overcome with him was marriage. It took me 10 years to convince him that marriage was special and meant something. Now the argument is over having children. I desperately want to experience motherhood and having a family of my own, and his answer is a firm no. I've tried so hard to convince him, but I just don't know if I will ever get through to him. Yesterday, I packed up the dog and left. Maybe us being gone will be the reality check he needed. I am at a loss for words, and my heart is broken. I just feel like yelling at the top of my lungs, "What did I do to deserve this???"

A few days later, Anonymous 87 commented:

A week after I left, my husband asked me to come back home and agreed to go to counseling. He said he cannot make me any promises as to whether he will change his mind about wanting kids one day, but he can promise that he will keep working on his underlying issues. So we are making some progress, but I do not want to get my hopes up at this point. I am taking it one day at a time.

JMC: I am on the other end of this dilemma, sort of. I'm 42, my amazing wife is 33. We have been married for five wonderful years. My second marriage (two kids, ages 18 and 15), her first. As time passed, my wife and I discussed her wanting children and I grew more toward not wanting any more. She always told me that she was okay without having children of her own, that our relationship was more important to her than having her own children . . . .

She was lying to herself and me. Now she's leaving, not even allowing me to discuss it. I told her let's just have kids. She thinks that I don't really want one, which isn't necessarily true. If I knew it was that important to her, I would give her a child. But I don't have that option now.

JMC posted a couple more times as he attempted to reconcile with his wife. It didn't work.

He says, "She is moving forward with the breakup. She is giving up on a loving marriage for the hopes of finding someone to have children with, all the while thinking I'll take her back if she doesn't find what she's looking for. My heart is heavy with sorrow at the moment. I'm losing my best friend."

THINKING OF LEAVING A CHILDLESS MARRIAGE?

Many of you agonize over whether to leave a partner who doesn't want to have children. Faced with that situation, here is what Victoria did and how it turned out.

I met the love of my life in 2012. I was 30, and he was 37. We didn't really discuss children too much, but six months after we met, over lunch with friends in France, he casually mentioned he did not want them. At that point, I was devastated. I knew I wanted children, but I had also not ever felt this way about anyone before. We discussed things at length, and he said he would think about whether he might change his mind. The years rolled by. We were so happy, and I couldn't coun-tenance leaving him. It seemed so wrong to give up someone I loved so much for the potential of a child that might never exist. The issue came up a few times, though it was always in the back of my mind. We ended up having some therapy together to try to get some sense of how to navigate life without resentment and guilt building up. Eventually after four years I decided that I could accept and embrace a childfree life if it meant keeping the man I loved.

I read your blog many times, often seeing the same theme: Should you leave the person you love in the hopes that you'll find someone you love just as much, who also wants children, and you're both able to have them? That could be a needle in a haystack. I thought I was quite at ease with my decision.

In 2017, we went on a holiday with a group of friends. One of the couples had a one-year-old baby. Watching them together was quite hard, and seeing how my part-ner reacted to the baby was equally as difficult. He just did not want to be around the baby at all, and it seemed to ruin his holiday. At this point, I had just turned 35. By now, the thought of being childless forever was in my mind every time I went to sleep. I thought about it all the time. Would I regret it? Did I even have any viable eggs left? I'd read so many forums, talked to friends, talked to my own therapist, and I just didn't know what the right answer was.

One Sunday morning, after quite an emotional night, I made a snap decision to end the relationship at that moment. My desire to have children and my fear about how I would end up hating the man I loved over time became too much. I decided to leave. He understood. There were a lot of tears. Many days, I almost went back, but I didn't. I thought I would look into having a baby alone. I had lots of tests, and I was lucky that at 35, I had a good ovarian reserve. I decided to give it a year and see if I met anyone. If not, I would go it alone. To be honest, at 35, meeting a single man who was of a similar age who didn't already have children but wanted them seemed a long shot.

Six months later, I happened to meet a lovely man. He was 36, single, no chil-dren, but he mentioned on our first date how much he regretted not having children. Eight months later, he proposed. Two months after that, we decided that as I was now 36 we should consider stopping birth control. A few months after that, I was pregnant. I honestly could not believe it. I spoke to my previous partner to let him know (he was now in a new relationship with someone who did not want children.) He was so happy for me, and said he felt a weight lifted off his shoulders, which was amazing.

In January of this year, I gave birth to my son. He is nearly six months old, and he is so perfect. I look at him every day and can't quite believe that after all the years of agonizing, I finally have him. Admittedly, motherhood is a lot harder than I thought it would be. I struggled after a very traumatic labor and then dealing with a young baby and the COVID-19 lockdown has not been easy, but everything I went through was worth it for him.

I wondered if my story might help others who are struggling with the stay or go question. I am not suggesting go is always the right answer, as I think for many people it isn't, but for me it was.

In a follow-up email, Victoria added:

You reach a point where all of your friends are having kids, pregnant women or people with babies seem to be everywhere, and I could hardly stand to look at them. I used to constantly imagine being pregnant, holding my baby etc. It became too much for me, and honestly I think the guilt became too much for him. We are both happier apart, I think, although I will always love him dearly.

We are undecided about another child at the moment after such a traumatic labor and being on the older side. Certainly not until next year if we do decide to, but I won't feel too bad if we don't or can't.

3

PARENTHOOD DELAYED

WOMEN IN THEIR 40S who are still trying to figure out whether to have children are not going to like this post, but they need to know the facts.

A reader sent me a comment today that fit right in with a recent news story I was planning to share. She's 42 and has a child from a marriage that went sour. Now she's dating a 28-year-old man she calls her soul mate. At first he said he didn't want children, but now he does, and she's stewing over whether or not to have a child for him.

The thing is, she's not likely to get pregnant at 42, even if she decides she is willing. Check out this article at cnn.com. "The 'Big Lie' in Putting Off Pregnancy"[22] makes it clear that while today's 40-year-olds may be as youthful as yesteryear's 25-year-olds, their eggs are old-school. A lot of the reason more than twice as many women age 40-44 are childless as in 1976 is that they're delaying parenthood while they build their careers and enjoy the unfettered life. Meanwhile their eggs are going stale. By the time they think about having children, it's too late.

The article notes that a woman in her 20s has a 20-25 percent chance per menstrual cycle of conceiving naturally. In her early 30s, the chances are 15 percent. After 35, it goes down to 10 percent. After 40, the number falls to 5 percent, and after 45, it's only 1 per cent. It doesn't seem fair, but that's the way it is.

You can just go to the doctor and start fertility treatments, you say. Unfortunately, most of the women who go that route do not end up having babies. They spend thousands of dollars, experience repeated disappointments and sometimes several miscarriages before they give up. Sure, we hear about celebrities and others having babies in their 40s, but for most of us that's not going to happen.

Last night, I lay in bed running the numbers. During my first marriage, I was in my 20s, but my husband wasn't ready for children. When I married Fred, I was 33. I had time, but not much. By the time we moved to Oregon, I was 44, and it was time's up. Scary.

A lot of readers who comment here are in their late 30s or early 40s, still trying to work out the baby thing with their mates. I hate to put more pressure on you, but there's no time to waste. Men can wait, but women can't. In your discussions, show them the numbers. Maybe they'll get the point.

Anon S: Yup, Sue, this does interest me. Sort of. At 39, I know my fertile years are in decline. The numbers don't lie. Still, I don't read facts like this and think "oops, I better do something—fast." I'm not sure why, but in this area of my life I behave almost like an innocent bystander. I have unprotected sex with my husband on a mostly regular basis. If it's going to happen, it will happen. If it doesn't, then I probably won't be a mother. The lack of burning desire confuses me. Maybe I know that I don't have it in me to go the fertility route. I know I would never do in vitro (no judgment—just not for me). I'm in debt and have no savings. How would I afford these sorts of avenues anyway?

We have almost 30 nieces and nephews, many of whom we are very close to. Maybe that is enough for us? I'll probably be relieved when these "maybe" years are over. But there still feels like a piece missing. Maybe it's because society tells me it's odd for me to not have children in my family-centered small town. Maybe I feel I've disappointed my parents. Maybe I'm just sad that I won't ever know how a child of mine would look or behave. Sometimes I see a photo of my brothers' children and I feel a thrill when their smile or a bit of their profile looks like me.

I'm shedding tears as I type (quite unexpectedly), so there is something that bothers me and I continue to look for that "I'm okay. I know I'm okay" moment.

SFL: Anon S, maybe the lack of burning desire is a protective mechanism. In my experience, the hardest time is where you're at, the "maybe" years. Once it's over, it's easier to relax. The tears will still come at unexpected times. Sometimes I get angry. But most of the time it's okay. And who knows? It's not impossible to conceive after 40, just a lot less likely.

Anon S: Yeah, Sue, it could be. For the most part, the times when I wish I had a child are mostly self-serving. Example, I wish I had a little girl. I'd throw the sweetest birthday parties (because I'm creative and fun and would do a really, really cute one). I can see those super cute family photos. Christmas morning. Taking kids to get ice cream. I welcome all this FUN stuff. I've found that tagging along at a niece's birthday party I'm happy when the younger sister wants to hold my hand. Dinners out with my brother-in-law feel good when the kids fight to sit next to me. Random hugs from my older niece are great. I love talking to all these children. I truly enjoy watching their excitement, joy, whatever. A few times, my heart pulls. When a favorite niece doesn't want ME but her mom when she falls down. That is when I know I'm just a beloved aunt and nothing more. Maybe that is enough. I certainly don't mind my childfree life when they pull out of the in-laws' driveway with howling children in the back seat. Or people post on Facebook about issues with their children. I don't mind getting to do lunch and a movie whenever I want. Sometimes even the dogs weigh me down. So maybe I'm okay just as I am. Maybe.

roddma: I just love these fear-monger articles. I think they are trying to scare women more than inform them. We live in an age where women have made progress. We no longer have to live like our grandmothers. It seems having a child has taken priority over a steady relationship because you'd better not delay or else. Yes, there may be a few more risks at advanced maternal ages, but what about the overweight drug-addicted 20-somethings? I would rather gamble with my fertility later in life than take a chance on being a terrible parent. I think this generation is being encouraged to marry and have kids early like no other options exist. It just burns society for some reason that more women are staying single and child-care free. I feel sorry for these baby-obsessed women. I was that woman once and finally realized I can live a happy life with no kids. Women don't need children to be women. I just wish people would put more thought into having kids if they want to do so.

SFL: Roddma, I debated about approving this comment because it's so mean-spirited. I think you're not quite getting the point about having babies after 40. The eggs are gone. You have nothing left to make a baby with by your mid-40s. That's not fear-mongering; it's fact. Also fact is that fertility treatments don't work in the majority of cases.

Should people think hard about having children and make sure they and their mates are in the right space before they do it? Absolutely, but I will not accept people bashing people who want children in this blog.

roddma: First, I was not bashing people who want children. I wanted them myself, but learned I am still a complete woman. Women are still pressured to have kids, and I just think it's sad. Second, this article blames fertility solely on women. A woman can indeed be fertile in her early 40s. I have read other articles that refute older motherhood myths. Note they never address the positive outcomes. Halle Berry had her first child at 43 and another recently at 47. Yes she's an actor, but she is in much better shape than most 20-somethings. Add Madonna and Lucille Ball to the list, too. Also, they fail to address the 20-somethings who need fertility treatment. I am probably done with this blog. Even if we want or wanted kids, not everyone has baby hunger. And childless women are the most bashed people.

SFL: Roddma, I'll be sorry to lose you. We need people who are willing to speak out and offer different points of view. People can get pregnant in their 40s, as you say, but you can't count on that happening. Most women are getting pretty low on eggs by then. And yes, even younger women—and men—can have fertility problems. Not everyone has baby hunger; that's true. Many of the readers here are in the throes of trying to decide what to do about babies, but certainly I know lots of childless women who are completely at peace with not having children. To be honest, if you handed me a baby now, I would not be thrilled. I wish you all the best.

Anonymous: I doubt Halle Berry used her own eggs at 47. The fact is that it IS much harder to conceive AND carry to term after forty. The miscarriage rate is much higher, too. I don't see this as fear-inducing but factual.

Anonymous: I believe that women have been deceived by media into thinking that they TOO can be "like the stars." Talk to any reputable ob/gyn and he/she will tell you point blank that the chances of a woman conceiving naturally AND with her own eggs at the age of 47 are essentially a million to one. Clearly there are rare cases of "change of life" babies, but they are the exception and not the norm. The chances of conceiving each month at the age of 41 are 5 percent—and that is not even allowing for miscarriage (which is higher)—so essentially, it's a gamble to wait.

Anon E: Sue, I did get pregnant at age 45 via donor egg, and honestly I didn't consider Roddma's comments to be mean-spirited. I feel that I'm giving my child a MUCH better life than say my husband's niece who had her baby out of wedlock, has always fought the baby daddy to deny him custody or visitation, and has collected money from the government. Sorry, but that's not mean-spirited at all. JMO. And to the other Anonymous, so what if Halle Berry didn't use her own eggs at 47?

Anonymous: I got pregnant within three months the first time I ever tried. That was three months after my 40th birthday. Completely natural and healthy conception and delivery. I'm not gonna lie; the pregnancy was a little rough on me. But I was healthier than I had ever been in my life before, so there's no way to know if it would have been different earlier. What would have been different earlier: motherhood. It would have been VERY rough. My life was full of obstacles and tragedies, largely in the form of bad relationship choices with fear-based-thinking men. I met the love of my life the day after my 40th birthday. So, it happened at the right time for ME. Another thing: I won't be middle-aged till my 50s. Women in my family who have had babies in their 40s tend to live past 100. We're a bunch of badass bitches.

SFL: Anon June 30, good for you! I love badass bitches and aspire to be one. I'm so glad it worked for you, and I wish you many years of happy motherhood.

IS CHILDLESSNESS THE NORM FOR MILLENNIALS?

In response to a request for ideas for the blog, I got this response from Crystal:

I would really like to see a post about childlessness being the de facto relationship situation for millennials. It says in the title in your blog "parenting is expected." Well, for me and my experience, I would disagree with that statement. My family told me to wait to get married until 25. I was expected to go to college and find a career path. I was asked at an early age, what do you want to be when you grow up? Not, how many children would you like to have?

When I got married, my husband was still in school, racking up an $80,000 student loan debt. He graduated and had every opportunity that he needed to have a career, have enough income to afford a comfortable lifestyle, and be able to pay his student loans. Nevertheless, he used the student loans as an excuse to "wait" before having kids. I asked how long, and never got a straight answer. This is a huge topic in other blogs and forums I visit. Millennials can't afford to have kids in many instances. They are waiting longer to have kids, or just not having them. Real estate debt, student loans, and credit card debt are putting stress on the family. And the *kicker is this: no one seems to care. I was never asked about when I was going to have kids. My parents never pressured me to have kids. I even went to my friends who are the same age as me and tried to talk about it, and they were like it's so hard to have kids, you know, but it's OK for us to because we have relatives in town to help us. I was like wtf?*

As I read Crystal's comment, light bulbs lit up in my head. I am not a millennial. I grew up in the "Leave It to Beaver"[23] era when all women were expected to become moms wearing aprons and baking cookies—or that was the illusion we were given to believe. Things have changed tremendously.

I had to look up the dates that define millennials. There are different definitions, but the most common is folks born between 1982 and 2002. They're between 18 and 36 years old now. The older millennials are edging toward the end of their fertility.

I see exactly what Crystal is talking about in my friends' children and the younger members of my family. They are marrying much later than we did and putting off having children for years if not forever. In the San Francisco Bay Area where I come from, nobody with an ordinary job can afford to buy a house. Rents are two or three times what I'm paying for my four-bedroom house in Oregon. And student loans can dog a person forever. When you're already struggling to get from one pay period to the next, how can anyone think about having children?

There is tremendous pressure for both men and women to get their education and establish their careers before starting their families, by which time it might be too late. Back in that different world where I grew up, the priorities were reversed for women. We were supposed to get married and have children. Whatever else we did was extra.

I'm not a millennial or even Gen-X. But I know that many of you readers do fall into those age groups. So let's talk about it. Enlighten me. Where are you in the work-education-money-babies conundrum? What are the biggest challenges for your age group? Where do you see this heading?

Read about it:

"Nine Ways Millennials are Approaching Marriage Differently from their Parents" by Shana Lebowitz, *Business Insider*, Nov. 19, 2017[24]

"Young Americans are Killing Marriage" by Ben Steverman, *Bloomberg*, April 4, 2017[25]

Migrainefreeme: This is so interesting, I never thought about it that way. I am an older millennial (35 this year), and so much of this resonated with me. Although health issues are the primary reason for my childlessness now, I know part of it is also because parenthood wasn't on the radar for a long time as I built my career, paid off student loans and bought a house big enough to have a family in. Now I am unable to work, the house feels way too big for just two, and the mortgage payments are massive for just one wage when we budgeted for my income, too. I have lost so much in my life due to illness, but not having children is the hardest to deal with. I never thought about it as a generational thing, and I don't regret the years I spent focusing on my career, but I can't help but feel it's come at a great cost. Thanks for sharing this perspective. I don't have any answers to your questions, but I am interested to hear more on this topic.

Crystal: Hi MigraineFree, I'm the original poster. I just wanted to say something because I am the same age as you. I liked how you described yourself as not making kids a priority while you focused on your career and then bought a house, presumably the house you could raise a family in, and then it didn't work out. I just wanted to say that I was the opposite. Parenthood was always on my radar. I had a job, got married, and wanted kids right away, and we were totally "ready." I don't believe in having to have a house to have a baby. Anyway, I did "everything right" and still nothing, even though no health problems. Isn't that crazy?

Laura: Hi, also an older millennial. For my generation and background (educated professionals), about half my graduating class haven't started families. For those of us who do want kids, it's a stressful race to fit it in that 30-35 window along with paying off your student loan, trying to buy a house, and meeting the one whilst establishing your career.

I was one of the lucky ones. We have one child, but childcare takes half my salary, and I doubt we can afford a second child

Have several friends going through IVF and have been reading this blog so I can support them.

Erica: I'm a Gen Xer, born 1978, and there are some similarities. Growing up, getting married and having kids wasn't stressed as much as getting an education and "being something." But then around our late 20s to early 30s there seemed to be a sudden switch. For most of us, we got the degrees as we were told, then the jobs, but as it turned out, the jobs were unsatisfying and going nowhere. Suddenly the message was "hurry up and get married and have kids before it's too late," and everyone scrambled to get that done in that five-year window. A lot of us weren't able to. Of the six girls I lived with in college, only two had children. One of them had to pretend it was an accident to her boyfriend to make it happen. One (me) married someone who refused to have children and couldn't bring myself to do the same as she did, another divorced after a short marriage, another never got married at all, and the other married what turned out to be too late and couldn't get pregnant, I suspect. We're not in touch, so I'm not 100 percent sure on the reason, but kids never came even though she had planned on them. We were supposed to be the ones to "have it all," successful career and a family. What a joke that turned out to be.

Money is an issue too. A lot of us could still get good jobs out of college in 2000, but many were laid off between 2004 and 2008. Most of my friends were never able to afford houses. I managed to buy a townhouse, but it lost a lot of value when the housing bubble burst, so upgrading to a regular house with a yard, the kind you would imagine raising kids in, would be difficult if not impossible. I'd probably go into debt if I tried it. Because I don't have kids, I should (hopefully) be able to retire someday. Those in my cohort who do have families probably will never be able to, which is another issue and reason younger people are opting out of having kids.

DJ: I'm an older millennial at 36. I was adopted when I was a baby and all I've ever wanted was to be a mother and have children of my own. I am an only child, and my mother wants to be a grandmother, too. I went to college, accumulated student loans and am still paying them off. I live in Southern California, and the cost of living is astronomical. I have a full-time job, but it's not enough for me to buy a house or invest with. I desperately want to have a child, but my boyfriend of three years does not. He doesn't believe in marriage (another millennial trend). My boyfriend owns a house, but depends on me for half the mortgage payment every month. We couldn't afford to do it alone. We have a wonderful life together. It's very peaceful, but a little too quiet. I always dreamed of having a house full of kids all running around, playing with friends, etc. If I stay with him any longer, I'm afraid I will age out of having children of my own. I'm not sure if I could even afford to have one by myself. I would probably have to move back into my mom's house. I love my boyfriend, but I have to make a tough decision VERY soon. Do I stay with him and never have kids? Or leave him and try another way. At my age, I would have to immediately start dating, hopefully find a partner who also wants kids, fall in love, get married, and then . . . hope for a successful pregnancy. After all of that, I'd be pushing 40. At this point, I feel like my best and quickest option is to go to a sperm bank and be a single mother. I feel paralyzed, and I can't make a decision.

All my girlfriends got married and had kids years ago. I do feel left behind, and it's very hard to look at all their cute baby pics on social media. It just makes me sad to think I will never get to experience motherhood. I feel like I wasted so much time on a career that didn't pan out and dating the wrong guys. I'm finally with a really great man, but I'm not sure his love can fill the void of having no children. I'm devastated. I know if I stay with him, I will regret never having children, and I will end up resenting him for it. I read this blog searching for advice to help push me in the right direction—either coming to terms with being childless or jumping off that cliff of uncertainty and starting over on a new path with no guarantee of having a child of my own.

Crystal: Hi DJ. I have advice for you. Take it or leave it, I guess. I am very much pro-baby. I had a baby last year, after a marriage with no kids. We got divorced because of that issue. You sound like a wonderful person who would be a wonderful mother. Also your mother, who wants grandchildren, would be a wonderful grandmother. When my older sister had her first child, and my mother became a grandmother for the very first time, even though I knew my parents were awesome, I was totally blown away by how wonderful my parents were at being grandparents. It was amazing to see that loving bond.

First of all, your boyfriend, who owns a house and can't afford this house without you and doesn't believe in marriage, is a tool. There is absolutely no excuse for him depending on you for half the mortgage payment, unless he is willing to give you a ring and properly wed you, AND make all your dreams come true. Since he doesn't believe in marriage, why should you believe in having a nuclear family? I think your sperm bank baby idea is the perfect answer to his non-belief in marriage, (while having ALL the benefits of a WIFE). It is 2018. If men don't want marriage, and they basically just want what they want all the time, then women should respond in kind. Also, an added benefit is if you and your boyfriend break up, and then you go and date again, there won't be any baby daddy drama. I'm not a lawyer or anything, but in the state I live in, I have seen how long-time boyfriend-girlfriend cohabitating people end up going through a divorce court situation where the ex gets half of the house that she lived in and helped pay for, just FYI. You are his common-law wife, okay?

I was going to write another paragraph about how having a baby really isn't as hard as everyone makes it out to be. But I don't have any way to judge your own situation. I say go for the sperm bank!

Rach: My husband and I are in our early 30s. Together for over 10 years and married for four. I always assumed I would be a mom and really do want the experience. HOWEVER, college left me with a crapload of debt, and while my job pays decent enough, I will still be paying these things off forever. Add that to my husband deciding he couldn't stand to work for someone else anymore and started his own business that makes very little (which I initially supported but really don't think it's worth the stress anymore). So here we are in our early 30s with mountains of credit card and student loan debt due to bad choices in our younger years. I am also the breadwinner and wouldn't be able to afford being out of work for any substantial amount of time. Add that to lack of affordable childcare in our area and a minimal support system. My husband thinks it would all magically work out if we went ahead and tried for kids but isn't begging to have them either.

We now have too much debt and never traveled or did any of the things I always wanted before starting a family. By the time we would be in a position that I would feel comfortable with, I'll be close to 40. I don't want to bring a child into a financially unstable home or one with older parents. We both have parents who died young, and due to health issues, being older parents probably isn't a great idea for us either.

What really gets me is the few times I have expressed my concern to a friend or family member as to why we have postponed having a baby, they usually respond with "There is never a good time," "Oh you'll figure it out," or something like "Babies really aren't that expensive" and "You can still travel with kids!" I do believe there are better times to bring a child into this world though, and I also believe in taking my mental health (and my husband's) into consideration. It isn't fair to purposely bring a child into this world when we aren't stable enough to feel comfortable with it.

So now I am trying to come to terms and reconcile my past choices and what it means for my future. While I really, really want to have a child, I don't want to continue the pattern of financial or emotional issues because I grew up in that kind of household and don't want to do that to another child. With the debt we have at this point, we won't be living it up without children, but at least I can find some comfort in knowing that I'm not projecting our struggles onto another living person.

ARE YOU WAITING UNTIL CONDITIONS ARE PERFECT?

I have heard that in nature animals will not reproduce if conditions are not right, if there's not enough food or a safe place to nest. Plants don't grow and reproduce without the right mix of nutrients, sun and water. What about people?

During the Great Depression (1929-1939),[26] birth rates dropped to 1.9 per woman in the U.S. Couples could barely feed themselves; how could they feed their children? The birth rate went up to over 3.5 during the baby boom that followed World War II. At that time, the economy was flourishing. People could get good jobs. They could afford to buy homes and raise children.

During the "Great Recession" that started in 2007, birth rates dived again,[27] back to 1.9, and they have not come back up.

I got to thinking about all this after reading an article at Jezebel by Madeleine Davies titled "With Environmental Disasters Looming, Many are Choosing Childless Futures."[28] She discusses how some people are deciding not to have children because they worry about the environment and the world into which these babies would be born. That world includes the wildfires, floods and hurricanes that have devastated much of the U.S. recently. I would add mass shootings, terrorist attacks, political upheaval, wars, and families living far from each other.

Workers in my dad's day were reasonably confident that they could stay in the same job and live in the same house until they chose to retire. Who can count on that now? In Silicon Valley, high tech companies pay high wages, but they also lay people off by the thousands. The cost of living is ridiculous. It feels like we have to keep changing jobs and keep moving just to keep up with the bills. How can we add a child to this situation?

But let's go beyond the big-picture issues. How many of us with reluctant-to-parent mates have heard variations of "conditions are not right?" We need to finish school, get better jobs, save more money, buy a house, etc. In other words, we need to make everything perfect. But time is passing, and perfection is impossible. Maybe we can have it for a moment, but then the job goes away, a tree falls on the house, or someone gets sick. Maybe we should try for "good enough."

I could be wrong, but I think men generally worry about the money part more than women do. They feel the burden of supporting a family, even when their partners provide half the income. Women, full of hormones and watching the biological clock, are more likely to say, "We'll figure it out." Am I totally wrong on this?

Let's talk about it. Are you putting off having children until conditions are right? What would need to change? Do you worry about the world into which they would be born? Do you know others who are having these feelings?

Erica: While this isn't the reason my husband refused to have children, I have thought of this before. Sometimes it makes me feel a little better about the fact that I didn't bring a child into this messed-up world. I feel like I spared "my children" from a future that isn't looking very good for anyone.

Anon S: In my life, I've always been waiting until things feel "right." Those who have lived with an alcoholic might understand. Who wants to be pregnant and have to get out of bed to pick up hubby/daddy-to-be at the bar? Right. Weeks of sobriety turn into months, and you start to feel "right." Then a family wedding or the Super Bowl happens, and you have to start all over again. And you are thankful that you didn't get pregnant that month that you thought you might have been. Months of that cycle turn into years and suddenly your clock is ticking louder than before. You lost track of time but your body sure didn't.

These days, my marriage is solid. For years and years, it's been solid and wonderful. I'm stronger and better than I've ever been. But somewhere along the line I must have conditioned myself into not playing that game. We seem to be holding our breath. Waiting for another week of good. Another month of sobriety. Another year of trying to save money.

I have a cousin who can never arrive anywhere on time. She tries hard, sets an alarm, puts her things by the front door, etc. But she's always late. Everyone knows she will arrive after the bride has been down the aisle. She slides in after the toasts at a retirement party. Her kid is always the last to shrug off his coat and "catch up with the others." Some people just can't get it together. I sometimes feel like the "expectant mother" equivalent of my cousin. I just never got it together.

There is a point in your life when a person at a party might reasonably ask, "So how many children do you have?" Then there is the point in your life where people feel comfortable saying, "So, you never had any kids, huh?" The timeline between these two gaps is full of possibility and uncertainty. I think I'm waiting to bridge that gap. To get securely to that other end. To know. To finally feel right.

4

BABY LUST

Last Saturday night at church, I played piano for the First Communion Mass. It's a big deal. The little kids, mostly Hispanic at Sacred Heart, dress up in white, sit up front with their *padres* and *padrinos,* and become big kids in the church, finally allowed to consume the bread and wine.

They brought their whole families, which included lots of crying babies. I became fascinated with this little guy sitting near the front. His mother and grandfather kept trading off, trying to calm his cries and squirms. I found myself aching to hold him, to hold any of the babies. Even if they were crying and drooling.

I rarely get to hold babies. The last time was at Thanksgiving when I cuddled my niece's six-month-old daughter for a while. So sweet. I loved talking to her, watching her smile at me, letting her wrap her tiny fingers around my big hand. Now she's a year old. I missed the birthday party because I was up here in Oregon playing the piano so other people's kids could have First Communion. I'll never get to dress a little girl in white, teach her the Our Father and Hail Mary and take lots of photos to treasure forever. You'd think I'd be over it by now. Nope. My friends, this is a hunger that will keep coming back.

At my age, I'm not anxious to deal with dirty diapers or sleepless nights. I just want to hold a baby. The child doesn't have to be mine, just one I could see often enough so that she or he knows who I am and feels comfortable in my arms. Like a grandma.

People not in my situation would suggest I find a way to spend more time with the little ones in the family, maybe even move back to California. It would be easier if I had a bigger family that I saw more often, with a bunch of siblings and their offspring who would come running to Aunt Sue. I think about that a lot, but I have a full life that I enjoy right here on the Oregon coast.

I could volunteer to do babysitting or daycare or some other activity that puts me in close contact with little kids. But somehow it feels too late. I was so busy avoiding babies in my reproductive years when I was trying to accept that I would never have one that I never learned the mothering skills that seem so natural to other women.

Of course babies don't stay babies. A friend who just came back from her grandson's birthday party complained that the kid paid no attention to her; he was glued to his cell phone the whole time. I'd probably snatch the phone away, and then he'd hate me. At least we don't have to deal with that.

What do you think? Is there a substitute that really fills the void for those of us who are childless? Do you get the baby hunger, too?

Dubliner in Deutschland: Here in Germany, there is an organization that matches up older people with young families. It's meant for people who either don't have grandkids or theirs live far away. It's a nice idea, as the older people can be lonely and young families are grateful for a bit of support.

SFL: That sounds wonderful. We need more of that in the U.S. So many older people are alone most of the time, even if they have children and grandchildren.

Laura: For those babies that you desperately want to hold for a minute, maybe find a local coffee shop that you could become a regular at and see if you can get friendly with other regular customers. When you see that mum who just wants a minute of time to enjoy her coffee, offer to hold that baby or toddler for her to give her a break. I often see my mum do the same for others in our cafe and whilst it helps that customers now recognize her as my mum, I see the light in their eyes for someone who's willing to help them out for just that one minute when they are sitting in their own midnight of crying babies, dirty nappies and other motherhood juggles. Sending you light and joy.

Stacy: I am 42 and a childless stepmom. I thought I was the only one who craves to hold babies. I tried to have a baby of my own, but many attempts and fertility treatments, even IVF, ended in a miscarriage and I never got that experience. My fiancé's children were 6 and 8 when we met, so I never had any baby experiences. Every time I see babies, I instantly want to hold them and smell them, everything. It's definitely a longing that I completely understand. Not being able to have children is a loss that is hard to deal with every day.

DO YOU FANTASIZE ABOUT BEING PREGNANT?

I've been watching "Jane the Virgin"[29] on Netflix. It's a fun show about this young Hispanic woman who was accidentally inseminated with sperm from her boss. The whole thing is a spoof on the wildly melodramatic Spanish telenovelas. If watching someone's pregnancy grow with every episode bothers you, you might not enjoy it.

I liked Jane, but it sent me flashing back to my first marriage, when I often fantasized about being pregnant. Sometimes I'd wear big tops and let people wonder if I was hiding a baby underneath. I'd feel my abdomen and imagine it was getting a little bigger. I'd even sit and stand as if I were carrying a baby. I crocheted a lot of baby booties. Even though we were using birth control every time, I wanted that feeling. I physically yearned to be pregnant. I also wanted to do what other women my age were doing and get the extra attention that comes with it.

I used to have dreams about being pregnant. Do you? Sometimes those dreams would be so real, I'd wake up expecting to feel the baby bump and be devastated when I realized it wasn't real.

Sure, I didn't long for the pains that come with pregnancy and delivery or the sleepless nights that come with a newborn, but I wanted to be pregnant. It was the 70s. I was 20-something and married. Everyone, including me, assumed we'd be having children.

Then my period would come, cramps would tear me apart, and my belly would feel flat and useless. For 40 years, I suffered through painful periods and PMS as my body prepared for pregnancies that didn't happen. What a waste.

Maybe women who never wanted to have children don't experience these feelings. Maybe their baby dreams are nightmares. There were certainly years between marriages when I did not want to get pregnant. Now that pregnancy is impossible, when my belly feels big, I think I shouldn't have eaten so many French fries. But in those early years, sometimes I could convince myself that it was really happening.

Men who might be reading this, I don't think you can possibly understand how this feels. Women's bodies are made for baby-making. Dramatic things happen inside for that purpose. All you have to do is provide sperm. So when your mate starts whining about wanting to have babies, be aware that their bodies are nagging them as much as they're nagging you.

I tried to find a link for you to read more about pregnancy fantasies and came up with porn sites about guys who get off on pregnant bellies. Not what I was looking for, but I guess that's a thing. I also found several sites that show how you fake being pregnant. Honest to God, there's www.fakeababy.com.[30] They think it's funny. It's not so funny for us, is it?

What do you think about all this? Male and female, I'd love to read your comments.

gr8southlandgirl: I don't remember fantasizing about being pregnant, but I often dreamed about my toddlers playing on the lounge room floor or my kids running around the back yard. I was never a clucky woman, but I did expect to have some of my own kids in my future.

I too suffered painful PMS and periods. It would knock me out for a day or three. Being a teen back in the 70s, you only went to the GP for serious health issues. When I did finally go to get it seen to, he mentioned that the first birth would usually settle the hormones, and the cramps would likely ease off or disappear. Ha ha, bittersweet advice, never to see the light of day. Nowadays, thank goodness for ibuprofen!

I wasn't overly invested in having kids (it would happen one day, I thought), so I couldn't understand how the grief and hurt I felt when I realized it would never happen was so raw and deep. As you say, it's our bodies nagging us as much as our brains.

mrsp: My doctor told me the same thing. Of course, no babies materialized, so . . . when I hit menopause, I was quite bitter about it—all that discomfort and pain for nothing.

I used to have baby dreams—I would dream I'd had a baby.

Once, I dreamt I had a gorgeous little girl—she looked about six years old. When I woke up, I realized that my (very early) miscarriage would have resulted in a child of about that age.

A.Roddy: While I think it's natural to desire kids, the desire often crosses into a mental illness. I recall a movie on Lifetime once where a woman pretends to be pregnant, perhaps after a miscarriage. I know in one scene the husband says, "I'm not taking you to the hospital." She pretends to be a nurse and takes a patient's baby. I want to say it's "Empty Cradle."[31] Fantasizing seems innocent, but as I said it can have a dark side. I point fingers at the pressure put on women, plus the controversy over whether there's such a thing as pregnancy addiction. I guess wanting babies is seen as natural and not something that can become sinister.

Navigating Childlessness: I can so relate to your article! I used to dream of being pregnant, too. One of the worst times during all of the infertility treatments I went through so many years ago was when I was approached by more than one person asking if I FINALLY got pregnant. I hadn't; I just blew up like a puffer fish during an IVF cycle.

SUDDENLY WE'RE ALL WEARING MATERNITY CLOTHES

I became an adult in the late 60s and early 70s, when women wore mini-skirts and platform shoes, peasant blouses and bell-bottom pants. In high school, I had some psychedelic-patterned, tent-shaped dresses so big you could have hidden another person in there. They seem hideous now, but that was the style.

Pregnant women wore "maternity clothes," stretchy bottoms and big blouses with Peter Pan collars, bows, and lacy sleeves. The object was not only to make room for the baby, but to be "modest," a word we don't hear much anymore. As desirable as it was to have children, there was something crass about showing one's baby bump in public.

I never had a baby bump. I had a my-period-is-late-and-I'm-so-bloated bump. I had a my-period-is-late-and-please-God-let-me-be-pregnant bump. And these days I have a can't-stop-eating-mayonnaise-and-French-fries bump, but I never had a baby bump. That did not stop me in my days as a young married woman from wearing big clothes and hoping people thought I might be pregnant.

In today's tight dresses, there's no way to hide one's pregnancy status, but back then, it was easy to pretend, to play mommy-to-be dress-up.

More than the actual baby, I think I wanted the public affirmation of my womanhood, the approval, and the excitement of entering the next phase of my life. Instead of maternity clothes, I put on suits, narrow skirts, slacks and blazers for my career as a journalist.

Why do I think of this now? I realized the other day as I put on my leggings and matching "tunic," that we're all walking around in pseudo-maternity clothes. I could wear that stretchy outfit all the way to my delivery date if I were pregnant. I don't know about where you live, but all the women and girls here in western Oregon are wearing leggings. They're only flattering if you have a perfect figure. They're not warm enough in the winter. Some derrieres are showing that shouldn't be shown. But they're comfortable, and if you wear a big top, who cares how many French fries you eat?

Ironically, the women who are actually pregnant don't try to hide their pregnancies. The other night at a concert, I saw a young woman wearing shorts and a tank top that stretched way out with her pregnancy of at least eight months. No frilly blouses and stretch pants for her. We have all seen celebrities flaunting their "baby bumps." There's no doubt what's going on in their uteruses.

When you're clothes shopping, do you ever accidentally find yourself in the maternity section? I rush out of there as if someone is going to catch me and point out that I don't belong. What do you do? Do you long for those Baby on Board tee shirts or try not to look at them?

Am I the only one who has worn big clothes and hoped people assumed for a little while that I might be pregnant? Do you know anyone who has?

I apologize if this whole discussion is making you feel bad. From my post-menopausal perspective, it's interesting. And now that I have Googled "maternity clothes," I will be plagued with ads for pregnancy-related merchandise by the heartless algorithms of the Internet.

Click here for a look at maternity fashion through history.[32]

SilverShil0h: I hadn't really thought of this. You are spot on, Sue. I guess the big question is: How does that make me feel? No matter what clothes they're wearing, I still feel like less of a woman around a pregnant woman. My insecurity, nothing they have done to me personally. I don't long for the more modest maternity styles. Although knowing me, I doubt I'd be purposefully showing off my bump if I were blessed to have one. It's just not me. Changing gears, I'm grateful for loose clothes—and French fries.

Jenny: I don't look at the maternity clothes. A friend who was pregnant 17 years ago bemoaned all the frilly-edged items on offer to her. She did have some nice embroidered jeans that I'd hoped to borrow when it was "my turn."

I do still look in the baby clothes departments. I buy baby and toddler clothes from charity shops for a charity near me that sends a container to Tanzania each year. It gives me a bit of a fix.

THE SOFT KISS OF A LITTLE GIRL

Every Sunday at St. Martin's Church in San Jose, a 4-year-old girl named Camille comes running to the row of seats near the back where my father sits and throws her arms around him. This stern 91-year-old man melts. "My girlfriend," he calls her. Camille is a beautiful child with long wavy hair, dewy skin and big blue eyes. Dad often talks about her, telling me how smart and fearless she is, how she already knows how to read, how she's starting school next year. Visiting from Oregon, I watch them, so jealous I could weep.

Camille has a 2-year-old brother and a 1-year-old sister (no Catholic jokes, please). They are all beautiful children and a handful for their parents. The mom and dad spend the Mass feeding them Cheerios, reading to them, shushing them, and taking them out when they get too squirmy. I don't envy them that part of it.

During the sermon, the littlest girl stares up at my father, raises her tiny hand, and Dad matches his giant hairy brown hand against it. In this sweet moment, I realize how much my father actually likes little children, and I could die for not making him a grandfather.

My father keeps the family's Christmas card, with pictures of all the kids, on the piano with pictures of me and my brother and my brother's kids.

Before Mass, Dad introduced me to the young parents, and the mother told Camille, "This is his little girl all grown up." Yes, I am my father's little girl, still going to church alone with him when I visit California and staying with the choir back in Oregon because otherwise I'd be going to Mass alone.

At the sign of peace, my father hugs me and then I see Camille reaching up for me. She kisses me on the cheek, the softest sweetest butterfly kiss. How I wish I could hold on to it forever. If only that perfect family were mine.

Know what I mean?

Anonymous: A beautiful and painfully honest essay. Yes, I do know what you mean. Your entire blog is full of experiences which are only too familiar to me. At various times, I have put a pause on attending church because of its aching emphasis on family life. I take comfort in the idea that God holds our hopes and imaginations in His heart and there, makes them real. He wipes every tear from our eyes, and makes each soft kiss from little girls our own to keep. Blessings.

DON'T KNOW NOTHIN' ABOUT BABIES

Some women can't wait to get their hands on a baby. If a mother brings her child to the office, they reach out for the little one, anxious to feel the magic of a child in their arms again. Me, I back away because I don't even know how to hold a child properly. Babies take one look at me and start crying.

My mother had the gift. Babies always seemed to know they were in good hands with her, but she had lots of practice. Her brother was much younger, and Mom was the designated babysitter. She had lots of younger cousins, too, so she knew how to handle babies, how to hold them, how to feed them, how to diaper them, how to get them to stop crying.

I grew up in a different era in a different kind of family. When my brother was born, I was still a baby myself. My parents didn't have any more kids. All the children on our block were the same ages as Mike and I. I did not have babies around to take care of—unless you count my Tiny Tears doll. When I tried babysitting in my teens, it was a disaster.

As a young married woman, I was surrounded by other young married women who were not ready for children. If they had had babies, or if my first marriage had lasted longer, maybe I would have gotten used to being around them. But I got divorced, and when I married again, I married a much older man whose kids were nearly grown and whose friends' children were already adults. I missed the baby train altogether. I got a small taste with the step-grand-children, but not enough to compete with experienced mom-types. I still can't put on a diaper so it doesn't fall off.

Dogs are a different story. I am a fully qualified dog mom. But I missed the training for people moms. How about you? Did you grow up with lots of babies around? Were or are you surrounded by women who have children? Are you comfortable around babies, or are you stranded on the Planet No-Kids like me?

Professionally childless: As a teenager, I'd say I was a professional babysitter. Comfortable around kids, their parents liked me, the works. But then I went to college and then grad school. I went through a phase where, as a 20-something, a baby meant the end of your career. Babies were to be avoided, not cuddled. They were simply not part of my life and I didn't think about them. I figured I had plenty of time to get back to that sometime in the future. Unfortunately, it didn't work out that way for me! I love babies, children. I have nephews whom I love spending time with, the crazy monkeys. It is the biggest regret of my life that I didn't focus on making a family sooner. I am in my 40s, married only two years, and childless. After six IVF attempts, it looks as though it will stay that way and I am heartbroken, in a state of despair. I am glad I found this site. I don't know what else to do.

Libby: I have been around a few babies, but I'm not entirely comfortable around unfamiliar babies. Years ago, I lived two doors down from my sister. She had three children, all spaced two years apart. I was there for all three births and was at her house every evening after work to help cook dinner, bathe kids, and just play. I could do anything with those kids. Then she moved to the other side of the state, and now I only see them a couple of times a year.

Other kids, well, I just haven't had a lot of time with them. And it seems to me like they must be able to pick up on that. The tiniest ones always howl when they are handed to me.

As for puppies? I'm a pro! I can take care of any dog, any size, any age, any temperament. They all love me.

Professionally childless: Thank you, Sue. My advice to you is, next time someone plops a baby in your lap, think of it as a puppy with a big head. Not too much difference, really. They both need food, sleep, and warmth. They may even like the same type of toys. The calmer you are, the calmer they can be. As you know, dogs, other animals, and human beings can sense fear and anxiety coming from someone. Whether an infant is capable of doing so ("I make babies cry"), I'm not sure. But it's a start to set your anxiety aside (if it's there at all) and to think of the lovely new "puppiness" in your presence and what joy it brings. The good news is that you get to hand it back to the parent when it starts to cry!

SFL: Pro, thanks for the advice. Puppy with big head. Got it. Next time I have the chance, I'll put this advice to work. Somebody pass me a baby.

THAT BABY'S A REAL DOLL!

I explored the toy section at Wal-Mart to find out what dolls girls were playing with these days. I'll admit that I wanted to play with some of those dolls. The baby dolls were so realistic I wanted to free them from their wrappers and hug them against my barren breasts. But I didn't. It's a small town, and I don't want people to think I'm nuts.

However, it seems some women actually do buy baby dolls as substitutes for real babies. They're calling them "Reborn" babies or "memory" babies. For the whole story, read "Fake Babies Ease Women's Anxiety, Sadness,"[33] published last week at MSNBC.com. Author Dr. Gail Saltz explains the therapeutic value of dolls for empty-nesters, women whose babies have died, and childless women. Unlike real babies, dolls never cry or need clean diapers, but in some odd way they provide some of the same positive feelings as real infants. "It fills a place in your heart," doll-maker Lynn Katsaris told Matt Lauer.

There's a British documentary called "My Fake Baby: New Life with Reborn Dolls."[34] A clip from the film shows a woman carrying her "baby" around a grocery store. People who stop to admire it are amazed to discover it isn't real.

I'm ready to call this just plain nuts, but then again after my dog Sadie died, I purchased a dog statue made of stone. It's about a foot and a half high and sits on my hearth gazing up at Sadie's picture. I call him Stoney and make jokes about how he's such an easy dog to care for. The idea was to purchase a memorial to my beloved pet, but before we got the new puppies (agh, wild mudballs!), I sometimes talked to Stoney and thought of him as my dog.

So who am I to say we're too old for dolls, especially as Chatty Cathy looks down on me while I type?

FreeSpirit: I am a 41-year-old woman from London. I have never been in a relationship where we were ready to have kids or the man wanted to. I have just found out that I am perimenopausal and whilst I knew it was getting a bit late to have kids, this news has left me very upset. I have never had a great urge to have children, but always wanted the choice. In my sadness, I saw these Reborn dolls and the urge to own one was overwhelming!! So I searched online, found one I loved the look of (that I thought looked like I might as a baby) and bought it, but I feel so ashamed!!! Like it's a dirty secret. It hasn't arrived yet, but I don't think I can show anyone when it does! I feel SO sad. The link you gave in your blog made me feel a bit better, but I still feel I have no one to talk to.

Dianne: I like your post, FreeSpirit, and I am in exactly the same boat. I hope the people close to me can understand that it may be "only a doll," but it does help fill a terrible void.

5

HOW DO YOU HEAL FROM CHILDLESS GRIEF?

MY 2007 POST ABOUT CHILDLESS GRIEF has been the most clicked and commented on over the last 13 years. Almost 300 comments at this point. Readers continue to pour out heartbreaking stories about being denied the chance to have children and finding the loss unbearable. They write, "I don't know what to do." "I can't go on." "My heart is breaking." I tell them I'm sorry. I tell them I'm praying for them. I urge them to find someone to talk to, whether it's a friend, family member, or therapist. I tell them to keep talking with their spouse; don't hurt in silence.

The pain is real. The loss is real. You are trying to figure out how to live without the family and the life you thought you would have. It's not just the children. It's not just grandchildren and descendants through the ages. It's a way of life, an identity as a mother or father, an experience that most people have and you never will.

How do you begin to heal? What do you do with this pain? Even if you do eventually have children, you won't forget the years when you thought you never would, so healing is needed.

The stages of grief outlined by Elisabeth Kubler-Ross[35] can be applied here: denial, anger, bargaining, depression, and acceptance.

DENIAL: He'll change his mind. I'll get pregnant by accident. We'll do IVF. She's 43, but it's not too late. We all do this. We think a miracle will happen, and we will have a baby. While we're waiting for that miracle, our lives are passing us by.

ANGER: It's his/her/God's fault, and I am so pissed. He cheated me out of my chance to be a mother. She's too selfish to give me the children I always wanted. I never should have married this @#$%. I'm an idiot. And God, you suck.

BARGAINING: I'll let him get his degree/sports car/trip to Europe, and then we'll get pregnant. If I get a second job, she'll change her mind. If we move to Cleveland, which I hate, he'll let us have a baby.

DEPRESSION: I am so sad I can't go on. I want to have babies. I want them so bad I die every time I hear about somebody else having a baby. My friends and my sisters are all having kids, and I feel so left out. They don't understand. Nobody understands. I'm never going to have children, and my life is ruined.

ACCEPTANCE: They say you have to hit bottom before you can start working your way out of your troubles. One day, you will begin to see that although you don't have children, life has many other good things to offer: a partner who loves you, great food, blue skies and green trees, work you enjoy, a house you love, hobbies, friends, God. You realize lots of other people do not have children and live happy, successful lives, and you can, too. You still wish you had children, but life goes on, whether you're a parent or not.

As anyone who has suffered the loss of a loved one knows, we don't progress through the stages of grief in a straight line. One day you're feeling acceptance; the next day you're back at depression or anger or denial. I still feel sad sometimes, and sometimes I cry and punch things because I'm furious at how my life worked out. But the acceptance grows with time until it becomes your usual mood.

Karen: I believe you've hit on a part of why so many childless by chance women stay quiet. It's not only that it can be perceived as "whining" by the rest of the world. It is true grief. No one runs around always talking about their dead mother, for example, if they know they'll be in tears after a single sentence.

Our triggers are omnipresent and offered to us by people who, even if they intellectually know of our pain, don't seem to see our repeated hurts and how something as "simple" as a sonogram is a saber blade.

Anonymous: We are entitled to have any feeling, including sadness over no children, but my stance remains solid that not having children is not death. It is a conscious choice. Medically unable? Adopt. No child by choice? Then let's fill our lives with positive fillers, or good juju as I call it, and look forward, and not dwell on what could have been. On a personal note, my mom told me once that anyone can make a baby, but it takes a real man to be a father. For those who cannot, or choose not, to have children, I encourage them to go fill their life with happiness in other ways. Adopt, volunteer at elementary schools or chaperone the local high school prom. Be a baseball coach, or become a youth leader in a church. We have the power of choice, and we can fill our childless lives with activities that will make us whole.

Anonymous: I grieve lots about the children I am never to have. I'm 42, and I fantasize almost daily that I will accidentally get pregnant and have a little miracle baby. But, alas, my husband adamantly does not want that (nor do I think it's wise given my age). Most of the time, I don't feel the extreme wave of sadness until something triggers it. Today that was a friend's announcement on Facebook that she is expecting, complete with ultrasound picture. I came home in such a happy mood, and now I find myself plummeting toward my dark, childless hole. I'm sure I'll be fine, but in the moment, it hurts!

SFL: And here we have both sides of the story. Childlessness is not death, you're right, Anonymous #1. But it is a loss, and it does hurt, as Anonymous #2 tells us. I think it's important to acknowledge that pain and know that we have a right to grieve. But I also agree that one can't stay in that grieving place forever. After a while, we need to move on and do whatever we need to do to fill the gap. If we just can't move on, it's okay to seek help in the form of therapy or whatever it takes.

Anonymous: SFL said, "And the grief will come back again and again, like any big loss." VERY true words, Sue! I'm 66 years old and single, childless "not" by choice, and most any woman and especially group of women my age will appropriately and understandably be talking on (and on) about children and mostly grandchildren. "Moving on" is hard enough, but the frequent "being a wife/ mother is what we're put on earth to do," "children/grandchildren are blessings from God" type expressions make me feel even more like an abject outsider and NOT "blessed" or deemed worthy.

Anonymous: "And the grief will come back again and again, like any big loss." My first loss was Aug 10th, 1987. I struggled with infertility until 1998 when I finally gave up and thought I put "closure" on my grief. Now, at 49, I am feeling a huge loss and emptiness as I watch my peers with their grandchildren. I never anticipated this would hurt as much. And I fear 25 more years and dying alone with no family around me.

Anonymous: I grieve the loss of ever having a real family more than the child itself. Besides my husband, the only family I have are my parents. As I get older, inevitably it will only be my husband, and maybe then eventually just me all alone if I'm unlucky enough to outlive him. I've tried in the past to create a "family" of sorts with friends, but it just doesn't work. They all have their own things going on, and don't have the time to indulge me in being my surrogate family. It seems as people get older, family takes up a larger portion of their lives, and as I get deeper into my 30s and start to get too old to hang at bars with the 20-somethings, I feel like there's just no place for me in the world. It's hard enough knowing that I'll never get to experience holding my newborn baby in my arms, but to think that as lonely as I am now it's only going to get progressively worse, that's what really hurts.

Fizz: This is going to sound strange, but I feel so sad because of the child I had planned with my partner but never had. We talked loads about having a baby after we got married. When we went shopping for gifts for my baby nephew, we'd talk excitedly about when we had OUR little baby one day. We had names picked out. I had dreams of this little boy. So did my partner. We talked about him a lot and were so looking forward to being a family in the coming couple of years. Fast forward a year, and my partner left me. We were supposed to be trying for our baby in the next six months. I think I'm always going to wonder what would have been. I'm pushing 35 now and I just don't DO love and relationships. I thought I'd found my soulmate and my happy ever after. I never even wanted kids before we met. Now, I feel so stupid for grieving for something that never even existed.

SFL: It's not stupid at all, Fizz. You have lost a child and a marriage, and it sounds like you have lost your belief in love, too. You are entitled to grieve. I wish you peace.

Anonymous: I am reading all of these posts as I sit at work, trying, again, to hold back the tears. I had to come to accept the four miscarriages I had, which I have. Then we started the private adoption process, and shortly after, I was laid off from work in 2012. This delayed the adoption process, since we were running low on funds in order to keep our home. Now I am grateful to have found a job. However, I am making much less, given the economy. After realizing things are still tight, I thought, "How can we afford daycare at over $1,000 a month?" So, we have made the painful decision to move on. Sometimes I feel more pain, even a little resentful because my husband has two grown children.

Everyone around me has children. It's not fair. What made them better parents than me? Why do people who mistreat their children get blessed with them? It is like a death. I am going through all of the different parts of the grieving process, sadness, anger, emptiness. I don't know how to start to feel better.

RITUALS TO VANQUISH CHILDLESS GRIEF

Dear friends, losing our chance to have children is a real loss, in many ways like a death. We lose the life we had expected to live, the identity of being a mother or father, and the children, grandchildren, and great-grandchildren we will never have. When you want those things and can't have them, it hurts down to your bones.

Previously, I wrote about the stages of grief. Today I want to talk about rituals, things we can do to help get past the grief.

After my mother died, my husband and I took two bottles of Mr. Bubble to a cliff overlooking Nye Beach. Fred thought I was crazy, but we started blowing bubbles. "Goodbye, Mom," I said. "Go, be free." Some bubbles landed in the bushes and some melted into the sand, but others kept soaring over the beach until they disappeared into the clouds. You know what? We felt better. Afterward, we adjourned to a nearby bar, toasting Mom's memory. Ten years later, on the first anniversary of Fred's death, I blew bubbles again from the deck in our back yard. I also sang some of his favorite songs, remembering the times he had been there, listening and singing along. It helped.

Writing can be a great way to let go of feelings. Even if you're not usually a writer, try writing a letter to your unborn children, telling them everything you would like to tell them if they were here. You can keep the letters in a special place or burn them as a symbolic way of letting the children go.

Talk to your children. Go somewhere private and say what's in your heart. For several years, I "met" with my mom at a gazebo overlooking the beach, bringing her up to date on everything that was happening in our lives. It felt like she was still here.

Try hypnosis. I used it several times when my grief became overwhelming, and it truly helped. It's not weird, it's not voodoo. I knew what was happening at all times, but I was able to relax and let go. My therapist led me through conversations with my loved ones, living and dead, pouring out all the feelings and words I could never release on my own.

Create a symbol for your pain and send it into the world. Put a note in a bottle and toss it into the ocean. Write the names of your would-have-been children on rocks and arrange them in your garden. Hang a streamer off a tree or a pole. Make an ornament to hang on your Christmas tree.

Create art expressing your feelings and honoring your unborn children. Whether it's painting, sculpture, needlework, or another form of art, working with your hands to put it into a physical form can help deal with the grief.

Hold a ceremony, complete with prayers, readings, food and music. Invite friends and family to acknowledge your loss and honor your unborn children. Having your loved ones' support can be a huge help in moving forward.

These websites offer more suggestions for letting go of childless grief:

"Leaving and Grieving Ceremony/Ritual"[36]

"Grieving Ceremony"[37]

There are lots of ways to symbolically let go of grief. Nothing takes it away completely, but these rituals can help you move on.

"I'M NEVER GOING TO BE A MOTHER"

Can you say "I'm never going to be a mother"? Calmly? Without tears? You're a stronger woman than I am.

Back when Fred and I were engaged but not yet married, he told me on a camping trip that he really didn't want to have any more children. I was upset, but I never really accepted the situation as permanent, and I married him anyway. As I say in my *Childless by Marriage* book,

"Despite Fred's declaration in the woods, I honestly believed that somehow I would still have children. But how did I expect that to happen? Immaculate Conception? One stubborn sperm that survived the vasectomy? I was 50 before I could say, 'I am never going to be a mother' and mean it. I have asked dozens of childless women if they could say it out loud. Most had no problem with it. But just as I delude myself that I can lose weight while eating muffins for breakfast every morning, I held on to the idea that I might still have a baby."

Crazy? Perhaps. When it began to dawn on me that it really might never happen, I felt sorry for myself, as if this terrible fate had been placed upon me. It took a long time to understand that I consciously married a man who neither wanted nor was able to make me pregnant. That situation was not going to change. I chose Fred over children.

So, I am never going to be a mother.

How about you? Can you say this? Do you foresee being able to say it?

If not and there's still time, you may need to take drastic steps to make it happen.

Anonymous: I can't say it. I want to be able to say it with acceptance, but for now I can't. I am childless due to health. At the end of May, I had a hysterectomy, and while it was a great move physically, the mental and emotional suffering is harder than I thought. I have many cousins having babies, and I am happy for them. I am also sad for what I will never have. I try to say it now, and I cry. A lot. Someday I will say it with conviction.

certainlydifferent: Depends on the day. Last night I burst into tears when I came across an article for new parents, and there was a picture of the classic new parent (mom in hospital bed and dad holding swaddled baby). I am childless by marriage. I knew he wouldn't be able to provide children before we were married, but I was in love, and we said we could always adopt. After seven years, it didn't happen, and then a diagnosis of Ankylosing Spondylitis[38] made my life 100 times harder. Having kids would be so much more difficult. But still I dream about bringing a baby home, and it hurts to wake up from those dreams.

ciciwright: I'm able to say it, but it's just been a recent thing. I'm so happy to finally be at this place of peace. I'm sure it will still come and go and some days will be easier than others, but for now, I'm enjoying this phase.

Anonymous: I can't say it—yet. I am pretty sure I won't be able to until menopause. My sister is adopting, but we can't adopt due to my husband's medical condition. We would need fertility treatment to have kids and sadly, although it's not crazy expensive since there's nothing wrong with me, we still can't afford it (My life is run by medical bills and student loans). So I always think, if we suddenly get more money before I get much older, it could still happen. Deep down, I know it won't, but I can't cope with the idea that I will end up not only childless but broke (and childless because of being broke). My mom and sister try to make it "better" by saying that if I don't have kids, it's not so bad because "babies are expensive anyway." (Yes. That's how it works. A huge life tragedy is totally mitigated because of a small impact on another huge life tragedy. Good one, Mom.) Saying I am never going to be a mother due to the lack of "something" that is all over the place . . . I just can't do that yet.

Holly: I'm never going to be a mother. It hurts. Most days I'm okay, but not today. Mother's Day is approaching. It just reminds me of what I don't have.

I love my husband and knew we would never have kids. He has two, but they have never been mine. I am so sad tonight.

OUR SECRET GRIEF

In *The Savvy Auntie*, a book and blog by Melanie Notkin,[39] she writes about the joys of being a childless aunt. I highly recommend you check her out. Even with the joys of aunthood, Melanie admits to grieving over the children she never had. Earlier this month, she published an article in *Psychology Today* titled, "My Secret Grief: Over 35, Single, and Childless."[40] It's a touching piece about that grief that people with kids don't always understand. After all, they think, we *could* have had children. If we didn't, it's our own fault. You and I know that's not always true. Melanie tells it well.

Last week, I went to lunch with a bunch of church ladies. Inevitably, much of the conversation focused on their children. People talked about their latest escapades, compared their ages, and remembered how they were growing up. A friend showed photos of her pregnant daughter-in-law's sonogram. I didn't have much to say. Finally, a woman across from me said, "You have kids, don't you, Sue?"

"No, I don't," I said.

"I thought you did."

"Nope."

And then there was this silence. You know that silence? Oh yes.

A woman who arrived late took the seat beside me. I noticed her sparkling engagement ring. She announced that she and her fiancé had finally set a date. They have been together off and on for seven years. She is anxious to have children, but now she's in her 40s and doesn't know if she can. "If it's God's will, I'll get pregnant," she said. I believe in God, but I wanted to wring her fiancé's neck. Does he not understand that if you wait too long, you lose the chance to have kids? Seven years. Grrr.

Thanks for letting me get that off my chest. You know what? It's okay to grieve, but it's also okay to just get mad. Then maybe we can do something about it.

[Note: My engaged friend got married, but they never did have children, and now they're divorced. Eight years later, she's with another man. They bring their tiny dogs everywhere.]

Sara: I get that too. "Ooh, I thought you had children." Chirp, chirp. I work out of my home and often have clients to the house. I have set hours, and oftentimes a well-meaning person will say, "Oh, isn't 7:00 too late? I don't want to get in the way of you putting your children to bed." Other times people will ask, "How many children do you have?" Not even "do you have any children?" It makes me sad because it's a clear insinuation that I SHOULD have children. When I answer "no," I can see them mentally taking stock. Maybe guessing how old I might be. And then considering WHY after nine years of marriage I do not have children. Then maybe speculating that my body can't.

One woman apologized for asking me, saying that she has a niece who is going through infertility and she should have known better than to pry into my life. It never occurred to her that medically I'm strong, but marriagewise I'm weak. I envy that ignorance she has because I assume it means that marriage, children and the whole thing was probably a breeze for her. A no brainer. Too much speculation into my personal life, if you ask me . . . .

Oddly enough, this happened again last night. Idle chit-chat with an older woman led to, "Do you have children?"

"Nope, we have dogs." (A bit of dog-related conversation followed.)

"So, you aren't going to have kids?"

"Don't know."

She nodded, thinking about this for a moment before revealing that she had a child late in life. A "surprise" really.

We were interrupted, and oddly enough, I was disappointed that the conversation was over. For once I felt like someone had something to offer. She was a genuinely lovely person and I appreciated the candid conversation. I certainly prefer that to the stilted "Oh, well. Don't worry, it will happen."

Dr. L: This post really touched me.

Today, at work, a colleague who recently fell pregnant was sharing her news with us. After a few minutes, one of the women with children turned to me, the only one without children, and apologized that I would have to listen to talk of babies for the next several months. And despite knowing that she did not mean harm, the secret grief you speak about hit me. Because how do you explain to people that you secretly hope that one day, you too will be allowed to excitedly talk about babies like that?

DON'T HIDE YOUR TEARS FROM
YOUR PARTNER

"My God, I cried and cried reading your post as I sit here in the dark outside griev-ing for what will never be. I love my partner, and I hate him a little too because he doesn't want children and I am left bound by that decision. I feel my time running out and wish every single day he would change his mind, but he is unwavering in his decision. And at the same time, I can barely acknowledge this pain and grief to myself because I am terrified of it consuming me. This is the first time I have ever really sat down and let it all wash over me. I can't stop crying. I don't know how I am going to walk inside and pretend I'm okay because he doesn't understand."

The anonymous comment above brings back memories for me. I too hid my grief from my husband. I cried in the bathtub, in the car, or in the garage, but not in front of Fred. Oh no. Mustn't make him feel bad. But looking back, I think that was wrong. I should have shown him how I felt instead of hiding my feelings and hoping some kind of miracle would occur.

I am also bothered by her statement, "I am left bound by that decision." Is she? It's so hard to see a situation clearly when we're in the middle of it. We can't see any way out. We think we have no options, but we do. To Anonymous, I say reopen the conversation. You can agree to disagree, but don't hide your feelings. They count as much as his.

I don't cry all the time anymore. Sometimes I just curse and kick things, but when you're at the time of life when you see your chances of parenthood disappearing with every passing day, it hurts like hell. Losing your chance to have children is a big loss, and we don't need to hide it. If people don't like it, too bad.

Anonymous: I am in the crying-all-the-time stage. I have ups and downs, so the waterworks aren't always on. I am in a down time now, and it is a struggle. The tiniest things set me off. My parish had a trip to Rome, and the priest brought home St Gerard medals blessed by the Pope for anyone who is a mother or will be a mother. Just call the office and he would get you one and do a blessing. It is so small and I feel so selfish, but that is what you brought back for the parish? I hope I move out of my down time soon and get back into not crying all the time. Life is better there and I hope that as time goes on, more time is spent there. But for now, that is not the case. Kids are shoved in my face all the time and people all around are having kids and here I am. Not going to happen. No one is going to look like me or take after me. No one is going to have my eyes or my face. No fun days of finding out what I am having or reaching all the milestones of life. A lot of people on here comment that it does get easier after a while—once you're past the everyone-having-a-baby stage. I hope that is true.

Dana: Every word you said described exactly how I feel. I can't begin to tell you how comforting it is to not feel alone in this feeling. I feel so selfish and sometimes crazy with the amount of crying and wanting for a child and the amount of bitterness I feel towards those who have them.

I really hope it does get easier, too. I'm tired of crying.

Anonymous: I'm sure my husband wishes I did hide my tears. I pretty much punished him every 28 days. If I was going to have a miserable period for no reason, he was going to be miserable with me. I am not one who hides my emotions or can keep my mouth shut. But over time, it just got old and it wasn't making him change his mind. We pretty much came to the understanding that I would forever resent him and that wouldn't change, just like he wasn't going to change, and we just moved on from there. I will never understand why the love of my life didn't want the same things as me. He is an awesome man who loves me dearly. I truly have never been loved like this before by anyone, even after 30 years of marriage. I just couldn't ever see leaving him when there were no guarantees that I could even have children.

Silver: I had a meltdown last night on this very subject. We are on vacation and my DH (Dear Husband) keeps saying that his son would like this, or such-and-such would be perfect for his son. The fact that his son is 35, married with his own two kids and (extremely demanding) wife seems to not enter his fantasy formula. Finally yesterday I'd had enough and began to cry alone. I debated, do I tell him how painful it is because I don't have my own child to fantasize about returning with me to this lovely place and creating special memories. Or do I keep it all in? My DH is terrible at comforting, often taking my pain and making it about him. Eventually, he asked me if I was okay and I just let it out. Hot tears and words that ripped my soul apart. But I felt like it was a disservice to him if I didn't tell him. He may not be a great comforter, and he may say clumsy ineffective words of comfort making it about him, but in his own way, he loves me the best that he knows how, and for that reason alone, I spilled.

Naturally his first words were comparing me and my childless situation to his grandmother who married his recently widowed grandfather and mothered his very young children as though they were her children (implying I should/could be more like her). I didn't expect much in the way of comfort, and I didn't get much. He continued on until he was on a roll, mentioning every member of his family and not a word about my grief or how faithful God is or how the plan God has for me must be so different and special (among the usual things I tell myself), until I interrupted him. I requested that he quit talking about his family and that he bring me a cold wet washcloth for my headache. I also told him that his going on and on about his son was like sharp glass poking my heart. I didn't hold back. After I requested that he shut up about his family, he was at a loss for words and said nothing, although I could tell he prayed for me. He went to sleep; I lay there sobbing, more or less demanding God to hold me since He could have fixed this situation but opted not to, since He held the answers that I sought, since He was the only One on earth who knew the precision and depth of merciless suffering I endure from those around me who quite unknowingly rub salt in my childless wound. The bottom line is I did open up. I lowered my expectations of his understanding and empathy and in the end, it was worth it. He seems kinder today although it's still early, but—more importantly—he is slowly beginning to get a glimpse into my heart to understand (even if only a small understanding) who I am at the core. How can he do that if I never share this fragile, sad, and huge burden with him?

Anonymous: This was my comment you posted and I can't tell you how much I appreciate the time you took to respond to it. I tend to bury my emotions about this, but then every now and then it rears back up. Last year, I did fall pregnant unexpectedly and had an abortion. I was more on board with the decision then. It seemed like poor timing for many reasons. When we discussed it then, he said, "Let's say one day." And I clung to that. I kind of thought there would be time down the track in a couple of years to revisit it (although I am aware I may encounter issues due to my age). But he is adamant that there is NO chance. He loves me. He wants a life with me, but he doesn't want children. And while I know it hurts him, he has said if children are that important to me then I need to make a decision about our future. But it isn't that I want a baby. I want HIS baby. I want to share that experience with him. I want to see him hold our child in his arms, and I want us to watch it grow. In my heart of hearts, I know this will never be. I know he won't be moved from his stance. But I also know that in years to come when it is Christmas or a holiday and our family gathers, I will grieve that there is no one there that we created together. A physical walking, breathing reminder of our love. More than wishing I could change his mind, I wish I could find peace with this.

IF YOU CAN'T BEAR THE CHILDLESS GRIEF ALONE

At least once a week, I get a comment to this blog that leads me to cautiously, timidly suggest that maybe the writer might benefit from seeking counseling. I am not implying that they are crazy, but I am saying it might help to talk to a professional psychologist, psychiatrist or family counselor. People are very sensitive about this, so I hesitate to say it, but sometimes I feel I have to. These commenters say things like "I see no reason for living" or "I just can't go on" or "I can't remember the last time I felt happy." These are red flags that a person may be suffering from depression.

There's no shame in struggling to deal with grief or confusion over facing the possibility—or the certainty—of being childless. It hurts. It's a loss, just as much as if someone had died. If you didn't feel sad, that would be unusual. If it's weighing you down to the point where you can't get up in the morning day after day, not just once in a while, maybe you could benefit from finding an impartial professional to talk to.

I've been in counseling off and on over the years. The first time, I was coming out of an abusive relationship and found myself too depressed to function. I had given my heart and soul to this man, and he trampled all over it. Having no money, I called the county mental health department and got an appointment with a counselor. That first session, this kind woman made me feel so much better simply by listening to what I'd been through and letting me know it was not my fault. She took the burden off my shoulders. Many years later, a wise counselor helped me work through my husband's illness and death. Believe me when I say it's okay to get help.

Many readers here are struggling to figure out what to do. They are often in a situation where their partners are refusing to have children or there's a medical problem, and they don't know whether to leave that person or stay and accept that they'll never have kids. This is a horrible choice in which no one will come out happy. You could talk to your parents, your siblings, your friends, or your co-workers, but they're all biased. Sometimes it helps to talk to someone who can see all sides of the problem, who will let you say anything you want in complete confidentiality, and help you work through your decisions.

There are various kinds of counselors. Psychiatrists are doctors who are licensed to dispense medication. Psychologists are PhDs trained in mental health and counseling. Licensed clinical social workers and marriage and family therapists have master's degrees and clinical training in counseling. I see a psychiatric nurse practitioner who not only can prescribe meds but also does hypnosis, biofeedback, art therapy and many other techniques. She also gives good hugs. Most insurances cover psychiatric care to some extent. I have never paid more than a minimal co-pay. Ask your primary care doctor for a referral. There are also government agencies and groups such as Catholic Charities that can help if money is a problem. It's a hard phone call to make, but you can do it.

I recently received an email from a woman named Bonnie who was so distraught over this issue and other problems that she had decided to kill herself. I tried to talk her into waiting and getting some help. I hope I succeeded. She has not responded to subsequent emails. I searched everywhere for her actual name and location, but did not find her. The pain truly can become unbearable. If you are at that point, please call someone, even if you think it won't help. Tell yourself to wait a little longer. If you look, you can always find at least one reason to live.

This is a huge subject for which I have barely touched the surface. Here are links to more information.

"Finding a Therapist Who Can Help You Heal"[41] provides solid information about what therapy is and the types available.

"Symptoms of Depression" from WebMD[42] will help you understand the difference between ordinary sadness and depression.

SURVIVING: IT'S ALL IN HOW YOU LOOK AT IT

"I hate this rainy weather. It's so dark and wet," I whined to my counselor the other day. I live on the Oregon coast, where it starts raining in October and keeps going until Fourth of July. We hadn't seen the sun in two weeks. I'm fully aware that other parts of the country have much worse weather, but I'm from San Jose, where it never rains more than a day or two.

She held up her hand like a stop sign. "Every time you say things like that, it plants a negative thought in your mind."

She was right. I can't change the weather, only my reaction to it.

It's like the fog. My friend from New England says she loves it. I feel closed in, as if I'll go crazy if I don't see the sun within the next few minutes. It's the same fog, just different ways of looking at it.

Life is like that. I've been complaining because the neighbors behind me just built this giant building directly across from my office. At first I saw bare wood sticking out through the trees. Then this week, they installed a bright blue metal roof. It's *so blue*. It's the first thing I see in the morning when I turn on my computer. I hated it those first few days, but you know what? I'm starting to get used to it. It's kind of a nice blue. In time, I might even like it.

Childlessness is a little like that. I think about Karen, one of the women I interviewed for my book. Physically unable to bear children, she grieved until she discovered the term "childfree." The concept changed her whole perspective. She stopped feeling as if she was missing something and started spreading the word that it was okay not to have children.

In a book called *Childlessness Transformed,*[43] Brooke Medicine Eagle describes how among the Crow Indians when a person has no children, all the children are her children, not just humans but every life form. When a woman, parent or not, passes through menopause, she moves into the Grandmother Lodge. These "grandmothers" are responsible for all the children of the earth.

I don't know about you, but that makes me feel better.

If we wanted children and we can't have them, we are entitled to grieve, but we mustn't let it rule our lives. By changing our attitude, we can see the good things we do have, like maybe a loving partner, and other ways we can use our mothering energy.

I'm not saying it's easy. That same friend from New England posted a photo yesterday of her with her new grandson, and I felt the familiar ache. When I took my dog to the vet for her kennel cough shot in the afternoon, an employee on maternity leave was in the waiting room showing off her four-week-old baby.

Annie stared at it, puzzled. "That's a tiny human," I explained. "I wish we had one of those." We both gazed in awe at the baby's tiny hands and feet. Then I took a deep breath and said out loud to the mother, "Congratulations. She's so cute."

After which, the technician called Annie in and my 77-pound baby dragged me into the examining room, where she knew there were dog treats on the counter. Who cares about babies when there are cookies to be eaten!

It's all in how you look at it.

Anonymous: Sue, this post of yours is an especially true "gem," imho. I'm printing it out for my "read this a lot" collection. Thanks!

Determine gender baby: How enlightening! My uncle and my aunt are also doing this, surviving childlessness. I think if they really want to have a kid after all the efforts they've done, they could adopt an orphan child. In fact, they haven't done that. But they look so happy and are enjoying their lives.

Anonymous: Thank you for posting this—I'm struggling with this now, and it helps to know others have not only survived this but found a new way of seeing the world in a positive light.

6

LEARNING TO ACCEPT CHILDLESSNESS

I DON'T LIVE EVERY DAY thinking about being childless. I know it has a huge effect on my life. While my friends are busy with their children and grandchildren, I spend my days writing, playing music, and maintaining myself, the dog, my home, and my elderly father. They post pictures on Facebook of their family gatherings. I post my latest publication. Come the holidays, most people my age expect to be with their kids. I usually play music at church, then go home to an empty house. But I don't think about it all the time. I don't wake up in the morning weeping because I'll never be a mom. I used to, but not anymore. I promise a time will come when you won't either.

I pray the first four lines of the Serenity Prayer[44] every morning. My lack of children is one of the things I cannot change that I need to accept. I wanted children, but it's too late now. I have a good life as a non-mother. I'd love to be one of those grandma ladies, but you know what? I feel much younger and freer than most women my age who have children and grandchildren. I like that.

Then I read this quote from actress Jessica Lange in the August/September issue of the AARP magazine.

"Having children gives you a perspective you didn't have before. You are no longer the center of the universe. It opened my heart, made me a different person. Every move you make is with someone else in mind. I loved being a mother more than anything else in the world, and being a grandmother is even more fun. There's the chance to do it again. It's in the perfect order of nature:

You raise your children, and then the next generation comes along. They are the redemptive force in nature. Plus, it's easier!"[45]

Here's the thing. I believe what she says. Every word of it. But I don't dare dwell on it or I'll go nuts. I tell myself I'm supposed to do other things with my life, and that's that. I need to accept my situation. That works better some days than others.

How does it make you feel? I apologize if I made you cry, but you don't have to hide your tears here. What percentage of your life do you think about not having children? Is it something you can change or something you need to accept? Let's talk about it.

Mary: Sue, it's not really a matter of thinking about it. I go along not thinking about it, and then something happens to remind me that I haven't gotten pregnant, carried a child full-term, given birth and raised a child. It could be a person's comment or an advertisement or an article or filling out a form at the doctor's office or the child screaming at a table 10-20 feet away from me in the restaurant while I'm trying to eat dinner, but it's pretty consistent, all day long. If my eyes are open, I'm going to run into it sooner or later. By the way, that's risky of you to put that quote up today. Full of triggers. I can't even say I agree with it. I've known for a long time I'm not the center of the universe, not sure giving birth is a prerequisite for that bit of information. Even if Ms. Lange loves being a mother, not all moms feel that way and others might argue it's not something they love more than anything else in the world.

SFL: Mary, I know that quote is full of triggers. I want to know what people have to say about it. And you're right. Reminders are everywhere. I have just gotten better at not taking all of them to heart.

Lacie S: I'm 39 and I've been working my way toward acceptance for the last few years. I'm really hoping that 40 won't hit me hard. My brother's wife recently had a baby and I can say that when I held her I didn't feel the same yearning that I had when my last seven nieces and nephews were born. I'm hoping that's a sign that I'm finding my way to the other side of grief. But I'm tearing up as I type this, as though letting go of the grief is somehow a whole other grief process . . . good grief! But you give me hope that I can grow into my older years gracefully and with an open, adventurous spirit.

Tamara: The less I think of these things and the less I focus on being childless, the easier it is for me to deal with it. I cried and I cried, and now I am at peace with it. I desperately wanted to be a mother, but it was not in the cards for me. My husband is wonderful. No, he did not agree to have a child with me, but he gives us an amazing life full of so many great things. I also try to fill my life with as much positivity as I can by doing things I enjoy and staying away from negative people and environments.

Sharilee: Sue, I love this post! It is so hopeful and encouraging. That quote would have triggered me a lot more in the past but not as much today. Even though I don't have my own biological children, I have still had children in my life that have shaped me and my viewpoint. I was a teacher for many years and a stepmom. These children are still in my heart and I am sure there will be more in the future.

You are so right about the day-to-day reality, and as a writer, I can relate so much. Yes! I post my writing instead of a day with my kids or grandkids. I do see, too, how not having kids has given me more time to explore writing and ideas. Take care!

MAYBE IT'S TIME TO REASSESS

Six people I know have died in the last month. Six! None were family members, thank God, but still, they were people I knew and cared about. Also, my cousin gave birth to twins. Plus, I've got a new boss who is, how shall I put it, insane. And my neighbor has a new rooster who never stops crowing. What a month. Makes a person think and reassess.

I've been whining a lot lately about being alone and childless. I won't lie. It's hard sometimes. Saturday, when I arrived at a funeral that was not held at my own church, I found myself alone in a sea of families. And when the folks in front of me told me all about their children and grandchildren, I felt awful. So alone. I went home and cried and only partly for my neighbor who died. But part of that is my own fault for being too shy to introduce myself to strangers and make them friends. I'd rather feel sorry for myself. My friend Pat talks to everyone. Within five minutes, she has new friends, so she's never alone. Yes, she has children, but they all live far away. She has a husband, but he's disabled and can't do things with her. Her own health isn't great. We've all got problems.

But you know what we also have? Blessings. One day last week when I just couldn't face my work anymore, I got in my car and drove to the beach. I hung out on the sand until lunchtime, then treated myself to an expensive lunch at a posh restaurant with a fabulous view. Later I went shopping, and I drove down some roads I'd never tried before. I did not have to arrange childcare or consult with any other human being. I just went, and it was great.

I watched 13 episodes of "Orange is the New Black"[46] in one week last month. I'm not sure that's good for anybody's brain, but again, no one to consult, no child or husband to feed, nobody whining that they wanted to watch something else.

My dog Annie and I walk almost every day through the woods or on the beach. Between us, we have six good legs and we're healthy. That, my friends, is a blessing.

I eat three delicious meals a day and have money left over. I am so lucky.

Many of you have partners whom you love. You might be making each other crazy over the baby issue, but stop for a minute. Set that aside. What do you love about this person? What does he or she give you? Sex? Love? Support? A hand to hold when you're scared? That's something a lot of people don't have.

Do you have a home? Your health? Parents? Siblings? Cousins? Friends? Pets? Do you have work that you enjoy?

I know. This baby thing has you all tied up in knots. You worry about the future. Will you regret not having children? Will you end up alone? Will your relationship last? Should you leave? Should you stay? It's hard.

But today, right now, count your blessings. Life is short, and we never know when it will end. My fingers are getting tired of playing funeral songs. But I'm grateful that those fingers can still dance on the piano keys and I can still sing.

How about you? Perhaps you don't have babies of your own, but what DO you have?

Danielle: It's funny when everything hits at once and can bring up a lot of mixed-up feelings about family, loss, no babies, maybe babies. Like you were, I am involved with someone older with three children of his own. While he has been clear about his hesitancy to start all over again with a family, I'm the one who has been muddled and confused. He asked me the other day, "When you first got involved with me, what was your plan about children?" GOOD question. I explained that I always wanted a healthy relationship with a man first and foremost. Children, I thought, would come later. I knew that when I met him he technically couldn't have any more and didn't want any more. I just didn't think it would matter that much. Well, it does, but at this point, I want both of us to be happy, and so I think we are not going to pursue children together, which would need IVF intervention.

This realization makes me sad, and I can't really see anything else but that. I'm being honest. What is good is that I am sharing more of my feelings about being childless with my partner, and he has promised to be there for me when I need him. Before, like you did, Sue, I hid behind my pain, refusing to show that it mattered.

What I do have is a wonderful honest relationship. I do have my health, I do have a job (but I'm not completely satisfied with that at the moment), and I do have a good relationship with my mother. However, these great relationships do not take away the honest pain I carry around that I did not become a mother. What I hope will happen is that the pain will come and go and that I will be able to come to terms with being childless. After all, I am the one who chose to walk down this road with a near impossible chance to conceive.

Your blog helps me tremendously and I do not feel so alone, so thank you for that.

SFL: Danielle, thank you for your kind words and for sharing your story. Yes, our situations were very similar. And yes, some days, the sadness is all you see. Me too, but not as often as I used to. It's good that you're talking about it. To be honest, when I found Fred, I was just glad to have somebody. After my divorce and a few failed relationships, I thought I'd be alone for the rest of my life. He gave me so much, just not children.

Certainlydifferent: I have hope. I know and understand what the Bible teaches, and I get to help others learn. That fills most of my days. It doesn't help at nights when I am alone. But I have a horrible and eventually crippling and slightly hereditary disease (Ankylosing spondydlitis). Some days that is my "blessing," because as much as my heart still aches when others have kids and I want them so much, coping with this disease is all I can do, so I am glad I am not dealing with a child, too.

I am trying to sell our home so we can move into something smaller so I can let go of "wonderful fantastical dreams of a miracle," usually of adoption. I no longer want to give birth but had wanted to adopt for 10 years. That hope is gone. We tried, and it's not going to happen. Even if we tried private adoption, I don't trust that the local CAS wouldn't find a way to muck it up for us.

Looking through the comments from Grief, I think that if I had accepted that we could never get pregnant and not held onto hope of a miracle for the first seven years of marriage, it would have been easier when adoption failed. I spent 14 years of my life preparing for kids, instead of just being a wife. Now I am trying to embrace that, but the emotional cost has caused huge cracks in our relationship. He is a truck driver and is not home six days of the week, and sometimes that is a blessing on its own, because he doesn't handle my grief very well. I am encouraged to know that it will get better, but my advice to others is if everything points to a childless life—and this may be cynical but it's my hindsight—ACCEPTANCE is the key. Learn to accept it now, sooner. I think it might make the pain of letting go easier. If you hold on so tight to something, when you finally let it go, your hands hurt. Same thing.

Anonymous: I have been so lonely in my feelings and have felt ashamed to feel the craving to be a mother. My husband is a wonderful man but doesn't understand the pain and depression that I go through. I am under care with a doctor, but feel that it does nothing for me. I was told by one doctor that the feelings will pass in time and my medical doctor told me (after he said I was too old) that I should be thankful for what I have and not want things that I cannot have. Those words were a knife going through my heart. Even my husband was shocked at what he said. I am thankful for my stepchildren, husband, dog—who adores me—and my career. Some days are harder; some nights are impossible. Thank you for allowing me write my feelings out without worry or judgment.

SFL: Certainly and Anonymous, thank you for sharing these difficult facts and feelings. It helps us all feel less alone and maybe to feel grateful for the blessings we do have.

Anon, you need to find a different doctor, one who understands better what you're going through.

Certainly, you're so right about it being easier once you accept it, and it's important not to ignore the man or woman in your life because you're obsessing over babies.

SO YOU'RE CHILDLESS; WHAT ELSE ARE YOU?

Happy New Year! Hallelujah, the holidays are over.

As we start a new year, I want to share a quote that set me thinking about all the things we are besides childless.

In the book *Motherhood Missed* by Lois Tonkin,[47] one of the anonymous women included there wrote this: "I don't want to identify for the rest of my life as a childless woman. I want to be something else."

That really struck me because we are more than our status as parents or non-parents. We have other gifts to give to the world. We might wish with all our hearts that we had children, that we could proudly boast of being mothers or fathers, but there is more. There's always more.

So I want you think about what else you are. If you were writing a Facebook profile or a bio to put on the back of your book and you were not allowed to say anything about having or not having children, what would you write?

For example, the bios at the bottom of things I publish usually say something like "SFL is a writer-musician-dog mom living on the Oregon Coast." I go on to name my books and other publications and mention my job as a music minister. Am I also a mother? Readers don't need to know; it's irrelevant, just like my age or my shoe size.

Childlessness does not define me, except in particular situations, such as this blog. If I find myself at a school or other child-centered place, I can focus on my reason for being there. Perhaps I'm volunteering, giving a talk, or offering support as a student's aunt. It's about what I AM, not what I'm NOT.

So what is your gift to share with the world? If you had a child, what would you be looking forward to doing once they got old enough to leave alone? You are free to do it now. That's no small thing.

The arts are not the only way to contribute to the world. You can run a business, share your faith, teach, train dogs, keep people safe, help the sick and injured, or provide food, homes, clothing, and other necessities. Are you a gardener, an athlete, a chef, or masseuse? You have way more to offer than just eggs or sperm.

At my 50th birthday party, which turned out to be the last event my mother attended before she died, she gave the most beautiful speech about how proud she was of me. She mentioned my writing and my music, but she said the best part was my loving heart. She didn't talk about how I had failed to have children; she focused on what I had accomplished. So should you.

I know this is hard, especially if you're in the throes of your baby-no baby crisis. But let's give it a try this year. What else are you besides not someone's mother or father?

Here's another New Year's resolution for you: If you're on the fence because of your partner's refusal to commit, let them know that it ends this year. If they refuse to give you a definite answer, you will take their non-decision as a no and act on it. No more waiting around. No one has the right to hold your life hostage.

So that's my New Year's sermon. I started the new year by being up all night with stomach troubles, followed by a migraine. Yesterday my dog swallowed a guitar pick which I pray will come out the other end and not kill her. But today we're both okay.

Parenting is no guarantee of happy holidays. My brother's kids and grandkids are all sick. My best friend had a fight with her grandson, who says he will never speak to her again. At least we don't have to deal with that.

I feel good about next year. Let's try to see the bright side. Tell me in the comments: What else are you besides a non-mom or non-dad?

Lara: This is an interesting thought to me right now. My husband has adult children, with whom I get along well enough. I have a deepening relationship with his oldest son due to my husband's recent cancer diagnosis. I came into this marriage with the belief that his family would become my family, and it is not unfolding that way. With my husband facing lung cancer, at age 46 I am looking at what my life will be on the other side of his walk on Earth. Cancer brings so many things to the forefront. I hate that. I hate having to rebuild, again. I hate not having the family I thought I would. I hate being wired so differently from his family. But I am more. I need to focus on my more.

SilverShil0h: Lara, you describe a raw and arduous journey. I'm sorry to hear of this development that your husband and you face. I find you to be a brave and selfless person.

GOALS FOR A NEW YEAR WITHOUT CHILDREN

So many of you have been writing to me about your childless-by-marriage situations. I feel for your grief. I share it. Although I like to think I have accepted my situation and moved on, sometimes I curse when I realize, again, what I have missed by not having children. I never really direct my anger at my husbands who didn't want to have kids with me. I'm more angry at myself for letting the opportunity slip by without taking action.

With my husband passing away, this will be my first year in a long time that I haven't been married, so I have a new life to build. I get angry that this happened to us. It's not fair that I don't have kids or a husband at this age. But you know what? Hanging on to the bitterness doesn't do any good. God gave me this life, and I need to live it.

Whatever your situation this year, let's set some goals for dealing with being childless by marriage.

Repeat after me:

1. I will discuss very honestly how I feel with my partner or spouse. I will not hold back, even if I'm afraid that what I say will make him/her angry or sad. They need to know. Silent resentment will poison our relationship.

2. I will decide once and for all whether I can live a life without children. Is this person worth giving up children? If not, I will do something about it.

3. I will find a way to include at least one child in my life as an unofficial godmother, auntie or whatever I want to call it. I can find this child in my family, among my friends' children, in volunteering in my community, or even one of those situations where I "adopt" a poor child in another country.

4. I will find something to be thankful for every day.

5. (This one's for me) If I am posting as Anonymous, I will start using a name. It doesn't have to be my real name. It can be serious or silly, but it will help Sue tell one poster from another.

Happy New Year to all.

Anonymous: Ha! Great post, Sue, and helpful advice for the beginning of the new year.

I am anonymous SPS whose husband put me on a rollercoaster ride in 2011. He has turned a corner, and we're actively working towards a happier 2012 (with or without children remains to be seen). I'm 37 and feeling that time is running out. But today I have peace that I'm exactly where God wants me. I can now be referred to as Anonymous Sara.

Best wishes to you for a Happy New Year.

Cara: Thank you for posting this. That is really all I can say for now. Thank you. By this post, you have helped in ways you do not know. You have given me a path to start from, and a hand to hold along the way. Not feeling so alone any longer. So, again, thank you.

Anonymous Newly Blue: Thanks for you and others in this blog for your stories and sharing. I am encouraged by you all (and my therapist) to attempt goal No. 1 this weekend. So nervous, but I can't hold back at my ripe age of 36. Any prayers help.

SFL: We're praying for you, Newly Blue. Try to stay calm and not place blame. Just tell him how you feel.

Anon S: I'm finally understanding that the sum of my life is all my choices.

Choosing work instead of interesting outings. Choosing fast food instead of a more sensible quick alternative. Choosing to bow down to friends with children instead of seeking out more balanced relationships. Choosing to ignore the stains on my carpet instead of making the calls to get quotes on new flooring (or even renting a damn carpet shampooer).

Is it any wonder that I face the new year feeling old, frumpy, lumpy and tip-toeing across my disgusting carpet? I shouldn't be surprised to have received zero New Year's Eve invites. Most of my family and friends are mingling with others with children or doing nothing. I shouldn't be surprised that I'm worn out, tired out and only longing for a bag of Doritos and Netflix on NYE.

Next year will be different. I'm not sure how yet, but it will be different. Or maybe I'll regress and better resemble the person I was at one time, the person who once sought out fun activities and fun people. The person who would never have let a coating of pet hair stay on the carpet, let alone live with stains . . . It might sound like I'm depressed, but I'm not. The last couple of days, I've read bits and pieces of helpful advice and I feel good. I'm excited. I'm sick of being sad. I know that 2017 will be a game changer.

7

CHILDLESS VS. CHILDFREE

APPARENTLY I'M A WANNABE "breeder troll," at least according to the Selfish Heathens site, which is firmly devoted to non-parenting. In fact, parents, aka breeder trolls, are strongly urged to stay away. If they even lurk at the site, they will be summarily deleted. The Satanic imagery and strong language scare the heck out of a mommy-lookalike such as myself.

I learned about the Selfish Heathens from a blog entry by Canadian Writer Jonathan Kay,[48] who started a flame war with his piece about bringing children to restaurants. One commenter threatened to throw ice water into the faces of Kay and his "broodsow" if they ever met in a restaurant. Luckily they will probably never meet in person.

I often hear mothers referred to as breeders, as if they were cats who went into heat and turned out one litter after another with no regard to overpopulation or to the way their kids are annoying little brats. But then again, others talk about children being the biggest blessing of their lives, that raising them is the most important thing one can do, far more important than any other occupation. Many who can't conceive spend thousands of dollars on painful medical procedures trying to unite one egg and sperm successfully into a baby. When the effort fails, they come away heartbroken.

Why is there such an undercurrent of anger between parents and nonparents? Must we split into separate societies, those with children and those without? Why can't we just accept each other's choices and move on?

[Twelve years later, the Selfish Heathens website is gone, but the animosity remains].

Magdalen [Tiffany]: I think it's a total red herring to assume that there are two warring, oppositional factions in the world: happy, intentional mothers and blissfully childfree women. With a little empathy and creative insight, it's easy to imagine that perhaps not everyone falls into these two extreme categories. Stepmoms, foster parents, women who are on the fence about whether to reproduce, women who at age 27 are totally anti-child but who may find their feelings softening a decade later, moms who have second thoughts about having stifled their careers in order to have kids . . . we're all in this TOGETHER. We ALL suffer from being lumped into some category or being associated with some crappy feminine archetype we've inherited from centuries of patriarchal dominance. The world told us for centuries that our job as women was to be: 1) an obedient daughter and virtuous, virginal maiden; 2) an obedient wife who pleases her husband and brings him an heir; 3) a holy and beautiful mother; and then things trickle off a little.

After you've brought the heirs up, society doesn't necessarily have that much use for you. You can be a delightful old crone, one of the few other remaining archetypes. If you fail to preserve your virtue, you can also be a whore. That's the sort of mentality which gets us thinking that there are only Mothers and Notmothers, and the two shall never meet, agree, or help each other. I am not living in a society where my family members will stone me to death if I am raped, which still happens in many cultures. I live in the U.S. We're still trying to figure it out, and we still make 70 cents to every $1 a man makes, but we can be moms, stepmoms, happy childfree women, occasionally regretful child-free women, miserably childless women, successful career women, artists, nuns, sexually active women, married, single, partnered, straight, lesbian, bisexual, transgendered—any combination of these things. It's a rich and delightful mix. Reducing ourselves to just "Childfree by Choice" and "Moms" and "wannabe breeder trolls" is yet another way of limiting our possibilities. Let's give each other—and ourselves—a break. The world, and our psyches, are much more complex than that. Sorry to rant!

CF: The reason Selfish Heathens and other similar sites exist is that childfree people need a place to rant, not against all parents, but against a group of parents that do a poor job parenting. The most frequent example that comes to mind is parents who don't teach manners to their children and let them run wild in public places, most commonly restaurants, and disrupt the meal of other patrons. Therefore they are called BNP (breeder not parent), because their job as a parent seems to have only been giving birth, and not undertaking the long tough process of raising a child to adulthood to be an active independent member of society. Of course, there are also raves for PNB, parents not breeders, who do a tremendous job. The problem is there are more and more parents who give up and let their children become monsters, thus prompting fed-up childfree people to set up sites like this.

'BREEDERS?' NO, THEY'RE PEOPLE WITH CHILDREN

Have you ever used the word "breeder" to refer to a human being who has children? Please don't. Somehow in this crazy time when one-fifth of us are not having children and many of us have chosen the "childfree" life, "breeder" is becoming like a curse word. I'm reading posts on childfree and childless websites where the writers, mostly women, complain about all those breeders posting baby pictures online, daring to bring their children to restaurants, or spoiling them at holiday celebrations.

Breeder is a term that should only be used when we're talking about people arranging for the mating and procreating of animals or plants, not humans. Wikipedia says: A "breeder" is a person who practices the vocation of mating carefully selected specimens of the same breed to reproduce specific, consistently replicable qualities and characteristics. This might be as a farmer, agriculturalist, or hobbyist, and can be practiced on a large or small scale, for food, fun, or profit."[49]

But this is how I'm seeing it used on countless childless/childfree sites and how it's defined in the Urban Dictionary: "1: slang term used by some childfree people for one who has a child and/or has many after that, refuses to discipline the child/ren, thinks the sun rises and sets for their child/ren, looks down upon people who do not have children, and are in general very selfish and greedy when it comes to their whims and those of their child/ren, especially if they can use their parenthood status or their children as an excuse to get their way. A female breeder is commonly called a moo, and a male breeder a duh."[50]

The definitions and examples go on and on. Each one offends me more. Not having our own children, by choice or circumstance, does not give us the right to use terms like these or to assume that every parent is a senseless idiot bent on destroying our lives by making babies and actually showing them in our child-deprived presence.

The usage has ramped up lately as people prepare, often with dread, to join their families for the holidays. I know it's a hard hurdle to get over, but let's try to stop feeling angry or sorry for ourselves and just enjoy the children around us, even if they're not ours, for the little miracles they are—even when they're crying, making messes or generally being less than charming. For Pete's sake, if our parents hadn't "bred," we wouldn't be here.

If you truly can't stand to be around kids, just avoid them. Unfriend their doting parents and grandparents on Facebook. Spend the holidays camping or on a cruise. But don't call their parents breeders unless they live on a ranch. They're not "breeders." They're people just like us who happen to have children.

One more point. This may sound silly, but think about it. If you wanted a dog and couldn't have one, and you went someplace where there was a dog, would you hate the dog or the dog owner for being there? No, you'd pet that dog and play with it and love it. Why can't it be the same with children?

Anon S: Great points. Sometimes I get wrapped up in my childless world and get annoyed with those with children. Until I realize that the reason they are distracted on a phone call, or unable to focus on a lunch visit is because they are in charge of another human being who needs to be protected and loved. Me, I just need to make sure my handbag doesn't get left behind. I can't always grasp that responsibility that parents have. Other times, I find myself at a loss for conversation with parents. Then I realize (like you pointed out) that they are people too—only with children. When I look past the children and attempt normal conversation, I usually learn that my party companion is an avid reader or loves to cook. I personally would never refer to parents as "breeders." Not even those that choose to have many children. I don't refer to their children as "a litter" either. Even if I did have children, I'd probably only want one or two, but I know many happy large families who are not "breeding" like barnyard animals. All that being said, I do find irritation with those who can't seem to understand that their children are not the center of my world. I'm certainly interested in your life, your family, your children. But I don't want to know everything about her bedroom decor, her bath habits, her babysitter. I don't want to sit in mid-conversation and watch you decide to gurgle and coo to your child as you "pretend" to have a rapport with me. (sorry, dealing with anticipated, upcoming family drama) Many might disagree with me but I don't fully adopt the comparison of dogs and children. Enjoying the presence of a dog (even if you can't have one) isn't as difficult as enjoying a child (when you don't have one). This is only my opinion, but I have three dogs which I love and respect very much. But for me they aren't close to being children.

Certainlydifferent: I agree totally. I felt myself thinking about what I would say to a friend who had a miscarriage, and who was complaining about not getting an anniversary card, and honestly all I could think was, "Well, at least your husband has sperm," but that's not who I want to be. You are correct—if we like dogs but can't have them, we love every one we see. We should do the same for kids.

Anonymous: "Breeders" is usually slang for those who reproduce mindlessly like Octomom.[51] I can't tell you how many times parents complain about "childless hipsters." That is as insulting as if you lack value, since, like myself, many are not this way by choice. Even so, why are parents allowed to criticize "hipsters" and not the other way around? Whether I had kids or not, if I am in a public place, I expect parents to control their kids. I would have never been allowed to act as some of these kids do now.

CHILDLESS BY CIRCUMSTANCE?

In her book *What No Baby?*[52] Australian author Leslie Cannold maintains that many women are "childless by circumstance." They wanted to have children, but life worked against them. In today's world, says Cannold, young woman, and also men, are busy getting their educations and building their careers in their most fertile years. They believe that good parents spend time with their children, but if they take that time away from work, they will lose everything they have worked for and never achieve their career goals. Although women are the ones who are usually expected to stay home with the children, men worry about these things, too. In a world where people who work only 40 hours a week are considered slackers, who has time to parent? Although some men are merely selfish, many who decline to become fathers are afraid they won't be able to bear the financial burdens or that they won't be good fathers. If the wife quits to become a full-time mom, will the man be able to support the family alone in today's economy? What if he loses his job? What if they get divorced?

Cannold insists that people who are childless by circumstance, in other words who are not infertile and have not consciously chosen to be childfree, are not childless by choice. She suggests that major changes are needed in society's attitudes and in the workplace to make it possible for people to work and properly care for families, too. Otherwise, the numbers of people who never have children will continue to increase.

What do you think? Does everyone have a choice? Do you?

Gemma: I think to some extent we are childless by circumstance. I have to choose between my husband and children; thus far I have chosen my husband. I think others need to figure out how far they are willing to go and if they are open to adoption or fostering if IVF fails for them.

Anonymous: I am 53 years old and am childless by circumstance. My husband is very happy being childless. He said for a brief moment he thought it might be fun to have children. That moment passed. He was infertile and refused to complete any process to either conceive a child or adopt a child. He says that he doesn't feel like he held a carrot before me, but he did. He had surgery, but no follow-up. We were selected as adoptive parents, but he didn't fill out the home study paperwork. My sister is blessed with three grandchildren. She is two years older than I. At 40, I thought I was pregnant and was elated. My husband wanted me to have an abortion. That was one of the saddest times of my life. I was not pregnant, and I grieved alone. The last two days, my husband has selected movies for us to watch that involve children and how wonderful they are. I'm grieving anew and afresh again. In the last year, I lost two horses and my beloved kitty. I've wanted to die myself. I know about not wanting to get out of bed. I do think it gets better . . . when we are in heaven because in heaven there are no more tears.

Amanda: My younger sister is childless by circumstance. She was engaged and living with her fiancé for eight years when suddenly he up and left with their 23-year-old employee. My sister at 35 had wanted kids, but her fiancé didn't . . .

My sister decided if she met someone, it might still happen, but she wouldn't just grab any man to have kids. She never met a life partner, so remains single. She's a busy professional and has moved on in life. Her ex married the 23-year-old and now has three kids. Seems she wanted them, so it was the price he had to pay to keep his new partner.

My sister isn't bitter about the kids, but it must hurt—there was a picture in the local paper recently—her ex and his wife with their three kids. I threw it in the bin rather than show it to her. She's a highly successful professional, but I know she wanted kids and if her partner had been honest from the start, she might have had them.

Don't let men mess you around. If you want kids and they don't, leave and find someone else.

WHAT'S WRONG WITH WANTING A BABY?

My Google alerts brought to my attention a scathing review of Madelyn Cain's *The Childless Revolution*.[53] Jessa Crispin writes on her Bookslut page[54] that "those who choose motherhood and those who choose childlessness are on opposite sides. Once you've chosen, you're alien to the other group."

Well, I have noticed a divide between the "childfree" and the "breeders," but can't we reach across and find a peaceful way to relate? A lot of us who don't have children wish we did, and some of those who have kids wish they didn't.

In her review, Crispin begins by telling us Cain isn't qualified to write about childlessness because she had a child when she was almost 40. The fact that she had trouble conceiving for all the years before that doesn't count. And the fact that she had an intense desire to be a mother puts her on the "other" side, the breeder side. Do you agree?

Crispin goes so far as to note how many pages Cain devotes to each of her three sections, the childless by choice, by chance and by happenstance. The childless by choice get the short end, she says. "This isn't really a book about being childless. This is a book about women who wanted children but didn't get them."

She also complains that Cain's book is poorly written and that it has too many personal observations. I disagree. The issue of having children or not having them *is* personal.

All this makes me sigh. I hate to see women dividing into enemy camps. Also, I happen to think *The Childless Revolution* is fine book.

What do you think? Can a mother write about childlessness? Are mothers and non-mothers so different they have to live in separate worlds?

Magdalen: I do think that a mother can write about childlessness, though her view will obviously be altered by the reality that she eventually wanted and had children. I, too, am troubled by this bullshit idea that the world consists solely of Happy Selfish Breeders and Happily Self-Righteous Childfree People, and they must fight to the bitter end. I say this as someone who spent most of her life happily childfree by choice, who wrote articles about childfree/childless living for books and magazines, and who took some flak for it. I also say this as someone who now understands a "little" more about parenting, because I have a stepdaughter who lives with me half-time. I also say this as someone who ended up "wanting" to have a biological baby, but who has chosen not to for reasons of health, circumstance, staying with my partner and family, and just plain life.

The Internet encourages us to be simplistic and one-dimensional in our arguments. The relative facelessness of encounters online tends to encourage shrill self-righteousness and cruelty that we'd never do (or put up with from others) in real life. Once again, I'd like to think my opinion on this can be backed up. Thanks for bringing this up, Sue.

John: Just as a childless person is unlikely to write a book about parenting, I believe ideally, a childless by choice (also known as childfree) book should be written by a CBC person, unless it is an academic type book rather than a supportive type book. So yes, I would prefer to read this type of book from a non-parent.

Magdalen: John, I can definitely understand your point. I recently called around to people in my city who specialize in childless and infertility issues—counselors and such. My first question was, "Are you a parent?" and they invariably were. I still think there's something to be said for learning from each other, even if we don't happen to be exactly alike. And I don't believe that it boils down to a world of parents and non-parents. Those arguments tend to ignore some of the similarities we might all have—and also leave very little room for adoptive parents, step-parents, etc.

WHICH IS WORSE, NO KIDS OR A DOZEN?

The novel I've been reading, *A Place of Her Own*[55] by Janet Fisher, takes place in the 1800s. It's based on the true story of a woman who came to Oregon by covered wagon and settled not far from where I live. The heroine, Martha, married at 15, had one baby after another, 11 in all. She'd probably have had more, but her husband died. I almost want to add "thank God." He was an abusive SOB.

But that's not my point. The story takes place in the 1850s and 60s. Martha has no access to birth control, abortion doesn't even occur to her, and there is no such thing as a vasectomy or tubal ligation. If you have sex—and her husband isn't going to take no for an answer—you have babies. She spends the 21 years of their marriage either pregnant or nursing. Think about that. One baby after another, with no way to stop them from coming.

There comes a point in the novel where she has had two babies die in infancy and discovers she's pregnant again. "I don't want to have another baby," she cries. She already has so many to take care of and she can't stand the thought of losing another one.

Her husband treats her horribly, at one point beating her with a whip. She leaves him for a while and tries to divorce him, but discovers the laws at that time allow him to take all of their seven living children away from her. So when he promises never to hurt her again, she goes back. She has two more babies.

Why am I telling you about this when you and I don't have any babies at all? Think about how few choices women had back then, long before they earned the right to vote. When Martha, as a widow, went to buy land, the guy selling it preferred to deal with her 11-year-old son because he was male.

Only in recent times have we had any say about whether or not we would get pregnant and have babies or when we would have them. When I was born in the 1950s, abortion and birth control were not legally available. Nor did women have many career options. Most became wives and mothers. They started their families young, long before age-related infertility might be a factor. We never heard about spouses refusing to have children. I'm sure it happened but not nearly as often as it does now.

Today we have so many choices it's frightening. We make those choices and then we wonder if we'll regret them later, whether it be birth control, abortion, vasectomy, or committing our lives to someone who is not able or willing to have children with us. In these days when divorce is common, we're often the second or third spouse, and our partners have already created families with their exes. They've had their children, but we have not. They want us to be happy taking care of their children, but it's rarely enough.

Sometimes I wish we didn't have so many choices. Life was less complicated in the 1860s. But to be honest, I would no more want to have 11 babies and have two of them die than I would want to have none. Also, considering the lack of choices back in the 1800s (when my great-great grandmother had 13 children who lived), why would any of us let anyone else decide this most important life choice for us now?

What do you think about this?

Anon S: Wow! What a life for that poor woman. I suppose if she had a loving spouse, she might have enjoyed and welcomed as many children as possible. Certainly I've known people who have had no interest in children, only to divorce, remarry and suddenly have a large family with the new dreamboat hubby. These sorts of things make me feel like if you have a good spouse you can enjoy or endure most anything.

I've always been hesitant to take the baby plunge. With my first hubby, I just don't think I loved him in the right ways in order for me to ache to have his baby. With my second (and current hubby), our first years were so difficult that

I got a little scared about building a family. Then it got even worse, and there was no question that I'd be waiting to have children. Now things are beautiful between us, and I think *if only I were 10 years younger.*

Anything is still possible for us, but at this point in the game the choices are: Do we accept things as they are and regret the coming years? Do we work hard to have a child and risk an older pregnancy and regret the outcome of a late in life baby? Do we pour money into adoption and hope for the best?

Choices are hard when we know we have them. I wonder if it was easier 100 years ago to just do the things you were expected to do and carry on.

A.Roddy: Thank you for this suggestion. While babies don't die at the same rates now, there is a movement you may have heard of called Quiverfull,[56] where the couple has double digit families or close to it. A 'quiver' is supposedly six or more. The goal is to out-breed "heathens," whatever that means. The Duggars (with 19 children)[57] are an example and an exception since most of these families live in poverty or near poverty. The Duggars' last baby Josie was born three months early and spent weeks in ICU. They miscarried a baby at five months gestation. Andrea Yates was another follower (the one who drowned her kids because she wanted to save their souls). Their friends the Bates also have as many kids. I think the worst part is they expect the kids to follow suit.

I don't get bringing back the times when women had kids with no options. As much as I would have liked kids, I can't see taking on more than you can handle, yet they believe God doesn't give you more than you can handle. Any prevention is seen as sin. I bet women from that time would have given anything for birth control. As far as what's worse, I think being without any option is worse.

Jenny: Surely it has got to be worse to HAVE to have them, endlessly. Especially when combined with the situation of possibly being unable to feed them all, trapped in abusive marriages and no health service to provide pre-natal care and maternity services. Lots of children were orphaned due to maternal deaths. Maybe that's where childless women would have stepped in? Having said that, we should not forget that this is still the case today in many countries around the world.

8

LOCKED OUT OF THE MOM CLUB

AT THE SOUTH BEACH, OREGON, post office, one of the workers brings her baby every day. I have seen this baby grow from newborn to just starting to walk and talk. She's a cute, smiley child. I watch her and her mom with curiosity, but I don't know how to interact with them. Yesterday as I was collecting my mail, I watched a white-haired man having so much fun talking nonsense to the baby that he couldn't seem to tear himself away. Clearly he's had years of practice talking to babies, his own, his grandchildren, perhaps nieces and nephews. I have never been around babies, and I don't have the vocabulary for it.

At the library, I encounter a group blocking the stairs, two young mothers and three little kids, so busy talking they don't notice me trying to get to the ground floor to sit alone and write for a while. I edge around them. The children's room, occupied by more moms and babies, sits at the bottom of the stairs. I feel as if I am not allowed to step into that room.

A friend is hosting a series of parenting classes. She keeps sending emails asking us to help, but I am no more qualified to teach parenting than I would be to give surfing lessons or teach Mandarin.

Many of my friends have children and grandchildren. When we work on common interests, such as music or writing, we connect. But then they suddenly start talking Mommy, and our connection fades away. It's a lot like when I walk into the chapel during the Spanish choir rehearsal. I know some Spanish, but they talk too fast and use slang I don't understand. They look at me like I don't belong in their world, and no matter how many Spanish classes I take, I never will.

I often feel that I'm from a country that has no children, only dogs and cats. One is not better than the other, just different. Does this sound familiar to you? As childless people, are there situations where you feel like you come from another country?

Anonymous: I so feel this way much of the time. I live in a smaller city in the south where everyone seems to have kids, usually starting very young, unlike the northeast where I grew up, where it seems most of my counterparts went to college and established careers before having babies in their 30s. But even my career-oriented peers listed their most proud accomplishment as their child(ren) in the 20-year reunion update book—and out of all those that responded to be included in the book, I was one of two classmates that didn't have children by the 20-year mark!!! The love of my life, to whom I have been married 10 years, is from Sicily, and his native culture values being a mother above all else, it seems. I feel like I will never truly be considered "family" unless I give birth to one of their bloodline. One of my sisters-in-law implied that my 10 years of marriage doesn't mean very much since we have not produced a child together.

Of course, I don't know what it would feel like to have created a new life with my husband, but on the other hand, to me, in this culture of divorce, I feel like our marriage commitment of 10 years almost means more since we don't have offspring as a reason to stay together. I am not close with my grown stepchildren, and now my husband just became a grandfather for the first time. I am sure this is the beginning of many grandchildren.

I just started a new job, and of all of the women in my training class, I'm the only one over 25 without children. At 43, we are still discussing options of trying, since my new insurance plan has more covered options, but I am so ambivalent about the entire thing and have read about the reality of the statistics of pregnancy at my age. I notice I tend to bring up the children issue before others when meeting new people so that I don't have to deal with the punched in the stomach feeling when people ask how many children I have, never thinking that possibly I don't have any.

I desire to move to a more progressive area, thinking there would be more women childless like me, but probably deep down know that the problem isn't geography but my own unresolved feelings on the subject. Just know you are not alone.

Ruthie: Yes, I feel this way every time I'm around my stepkids and my husband's ex. I'm the only one who hasn't had kids. The best word to describe it is invisible. I think they've tried to accept me, but there are just moments they don't know what to think of me or do with me. Like just relaxing and accepting me where I am is so difficult. I have talked to my stepdaughter about my fertility challenges. She has never been one to be sympathetic, however. Her mantra is "you just got to GET OVER it." I didn't talk to my daughter-in-law though; she is even less sympathetic and a chronic interrupter to boot. I didn't open up about my infertility till my third miscarriage; then I decided to go public and posted it on my Facebook status. I'm so glad I did. There were only two people who had the gall to suggest that I try surrogate motherhood. That's not too bad for the number of people I told. Everyone else had manners and offered words of consolation and comfort. I know people (usually) mean well, and are trying to help fix my "problem," but this is an area where offering unsolicited advice will cause more damage than good. Dear reader, if I have described you, remember that after all, the woman has a doctor who has already discussed options with her. Offer sincere sympathy and stop talking. Let her drive the conversation.

HAVE YOU EVER PRETENDED TO BE A MOM?

"Our kids." "My son." "Being a mom . . ."

I have been going through old writings from the 80s and 90s. Most are columns or essays, some of them published in the community newspapers where I worked or sent out as freelance pieces to various magazines and newspapers. In addition to being embarrassed—I really thought that was good?—I'm surprised to read frequent phrases like the above that implied I had children. Did I really consider myself a mom or was I trying to fit in with the rest of the world?

I had three stepchildren. The older two, in their teens when Fred and I got married, did not live with us. The youngest, only 7 when we met, lived with us from age 12 to 20, flying from California to Texas to spend time with his mom for holidays and summer vacation. Sure, I was doing full-time mom duty for a while, but did I really think of myself that way? Certainly not on Mother's Day when the honors went to Fred's ex. Certainly not when it came to decisions about "our son's" religion, extracurricular activities, or his future. Certainly not when other women talked about their children's birth and younger years. Certainly not when I tried to hug my stepson and he backed away.

I was kind of a mom, but in my writing, I seemed to imply that I was a full-fledged just-like-everybody-else mom. So why did my "son" call me "Sue?" Maybe it was just too complicated to explain that these were stepchildren, that I had not given birth to them. Or was I embarrassed, feeling that I had failed?

Who was to know different? Not the photographer who kept calling me "Mom" as he posed us for a family portrait. Not the school secretary who called to tell me young Mr. Lick had not shown up for class. Not the Boy Scout leader who wanted me to bring two dozen cookies. Not the other moms who sent their kids to our house to play. In most cases, I did not set them straight.

It's as difficult to put myself back in that head space as it is to fit into the skinny clothes I wore then. I know I wanted desperately to be a mom. I guess I claimed as much of that status as I could, aware that it could be taken away at any minute.

These days, with Fred gone and no contact with the kids beyond Facebook, I just tell people I never had any children. That's not quite true either, is it? I still love Fred's kids and pray for them every day. But they've got a mom. I'm just Sue.

Have you ever pretended to be a mom or dad when you're not? If you have stepchildren, do you feel like their parent? Do you claim that status among other people?

SilverShil0h: In 20 years, I think I've said "my son" or "my kids" once, maybe twice. They have a mom they are close to, and I try to respect her boundaries. Plus, they do distance themselves from me, and I from them, from time to time, with the ebb and flow of family drama.

What I don't get is this "bonus son" or "bonus daughter." Or even "daughter in love" (replacing daughter in law).

I want to say to women who say that, you're not fooling anyone. I mean, what inside of them causes them to think they have to use a fancy label or be ashamed of the normal words people use? Do they think the rest of us who don't use those words are not as devoted, caring or loving? I just see the usage of those words as fake, I guess.

Mali: You may be Sue, not Mom, but rest assured you're not "just Sue." You're a Sue who was tremendously important in the lives of your stepchildren, especially the youngest. Everything you did for him in those eight years was, in fact, being a mom. Don't downplay your role just because you didn't have the label. You don't deserve that. And neither does your relationship with your stepsons.

And anyway, a stepmom is a mom but slightly (ever so slightly in some cases) different.

Anon S: I never had much of an opportunity to pretend. Once, we took some nieces and a nephew on a little day trip. I guess I pretended inside my head.

Probably my husband did, too. When I took my niece to the bathroom, someone complimented her boots and asked me where I got them. I sort of shrugged and looked to my niece to answer. The other person assumed I was her mom and had purchased the footwear. I was a little surprised and very happy to think that I pulled off the illusion of motherhood. Years later, I still remember the boots, the funny little bathroom and that whole day with pleasure. It meant something to me then, even if it makes me a little sad to remember that part of it.

I agree with Mali, who says that you are not "just Sue." I think of you often, especially now as I deal with my own health issues and looming childlessness. (I'm feeling especially unhinged today). This blog has been a "safe place" for me over the years. The work you do and the way you put yourself out there is important and meaningful. Thank you!

FAKING IT IN MOMLAND AT THE MALL

When we went shopping yesterday, I'm sure my friend had no idea she was taking me places I had never been before. I'm used to her chatting with everyone she meets and showing them all pictures of her grandchildren. I'm happy for her. At the clothing store where she talked me into a new Easter outfit, I smiled and nodded as she talked about childbirth with the store manager whose second child is due next month. It was hard not to stare at the woman's "baby bump" in her snug knit ensemble and to wonder who would take care of the store when she left on maternity leave. But hey, whatever.

Then my friend took me to The Children's Place.[58] Oh my gosh. Miniature clothing everywhere. Tiny shirts, tiny argyle vests, tiny bow ties, onesies, twosies, threesies, I don't know. If I had a child to shop for, this would be Disneyland. The sales prices were amazing. The merchandise was in disarray, as if a herd of rabid monkeys had come through, but my friend quickly hit it off with the clerk. Out came the baby pictures again as they compared babies and sizes and family situations while I wandered around feeling like a visitor from another planet. I have never seen so many children's things in one place. For me, it was like a whole store full of doll clothes and I wasn't allowed to play. Not only will I never have children or grandchildren, but nobody in my life is having babies these days. They're either too old or they have put off marriage so long they may never get around to it. My friends' grandchildren all live far away, so I'm not likely to ever see them except in photos on the smart phone or iPad.

I didn't say much at that store. I let them talk while I looked at things and made color suggestions for her grandkids' Easter outfits. As they continued to talk while my friend signed up for their rewards club, I rested on a chair near the cash register. I couldn't say anything about my own children or grandchildren, and there seemed no point in telling them I didn't have any kids. I just waited until they were through and we could go on to the Nike store.

I love my friend, and I'm grateful she includes me in her life, but when I mentioned that I had never been in a store like that before, it didn't register. Her mind was busy thinking about her babies. So I pretended I belonged, just like the other women.

Have you had an experience like this?

Jade: I sometimes "treat" myself to a look in the baby department in the shops. I look at the little girls' cute dresses and cute shoes. I let myself think about how lovely it would be to have a little one to buy these for and watch her run around. As an ex-foster caregiver of four pre-teens to teens, I know reality differs from the "dream" though. We shopped for the kids we cared for. It was often enjoyable, but the reality was you still couldn't buy just what you liked the look of. There were (boring) practicalities to consider. It was halfway through summer and the dress would only fit until the end of the season. They will have outgrown it by next year. They have dresses very similar to it already. The shoes don't match any other outfits they already have. They are cute shoes but won't last two minutes for walking to and from school. As pre-teens, they want to have a big say in what they want (and it's never what you want them to have!). And the really difficult one: that the item of clothing you want to buy is for the child who it is always claimed is "your favorite," so if you buy it what are you going to get for the others so it's all fair? But, yes I do still look. Always on my own for a bit of a dream. On a good day, I could manage a browse with maybe one other friend who would be shopping for her daughter and son. Or with my cousin who would be shopping for grandchildren. I would seriously struggle with a group of contemporaries all shopping for their kids. I'd probably go home.

Anonymous: Sue, dear heart, life can frequently be like lurching from a couples-only resort (and I'm the only single person there, inexplicably) to seeming like being on a Grandparents/Grandchildren Disney Cruise (and somehow I'm there with NO children or worse, NO grandchildren). By golly, I get to the point where I don't care about shark-infested waters. I'm headin' overboard and swimming for some island! To answer your question specifically re: felt that way? The Carl Sagan misquote "billions and billions" comes to mind.

SFL: Jade and Anonymous, you are both so right. I usually stay on my own island, but sometimes I get swept up with the crowd. I know the reality differs from the dream. Even when we were shopping the other day, my friend was having a hard time finding clothes that would fit and that would not irritate the babies' parents. And I have been shopping with a teenager. Not a dream situation at all, but still one feels left out sometimes.

We're not alone. We have each other.

MOM'S FACEBOOK POST SETS ME OFF

I'm scrolling through Facebook and here comes one of those picture posts with a saying about the glory of motherhood. This one proclaims, "Having a daughter is God's way of saying, 'Here. I thought you could use a lifelong friend.'" It goes on to say, "I love my daughter with all my heart. Share if you do too."

Just jam a knife into my heart. I've gotten this one twice this week from women I love and whose daughters I cherish, but they don't understand how these posts affect women who never had children. They have every right to glory in their children, and I'm happy for them, but it hurts and I'm not sure how to react. Not having a daughter, I can't "share." Do I "like" it when I have trouble even looking at it? Do I try in the comments to explain how it makes me feel? In at least one case, I don't dare. One friend would send me a hug, but the other would scold me for whining and tell me it's my own fault if I don't have kids.

Is it? Hello, God? Is it my fault? Did I free-will myself out of motherhood? Should I have stopped using birth control in a failing marriage? After that, should I have not married a wonderful man with three kids and a vasectomy in case someone else showed up to give me children? I have never met any other possibilities.

I was young. I didn't want to be alone. I didn't know all this would happen. I thought I could still be a mom right up until I realized it was too late. It took another decade before I could say the words, "I will never be a mother." So it's my fault?

No. I don't want to "like" this post, and I am not going to comment, so I scroll past and read some more junk about Trump [then a candidate for president]. Let my loved ones assume I was busy and missed their posts.

To be honest, my initial reaction to the Facebook post was a wistful "if only." Then I got mad.

Today there was a different post: "Share if you have a handsome son." Uh, next. We've all seen them, the shout-outs for daughters, sons, granddaughters and grandsons. Good for them. I'd probably post the same things if I could. I'd be disgustingly proud of my kids. I'm bad enough posting pictures of my dog.

Okay. Thanks for letting me vent. My life is good. I'm out to lunch, the ocean view is gorgeous, and my Caesar wrap is delicious. Also, the kid in the next booth is driving me nuts. She won't stay in her chair. She is not eating her kid-size fish and chips. At least I don't need to deal with that. So what if I'm eating alone? The book I'm reading is great.

Two old women in sweatshirts and jaunty hats pass by. They're laughing. I can be like them.

Keep saying it: My life is good. My life is good. My life is good.

Whew. See what one little Facebook post can do? Okay readers, what sets you off?

Anon S: I hear ya. Lots of memes about that. Scroll baby, scroll!!

It's the local "women's groups" that get me. A night out of the house? Try a new restaurant? Check out this new location? Catch a movie? That all sounds great until you read it and it says, "Join other Moms as we . . . blah, blah, blah."

Like seriously, people—you couldn't have just replaced "mom" with "women?"

I feel like leaving a comment such as, "Sounds like a blast. However, I noticed that this invitation is for MOMS. It's too bad your club isn't extended to witty, creative, accomplished women of all walks of life. I'd attend for sure if it was."

I agree. Life is good, life is good, life is good.

Laura: I tend to ignore those posts, just like I ignore the ones that say "my husband / boyfriend / _____ is the best in the world and bought me that latest Tiffany whatever with a bunch of red roses." I put those down to people wanting to fill their own void of insecurities, making them feel better to put that up and show off how great that one moment in their life is compared to the other instances where they could also be saying "my husband / boyfriend / _____ annoyed the crap out of me this morning for not _____" (we could all fill in the blanks!). I have this very firm opinion that if you are going to use Facebook as an open book into your life, then those sorts of posts need to be balanced with the other not so great stuff that goes on in your life. Which nobody does (or very few people do) and which is why I now find it a pretty useless social media tool. Put up your family photos, sure. Share a funny story about something your child said or did that makes people laugh, sure. But rub it in other people's faces that you have a better life because you have something that not everyone can have? No, I draw the line there. Then you're just being insincere. I also have an opinion that if I was to see you on the street and not be inclined to stop and talk to you, then we shouldn't be Facebook friends. And if we are Facebook friends and you were to say such a thing to my face (that is on these posts), then we probably wouldn't be friends for very long. Either that or we'd have a very long conversation about how it makes me feel and we'd know from there whether we were friends or not.

On the flipside, if you've put one of those posts up and the day after, you follow it up with one that says you threw your husband's shoes in the bin because he kept leaving them in the way to be tripped over even though you've told him a million times before not to do that (yes, I may have done that in the past), then I would tend to think you are being sincere on Facebook and we could very well be friends.

My life is for me to live, and not for others to make me feel bad for living my way, by choice or not.

WHEN PEOPLE ASSUME WE HAVE CHILDREN

I sit in a windowless conference room at the Tucson Doubletree Inn listening to yet another speaker talk about finding time to write. Children, especially little ones, seem to be the biggest obstacle for most. So needy, so 24/7. You can get up before sunrise or write late at night. Write while they're at school or napping. Write in waiting rooms or on the bleachers during their sports events. Hire a babysitter for an hour. Steal whatever time you can.

My mind wanders off. I know all that. I just never needed to worry about it. I never had a baby to take care of. By the time my youngest stepson moved in, he was old enough to take care of himself—and he preferred it that way. In one of my favorite memories, Michael trooped through the house with his friends. As they passed my office, where I was writing, he said, "There's my mom. She's a writer."

Sure, there were school activities, Boy Scouts and such, but they were no big intrusion on my work. I wrote for three different newspapers and worked on the novel du jour unfettered. Ironically, the walls of my office those first few years of full-time step-motherhood were wallpapered with Care Bears. I suppose the room was intended as a nursery. I enjoyed looking at the bears while I nurtured words instead of babies.

Husbands can be a bigger interruption. They need attention, too, but for me, husband number one was never around, and husband number two found it amusing when I raced off to throw words on paper. He had his own work during the week, and on weekends, it was TV sports all day long. When he got sick with Alzheimer's disease, finding time was more difficult. I wrote after he went to bed, while he was watching football, or while his caregivers took him to lunch. I talked my stories into a voice recorder in the car. I got it done.

Back at the Doubletree, the speaker drones on and on. He assumes we all have children and spouses to care for, that we are all just like him, but we're not. We might wish we were, but we didn't ease into a "normal" family situation like he did. We don't have family dinners, soccer games, and trips to the beach. We don't buy school clothes, throw children's birthday parties, or nurse children with chicken pox. It's just us, writing, and we'd like him to please change the subject.

People assume. A childless Facebook friend recently told about how an older woman started talking to her at a coffee shop. The woman gushed about her six grandchildren, then asked the writer how many grandchildren she had. She had to admit she had none, which brought the conversation to an awkward halt. She found the encounter terribly upsetting. You all would understand. But the grandmother didn't mean any harm. She just assumed that all women of a certain age have grandchildren.

We don't. With one out of five of women not having children, there are a lot of us who won't have grandchildren either.

A few days before Easter, I made the mistake of going out to lunch at one of our most popular local diners. It was spring break, and people were lined up waiting for tables. Lots of kids. So many kids. When I went to the restroom, I found myself waiting with a woman in her 30s. We could hear a mom in one of the two stalls talking to her kids. We heard yelling and whining. It took forever. When they came out, the other woman and I stared. The mom had three girls under the age of four in that little stall.

When the door shut behind them, the woman said, "My worst nightmare."

I nodded. "Really." This was not the time to explain my childless situation.

She probably assumed I was a mom. I assumed she didn't want children, but when I came out, her husband and son were waiting for her.

Never assume.

The good news is I'm free to write here in my bathrobe for as long as I choose and then share it with you while my dog takes a nap . . . Oops. Here's the dog, needing attention. Yesterday she chewed half a pen, and I still don't know where the other half went. Gotta go.

Mali: I love your story about the bathroom assumptions. It's a good reminder that we all assume, and we really shouldn't.

I also laughed at the comment that "husbands can be bigger interruptions." Too true! My husband was made redundant a few years ago, and has only intermittently had contract work. Whilst I do appreciate having him around, he does really cramp my style!

Sharilee: Sue, I loved this one! It is so true that people just assume everyone has children—in books, too. I have thought about that many times. Sometimes, it is in women's self-help books. The writer goes on and on talking about how hard it is to deal with kids, etc., and never once acknowledges the ones who don't have kids. It's almost like we aren't quite real. Thanks for articulating the things I think so well. Have a wonderful evening.

REUNION RAISES QUESTIONS ABOUT BABIES

Cleaning house on Saturday, I came across the video from my 20-year high school reunion. Blackford High School, San Jose, California, class of 1970. I shoved it into the VHS player (yes, I still have one) and settled in, mesmerized. The sound and picture were not good, but after all these years, it was fascinating. Look at those hairstyles, those clothes, and the facial hair on the guys. Look at how gorgeous I was with my big permed hair, contact lenses, and the sexy black velvet dress I used to wear for concerts. Where did that woman go?

As the cameraperson went from table to table, people answered a questionnaire about their lives. Most were married with children. Even those who were single had kids. Many referred to "having a family" instead of saying they had children. Only a few said they had no children. They said it almost apologetically. Randy, bless his heart, said, "I have no kids, but I still have a family." Rosanne, a school principal, said, "No kids, but I have a darling dog, Molly."

I cited my three stepchildren and two step-grandchildren. Gosh, my family plate appeared to be full, didn't it? I also talked about my writing and music, but that part was fuzzy on the tape. Fred, my handsome new husband, sat beside me, sipping his wine. He may have been the oldest person in the room, just as I was probably the youngest at his reunions.

I got to thinking about how times have changed. It's not just the hairstyles and music. In the 70s, having children was the norm, but now one in five women never have children, either by choice or by circumstance. Those 1970 grads started their families early. At 38, quite a few were already parents to teenagers. One woman was a grandmother. Today's 38-year-olds might not yet have started having children, and some wonder if they ever will.

Birth control, although legal, was a lot trickier to get in the 70s, and the girls in my class who got pregnant before graduation disappeared in shame. Yes, things are different now.

At 38, most of us were peaking in our careers. Our families were blossoming, and we were still healthy and attractive—more attractive than we were in high school. Several, like me, had gone through heartbreak and were in the first blush of new love, but most were still enjoying their first marriages.

Only one person talked about hard times on the video. He said he was finally sober after many years of being an addict. God bless him. A half-dozen grads had died, mostly in Vietnam. But overall, we were doing well. I guess if we weren't, we wouldn't be there. I missed the 10-year reunion because I was in the middle of getting divorced and I couldn't afford a ticket to the reunion.

I also had the video from the 25-year reunion, which I did not attend. A lot of people skipped that one. More were divorced. More admitted to not having kids. Several talked about their pets. One said she had adopted a daughter. A prize went to the grad with the most children—five—but at 43, we weren't likely to produce more babies. People talked about sons and daughters in the military and grandchildren on the way, but most of the emphasis was on their careers.

The 50-year reunion is two years away. I imagine those grads who are still alive and able to get back to San Jose will be talking about grandchildren and great-grandchildren. Most will be retired. I will still be the one talking about her work because I'm not retired, I have no children, and the stepchildren are no longer part of my life, except for Facebook posts. I'll still be the nerd.

Enough about me. I want to know about your reunion experiences. What is it like for people who graduated in the 80s, 90s, or 00s? Did you go? Did you feel left out because you didn't have children, or did you find others in the same situation? Did you/would you stay home for fear you'll feel bad among all the moms and dads?

Looking at those reunion tapes led me to thinking about what I have done with my life. When the camera focused on them, the grads summed up 20 or 25 years in a few sentences. What would you say?

The life we lead: Thank you for your blog. I needed to find this today. My husband is 15 years older than me with two sons from his previous marriage. When we got married six years ago (and I was 31), I was sure I did not want kids. Suffice to say my feelings on that have since waivered. I struggle with accepting my situation, mainly because I feel so invisible when with other women and alone in my fears of what my future will be like with an older husband and no kids. Because his kids were middle/high school when we met and married, I have a very minimal relationship with them. I also never considered the memories we

They do not list two loving partners sharing a home and life. They do not list childless couples.

Have people asked you, "When are you going to start a family?" Have you heard people say, "Without kids, you are not a family," or, God forbid, "They're not like you. They've got a family."

We all have (or had) a birth family, consisting of our Mom, Dad, grand-parents, siblings, aunts, uncles and cousins. But can we form our own family without children? Is it not a family if we don't have babies?

"Family" seems to be code for children. Family-friendly movies, restaurants, and TV shows are designed to amuse the little ones and keep them safe from grownup language, sex, and other dangers. I have learned to avoid these things because a) I don't have children, so I'm not qualified, and b) I don't like little-kid stuff.

As I write this, I keep hearing Sister Sledge's song "We are Family"[60] and seeing the last scene of that great not-child-friendly movie "The Birdcage"[61] (Robin Williams, Nathan Lane, Hank Azaria, Gene Hackman, Dianne Wiest, Calista Flockhart, Christine Baranski. Such a great movie). The only children there are the adult offspring of the main characters. As the movie ends, everyone is dancing with the female impersonators at the gay nightclub run by the Robin Williams character. Their definition of family is just a bunch of people who love each other.

So what is a family? Let's look again. The Urban Dictionary[62] lists some much more comfortable definitions. Says Lola5544 April 29, 2011, who wrote the featured definition, "family is a group of people, usually of the same blood (but do not have to be), who genuinely love, trust, care about, and look out for each other. Not to be mistaken with relatives sharing the same household who hate each other."

If you scroll down, there are some really funny definitions of family by peo-ple who are clearly not enjoying their relatives.

I'm not the only one thinking about this subject this week. Check out this article from Nigeria, "On Whether a Married Couple without Kids Should Be Considered a Family or Not."[63] The writer insists that the second a couple get married, they are a family, kids or no kids. I like that.

So what is a family? Can it be me and my dog? Me and my church choir? You and your partner? Do you have to have children to be a real family? What have people said to you about this, and what do you think?

Lynne: I declare my dogs and my cat fur children ; ergo, family. Nuff said.

Sue: I had the great fortune to go camping in Canada recently with my husband. We pulled up at a campsite which had a sign saying "Families only." For a second, I stopped to think "oh my goodness, this doesn't include us!" We had a chat and figured they meant no groups of guys and girls. But it was disconcerting. It got me considering what "family" means. I've concluded that it can be anything you want it to be. My husband, myself and our dog are my immediate family. My mum, brother and his brood are my family. My circle of friends are my family. Whilst at the campsite, one woman was talking about missing her grandkids back home and said to me, "You understand, as you must have family back in the UK." I said "yes" because it is my definition of family, even though I knew exactly what she meant.

SilverShil0h: At this point, family to me is whoever has my best interests at heart.

Jenni: I can't bring myself to feel that my husband and I are a family. To me, we are a couple. I feel inferior to families. I can understand that some childless couples get comfort from calling themselves a family. Each to their own.

WHEN YOUR FRIENDS BECOME GRANDPARENTS

"I'm going to be a grandma!" my friend shouted over the phone from Texas. We hadn't talked in almost a year, but now here she was telling me that her daughter was eight months pregnant with a little girl.

My friend went on and on about the baby, about baby clothes and baby furniture. I couldn't get a word in edgewise. She had no clue that while I'm happy for her, it felt like another rock piled on the mountain of gloom already crushing me. What did I have to report? Car crash, dog limping, crazy new boss at work, and I felt like I was getting a cold. Babies? Two of my cousins keep posting pictures online of their adorable young ones that I have never met. I hear babies crying at the back of the church. I see parents with their children everywhere I go. But I don't get to buy any baby clothes. I'd just like to hold a baby sometime.

This sounds way too sorry for myself. But here's the thing. My friend and I grew up together, always best friends. Except for going to different colleges, our lives had a lot of parallels. We both married divorced men with three kids. We both lost our husbands a few years ago, mine to Alzheimer's, hers to a heart attack. We both struggled with loneliness, aging, and dying relatives. The only difference was that she had a daughter.

When she finally took a breath, I mentioned that this was something I could never share with her. She responded, "But you're a grandmother through Fred's kids."

Not really. Not the way I think about grandmothers and grandchildren, certainly not the way my grandmothers were to me. I talked about how I don't see my stepchildren, have no connection beyond Facebook with them or their children since Fred died. I wish I did. All those years living in Oregon while they were still in California took a toll, plus they have their own grandmother and great-grandmother close by.

My friend admitted that she has lost track of two of her husband's kids and the other one has no plans to have children, so she kind of understands.

Exactly. Sometimes I hear about stepmothers who are so close to their stepchildren and step-grandchildren that all the barriers dissolve and they feel like family. But it didn't happen for me or my friend. Oh, we took on the titles, laughing at how odd it was to be "grandmothers" in our 30s, but only now with her biological daughter having a baby, does it feel like the real thing. I am so jealous.

I know a lot of you are still at the age where your friends are just becoming mothers, and I remember how hard that is. It doesn't help when people keep asking when you're going to have your baby. It's still hard when you get older. I was just thinking how great it would be to have the phone ring and someone say, "Hi Mom, how are you?" Or, "Hey, Grandma, I'm coming to see you." These are the kind of thoughts that will make you crazy.

Meanwhile, this morning I was sitting on the couch with my dog sleeping in my lap and I got to thinking that maybe God was wise to keep me from being a mom. My dog has fleas and another ear infection. I rarely groom her, and her collar's worn out. If I had human children, they'd probably be running around with crooked teeth, untied shoes and outgrown clothes because their mother was always so busy writing and playing music. And God knows what I'd put in their lunch bags: frozen meatballs and cold tortillas? On the other hand, my dog felt completely safe and loved in my lap. Maybe that's what counts the most.

SilverShil0h: Sue, this was quite poignant. I felt your inner struggle, yet I also know something in you is genuinely happy for your friend to experience the luxury of being a biological grandmother. And if your child had crooked teeth and all that, sooner or later you'd get that taken care of; we all know the main thing is that the child is loved, healthy and safe from harm.

Your transparency is so empowering for those in our shoes.

In my 20s, I lost my friends as they announced one by one, and repeatedly, "I'm pregnant!" Now in my 50s, after waiting decades to spend quality girlfriend time with them, and now that their kids are grown and out of the house on their own, I'm thinking, yay, we can finally do a girlfriend getaway or whatever fun event they want to do, and poof: "I'm going to be a grandmother!" And so for the second time, I've lost my friends yet again all these years later after waiting so long because I can't and I shouldn't compete with their grandkids for their attention.

Like you, I'm genuinely happy for them and want the best for them but I would be lying if I said I wasn't jealous.

I'm happy for your friend, but it struck me as clod-headed that she literally expected your two situations to be the same. This is truly a journey one has to experience firsthand to understand even the most basic concepts.

SFL: Shiloh, thank you for your kind words. You're right. Now we're into the grandma club business. I am happy for my friend. She has gone through a lot of bad stuff, especially in the last few years, and is finally having good things happen. I'm sure if we lived closer, she would share the grandmother journey with me, but here I am with my dog.

Lara: Omg. I would love to be eloquent in my response, but it won't be. I love the honesty of this post; I love to read somebody else say what I am feeling; I am grateful to not feel like I am a bitter self-centered b!+@# for what I am feeling/thinking simply by seeing someone understands it. I have been in a funk, as my husband's family is so child-centered, and trying to explain my experience to him falls on deaf ears. I have adult stepchildren. Let's just call that situation complicated. It is so difficult for me sometimes—keeping my mouth shut when I disagree with choices made in raising the grandchildren—and it just leaves me feeling more like the oddball. My best childhood friend's wife had a baby. He was always a support in this childless "thing." He is now that parent that is all about the baby. Too many baby things going on too close to me with no one around that understands. Omg. Thank you for this post!!

mrspolyglot: Okay, I'm late to comment here.

You can't necessarily be a grandparent through your spouse's kids. I'm not allowed to be grandmother—there's an age gap between me and my husband, and my stepdaughter (only a few years younger than me) "jokingly" said I was too young to be a grandmother when she had her daughter. (It's been quite clear that DH's first wife has influenced this.)

Give him his due, DH suggested I could be an honorary aunt, but that suggestion was knocked back by his daughter.

Cut to 14 years later, and we finally got a Christmas card that addressed me as "Aunt." I'm afraid that by then, I reckoned it was just too late. I'm pleasant with the family, I organize the birthday and Christmas presents, but that's it.

My husband has been an invalid for a few years now, and my stepdaughter has been kind enough to say how glad she and her brother are that their dad has me, but there's no real family feeling there.

I once got a joint birthday card from them when my DH reminded them, and I do get a joint present of toiletries from them at Christmas now, so I suppose that's some acknowledgement of being part of the family. I've been married to their father for 22 years. I reckon that if (in all that time) they can only manage one birthday card between them to me, then I know where I stand.

joannie1q2w3e: I love the one about "I just want to form a club for those like myself! The No Grandchildren club. " We couldn't have children in 1980, really no great fertilization methods abounding, so we simply didn't. My husband and I led professional careers. Now we are both retired. He is 72 and I am 68. What irks me is social media and the likes of it. Please don't throw your grandkids in my face every other day with multiple pictures. Yes, they're cute but they look the same as last week! And I have a very best friend since I was 18 years old, since nursing school days, who has five grandchildren, who doesn't throw her grand-stuff down my throat. Yes, we see one another every month for lunch. She sometimes says she is jealous of me for not having kids, never having to worry or see them sad. I told her, "You don't know what I've been through all my life!!" Always when I meet a new woman, one of the first questions is "Do you have children? Grandchildren?" After a simple "No," the look of the asking-woman is one of sheer pity. I want to hold her and say it's okay.

FOR A LITTLE WHILE, I WAS NOT CHILDLESS

On Fourth of July, I was walking the dog down a nearby street when this boy came out just past where someone had chalked "party" on the pavement with an arrow. There was no party now, just this kid about 10 years old with nothing to do. I had seen him before, remembered an awkward conversation about his missing model airplane. He's a loner, geeky with thick black glasses, possibly autistic. He has two sisters who are busy with their own lives, but I'm pretty sure he's the only boy on the block.

Without asking, he joined us for our walk down the paved street on our way to the wilderness trail beyond. His speech was slow, coming in spurts, worked around his crooked front teeth. "Going for a walk, huh?"

"Yeah."

He dodged nervously as Annie darted over to sniff him. "She's big."

"She is. But she won't hurt you."

"Is she gonna have puppies?"

I stared at him. What? "No. She's been spayed. She had an operation. And she's too old now anyway." Suddenly the whole idea of taking away a dog's ability to reproduce seemed ludicrous. Why would we do that? But he didn't ask. He just said, "Oh."

Annie paused to sniff a grass area where all the neighborhood dogs stopped to relieve themselves. The boy paused, too, then went on with us. It was nice having him along. I had been feeling especially lonely, this being another holiday I was spending by myself, my family too far away and my friends too busy with their kids and grandkids.

"Is it just you and her?" the boy asked.

I swallowed. "Yes."

"Oh." No judgments. No "where is your husband?" or "why don't you have kids?" He's alone, I'm alone, just fact. He reached out shyly to pet Annie's thick tan fur.

"What's your name?" I asked.

"Gavin."

"Nice name."

We walked on, Annie stopping between houses to pee.

"I know where there's a trail."

"Oh?

"I'll run up ahead and show you." He took off, streaking toward the end of the street to where the wild berries and Scotch broom have grown so thick you have to look hard to find the path.

"Is this your trail?"

"Yes. That's it."

He hesitated. "I'm not allowed to go past the end of the street."

With, that we said goodbye. I heard Gavin's shoes slapping the pavement as he ran home while Annie and I went on along the trail marked with the footprints of deer, dogs and tennis shoes, feeling much less lonely.

My dear childless friends, there are children who would love to hang out with you if you let them. Don't give up.

SilverShil0h: That's sweet, Sue. I could imagine Gavin walking alongside you, and both of you in total peace, just enjoying the day and the company. Isn't it cool how animals tend to bring people together? It's so special and warms my heart even more that Gavin wouldn't go down the path because he was told not to. A young man who understands obedience.

Technically I'm not childless by marriage, more like a weird mixture of infertility and doctors that gave up on me way too soon and I believed them at their word. Still, I've followed your blog for a long time now. I hope it's okay that I tag along even though technically I'm not childless by marriage.

Candy: I have often thought of becoming involved with the Big Sisters organization. However, when my thoughts deepen, I end up reminding myself that this would just be like having another stepchild. You devote time, energy and love to the relationship, but a resentful ex-wife is still in control and can take it away from you at any time. And then my thoughts end on pursuing it. I'm just tired of there always being someone else who is the parent and making the decisions and I have no say-so in anything at any time.

Today I bought a baby shower gift for yet another woman getting what I want. I was doing okay until I was driving home and envisioned her walking through the store picking out all of the items on her registry, and then I started to cry. Fortunately, my company called me out of town the day before the shower. I hate showers and never go, but was having a hard time coming up with an excuse for this one.

WHAT HAPPENS WHEN ONE OF US HAS A BABY?

Childless by Marriage readers are a diverse group. Some are married, some are single. Some have fertility problems while others are healthy, but they aren't sure they want to have children. Many are married or engaged to men who have already had children and don't want any more. Those men have often had vasectomies, making it difficult to change their minds. Some talk of adoption, fertility treatments or vasectomy reversals, while others like the woman who calls herself "Oh Well" are just trying to accept a life without children.

One commenter, Jennifer, tells a happy-ending story in which she finally convinced her husband to have his vasectomy reversed. Now they have a baby girl. She said she will probably unsubscribe from the blog soon.

I have a question for you. I know that most of us are struggling with the idea that we will never have children. But if one of us does have a child, do you think that disqualifies her (or him) from participating in Childless by Marriage? She knows how it felt to be childless and fear she would never have children. I think we should celebrate with her. What do you think?

I know that many of you are uncomfortable being around happy parents and children because it reminds you of what you don't have. Also, too many parents become so obsessed with their children that they forget their childless friends exist. They make new friends with people who have kids. I hate that, even though I understand how children can take over a person's life.

But our friends are still our friends. Way back when my best friend Sherri had her one and only child, we were both already in our mid-30s. I knew she went through a lot to become a mother. She never made me feel left out. We have never stopped being friends, and I'm glad to know her daughter.

So this week's question: What happens to our friendships, online or in real life, when our friend becomes a parent and we're still childless? Please share your opinions and experiences in the comments. If men are out there reading this, please join the conversation and feel free to comment on past posts, too.

Tony: Sue, in no way should our readers who have a child, albeit later in life, be disqualified from posting here. I believe they have much to contribute. To the people who are on here and have children in the process, for the love of God please keep posting. I'm getting ready for law school (at 66), and my young girl-friend wants kids. I do, too. What I'm learning is that we men have biological clocks too.

Polly: I think it's a question of sensitivity. My sister went through infertility and became pregnant unexpectedly. While I was happy for her, it was hard on me. She knew and acknowledged that, and it made a world of difference. She didn't forget what it was like when she was struggling.

SilverShil0h: My challenge is that—in my experience—moms who struggled the most to finally get pregnant end up flooding their friends and family members with pictures of their bellies, babies and kids as they grow up. A co-worker's wife struggled, got pregnant, inundated her Facebook feed with kid pictures, offered to have lunch with me to review my situation then never responded when I asked her for a good date and time, complained briefly in person about how exhausted she was, didn't recognize me in the grocery store due to baby fog, and then breastfed in our office bathroom. It's not that I don't care; I'm happy she has what she wants. It's the insensitivity.

There is a reason the infertility support groups I'm in don't allow anyone who struggled and then conceived and delivered. The women quietly bow out of these groups without saying a word to anyone but the admin. Sue, to answer your question, I wish I were stronger, but the reality is it hurts my heart too much when someone who had their dream baby thinks they know what I'm going through. They only know a part of my story and endless tears. If they continue to read, that's good, but if they choose to post, I hope their words are enveloped in love and compassion, with a tendency to leave out the happy ending bit, understanding that this has been historically a safe place to vent. Even if they do share the happy ending bit, I have the option to no longer read here and retreat to the safety of the infertility support groups I've joined. So in the end, it's on me. But since you asked, I was raw about it.

SFL: Thank you for being so honest about this, SilverShil0h. You make some excellent points. I do want this to be a safe space, and I for sure don't want to lose you.

Candy: Although it is lovely for women in this group to finally get what we all want, I just don't want to hear/read about it here. It was my hope with this site that it was free of all the crap we have to deal with in everyday life. The minute they have their baby, it makes them different from those of us who have zero hope of having a baby. Yes, they may have struggled just like me in their beginning, but at the end of the day they got the big prize and have no idea what it is like to be truly childless for life. I have always felt "moms" are the most insensitive people, and when one posts on this page and brags about how they now have their child, I feel my opinion has been confirmed. With all that being said, when I start to read a comment like that, I just stop and move on without finishing it. There are always other really good comments to read by women who truly cannot have children.

SFL: Wow. Strong feelings here. So apparently the woman who had the baby and was planning to voluntarily bow out was doing the right thing. The readers have spoken.

Crystal: I have also recently tried to bow out, as I do understand this exact issue. Even though I feel the same way, I feel like I earned my not-mom card, and I am totally different from the other moms out there. They have no idea what I've been through. I worry that I'm doing the same thing to us here. I do not understand what it is like to be childless for life, but I agree with Tony on this one. I feel this blog is about being childless by marriage, and I have taken that loss.

Divorce is much like a death in the family, except everyone tells you to move on and totally forget that person and that part of your life, so there is much loss.

I would also like to say that there is hope of healing. We have to grieve. There are stages to grieving, and then finally acceptance. I do feel that I got to that stage at the age of 33, where I was just okay with my life with no kids, and I very much hope that for all the not-moms out there.

Léa: It is a difficult question. My experience is that infertiles don't forget what they have been through and are often able to keep their sensitivity towards people who were not as lucky as them, even though they finally became parents.

But maybe your reader doesn't feel "legitimate" anymore to be part of our community. I recently also wondered if I would still feel comfortable writing in the name of childless people if I got the chance to become a mother one day (I feel I still have so much to write, but how would my readers react?).

On the other hand, I am convinced that the topics we are writing about would benefit from being read by a broader circle of people, including parents. My opinion is also that we will not achieve anything if we always try to oppose childless people and parents.

SFL: Thank you, Lea. I agree with you. I'm not going to make a blanket declaration that anyone with children can't comment here. Sometimes they have valuable things to say. I approve or disapprove every comment that comes in. If it seems hurtful, I just won't approve it.

9

MALE POINT OF VIEW

THE ONLY CHILDLESS MEN I KNOW are my younger relatives. All the men of my generation and older have children, although they may not have acquired them with their present wives. Childlessness comes with the second wife syndrome; he's done with kids, and you missed your chance.

But sometimes it's the woman who doesn't want to have children with the new husband. Either she has hers already or she never wanted to be a mom. Same problem. Or is it?

Men have more time. Women need to get pregnant no later than their early 40s while men have decades longer, so the need to hurry is less urgent. But once they're committed to a relationship with no babies on the horizon, don't they grieve the loss of children, too?

Man or woman, it always comes down to a decision. Did I always want to be a mom or dad? Do I love this person enough to sacrifice the children I might have had? There are no easy answers and no way for both people to get what they want.

I sometimes read a blog called Him + 17,[64] written by a man who married a woman 17 years older than he is. They were unable to have children together. In a 2009 post, he wrote, "I know I've missed out on something fundamental to human experience. Sheri has, too. Though I would not change a whit of my past if it meant losing Sheri, I sometimes try to understand who that young man was, and why he made the decisions he did."

A few years ago, an anthology called *Nobody's Father*[65] was published by Touchwood Editions in Canada. It offers some good examples of the male perspective. Some of the men are content with their situation while others are clearly in pain. One writer admits to conflicted feelings when a child has a tantrum over something he wants at the store. While he is grateful he never had to deal with that situation, he simultaneously wants to hold and comfort the child, giving him everything he wants.

If you wanted kids and don't have them, it hurts. Even if you never thought you wanted them, you might sometimes feel that something is missing.

Men out there, what do you have to say on this?

Downs: Thank you for writing this post, and for acknowledging that men also sometimes want children and are denied. The last lines of your post certainly pertain to me, as do a few earlier lines (I'm the fellow from HimPlus17). The struggle, I find, is understanding the various shades of my reactions to childlessness. Likely, this is an ongoing, never-ending effort. There's the honest grief that I'd have loved to bring forth a child with my wife, watch the baby grow, and then enjoy (I would hope) a subsequent friendship with the adult I helped make. There's also the part of me that just feels plain left out in a societal, cultural way. At family events, with friends who have children, I'm partly the odd one out. Of course, everyone feels left out in some way: the family that only had daughters or only sons, the man or woman who never married.

Perhaps people with kids sometimes look at my wife and me and think, "We could have had a life as free as theirs." I guess I'll stand by what I wrote on my blog, which you quoted. I'm missing something; I'm not sure exactly what. I've tried to fill that gap by spending time with young people, by being a mentor through teaching and as a volunteer with Big Brothers. It helps, but truly, I'll never understand on the most fundamental level what it means to love one's own child. As I age, as I learn to live with the reality, this reality remains a grief, sometimes sharper, sometimes less so. I suspect it will never fade and never become something to which I grow accustomed. Thanks for the post, Sue, and thanks for your blog.

lifewithoutbaby: Thanks so much for this post and, Him+17, for your insightful comments. I think that women have more outlets to talk about this issue than men, so I'm really glad to hear this perspective.

I am not sure that hole can ever really be filled. Then again, I wouldn't trade my amazing (15 years my senior) husband for the chance of a child.

Anonymous: So grateful to find this blog. I am an African-American male, age 40, still childless. While everyone has a different story, mine started at age 23 with an abortion and various miscarriages, concluding with several failed IVF cycles at age 40. The hole of so many disappointments can't be filled. Anyone else out there have any help when everyone who isn't gay, in jail or chooses not to have kids seems to have them?

Hopefulpapa: Glad to find this post. I am an Asian M, 40 and childless. Wife had three unsuccessful IVF cycles, due to multiple factors. I think a man's thought pattern is similar to a woman's who doesn't bear a child. Emotionally difficult indeed. Really helpless state, especially if one truly loves his wife. The tragedy is the thought that there won't be a bloodline hereafter. Does it really matter to us? I don't know. Surrogacy or adoption is not for everyone. Not an easy option, I think. My wife and I don't discuss this topic, as if we presume this issue is not an issue at all, but we silently brood on this. Prayer is my hope. God will one day hear our prayers. I am eager to be a father so that I can show my child this beautiful world!

Anonymous: It is a truth that every person at some point of time wishes to have a child, irrespective of being a man or a woman. I am male, 40, from India, where women are more oriented towards having a child. My situation has been very different. I have been married for the last four years. Of late, I am realizing I am missing something very important in my life. But my partner is not concerned about it. I wonder how and why, particularly when you belong to a country where having a child is very important for a woman. But my woman is uncertain. She is satisfied with the way she is going, a free married woman, and I am left with a childless marriage. Adding to the woes is the legal system that advocates for women, where divorce is a time-consuming and complicated process. Thus, men like me die silently. I want the legal system to be balanced.

Anonymous: Right now I'm going through a scenario where I have been in a relationship with a woman I love for two years. I am 33 and she is 31. When we met, she had a 1-year-old son from a previous marriage. While the biological father seems to be a good guy on the occasions we have met, she paints a portrait of him being absent during the pregnancy and early life of the boy. I have loved the child as if he were my own for two years now. However it is not the same as seeing a bit of yourself in a child's smile. She believes it is a deal breaker to ever, even in the future, consider having a child.

While I do not want a child now, I would like to approach the topic in two or three years. She does not believe her mind will ever change and even blames the first child on pressure from his father. The concern she voices the highest is that her son will feel replaced and without a family if there is a second child.

Second is that she never wanted kids at all. She has also raised the concern that she will have two children with two guys and that may be a hard societal pill for her to swallow. My hope is the 21st century "modern family" will help get the pill down. I just don't know if her feelings are truly genuine on this topic, or if some irrational fears and lingering doubts about being in a committed relationship are driving the conversation. What do you guys think is the best course of action; move on to somebody whom I may not love as much or at least in the same way (boy included) but who is open to the option of kids in the future? Or stick it out and deal with that feeling of impotence which accompanies any life goal lost? Maybe this too shall pass?

SFL: Anonymous, I wish I knew the answer. It sounds like everything is perfect except for her not wanting another child. How can you convince her that having a brother or sister would be the best thing for her son? I don't know, but if everything else is good, maybe you should stick with her. What do other readers think?

Anonymous: My wife and I have been trying for a child for the best part of the last decade. We are now 34. After several IVF/ICSI cycles, a couple of miscarriages, a serious bout of hyper [egg] stimulation where my wife was admitted to the hospital unconscious for two weeks and a rollercoaster of emotions, we have almost come to accept that we may never have our own child. Yes, it hurts like hell! I don't really know where I'm going with this post, but sometimes it just helps to get it out. Every day gets harder and the prospect of being a dad gets farther away. Being a bloke's bloke, I don't talk about this, but just grow older and farther away from my friends who all have their own families.

Paul: Very interesting article. I didn't/don't want kids, and told my wife that before we were married, but she thought I'd change my mind. I was open to it for a few months one year when I was younger and crazy. Now, after 20 years of marriage, I don't regret it, but my wife does. There are emotions involved, but personally, I've never felt I am missing out on anything. Maybe I am just strange, but the desire to reproduce is not there. I do find it annoying at church that everyone just assumes you either have kids or can't for medical reasons, rather than by choice, and I don't go to services on Father's Day as I don't like being made to feel like a second-class citizen or bad Christian for not having kids. Just my opinions. I wonder if other men, especially Christian men, feel the same way.

Anonymous: I was pleased to see this topic, and I am hoping to get things off my chest with this comment. Forgive my complaining, please. I'm a 34-year-old childless man. My wife has two boys from her previous marriage, and due to health issues is infertile. Though I've always wanted a child, I delayed it, as some do, waiting for the "right" time, financial stability, etc., etc. However, the older I have gotten, the stronger the desire has grown. Now, the powerful sadness of not having a child, of not feeling a real part of our family, and the resentment and feeling second-class to my stepsons' father and my wife as the biological parents has begun to consume me and bring about a depression that I didn't know was possible. I have always had a great desire for us to be as close to a conventional family as possible. I've poured my heart, soul, years, resources, and time into it, yet the results I hoped for always eluded me. The father pays no child support, and it falls to me provide, clothe, and care for the boys, which I happily do. Doing homework with them but never being allowed to attend a teacher conference, maintaining all the responsibilities of a parent but not being called "Dad," is torture. Simply, I feel resentful, hurt, and lonely from what I perceive my role to be: second class, outsider, not good enough. No matter what I do, I'll never have the bond my wife does with her ex. I'll never have those experiences with her, and it's hitting me for the first time that this is my reality. I love my wife dearly, which is perhaps an aggravating circumstance to my emotion. It's my own fault for making the choices in life I have. I just hoped for more, and I'm understanding that that hope was foolish. Thank you for providing a venue to vent. This has been eating me alive. I've browsed your blog, and it helps to know that it isn't just me, that maybe I'm not completely weird in my feelings.

Anonymous: To the anonymous 34-year-old childless man, I am sorry for you, but it seems you are carrying around the idea you must have a bio child to feel complete. Many people have children young, and it doesn't always turn out well. Stop beating yourself up. Maybe you should sit your wife down and tell her these exact things.

Anonymous: You might be surprised to learn that some men would prefer to marry a woman that is past the age of having children.

SFL: Anon, I can see that. No eggs, no drama.

Anonymous: Sue, marrying a woman who is past the age of having children makes a certain amount of sense for someone who is sterile naturally or is sterile as a side-effect of some medical treatment (such as hernia repairs, nerve blocks, etc.). Varicoceles, repeated cases of epididymitis, and anejaculation are things that naturally occur in a certain percentage of the male population, and some of us have multiple issues that make having children impossible. I was touched by a few stories I've read where girls had premature menopause in their teens or twenties and didn't think anyone would ever want them and wound up marrying someone who loved them and accepted them as they were. Some fellows will marry someone who can't have children because of "no eggs, no drama," and some marry because of love and because other women wouldn't touch them. Marrying for love and accepting someone as they are is the best. Two folks falling in love and realizing they accept each other when most of the rest of the world considers them to be rubbish brings those two people together in a very special way.

George: I am a 36-year-old male, in a relationship with a 38-year-old female. She has four children, ranging in age from 10 to 16, from a previous marriage that is still not totally over, due to some dragging-ons in the legal system, and by her hopefully soon-to-be ex. When we began our relationship, I was very open about my desire to have a child of my own. At the time, she was agreeable. Now, fast forward four years, and things have changed. She wasn't willing to have another child until her divorce was final, which still hasn't happened, and now she is saying flat out that she will never have another child, due to age, physical toll on her body and some other reasons. She just told me this almost three weeks ago. I have not been handling the news well, not eating, feeling angry and resentful towards her, not finding happiness in the things I normally do. Everyone I know either has kids of their own or never wanted them, so talking to them about this seems like a dead end. It feels like I have nowhere to turn for help and advice. The emptiness inside me with the realization that this dream I've had for years of being a father just up and evaporated has been heartbreaking, to say the least. Finding this, while not totally taking away the pain and suffering, has helped.

SFL: George, I'm sorry this has happened to you. It doesn't seem fair. I could recommend counseling or talking to a close friend, but I can't help wondering why you don't think about getting out of this relationship. She's still not divorced and she doesn't want to give you kids at this age and stage in her life. It's something to consider.

George: First off, thank you for taking the time to reply. Just knowing someone is listening, or in this case reading, means more than I can express.

I have been running the thought of leaving this relationship through my head over and over. But I always come back to the same feeling. Will going back into the single life and dating scene be any better? While I know that medically men are able to procreate much later in life than women, how would it be to have a child when I'm approaching 40? Could I even find someone who I could see having children with? While the simple act of at least attempting to convince someone is easy, finding a partner that you could envision raising a child with and building a family with is much harder for me.

To me, the thing I keep getting stuck on is my love for my current partner. I love so many things about her, and yet lately, I've found myself hating the situation that she has put me in. I hate the fact that I've become so close to her children. I hate the fact that over the past four years, I've invested myself in this family, and now she changed her mind and has put me in this position of having to make this difficult decision.

I still love her and her kids, but I hate feeling like I wasted the most precious thing any of us have, and that's my time. I've always wondered exactly what a love/hate relationship was all about, and I think I have now found out.

IS 49 TOO OLD TO BECOME A DAD?

He thinks he's too old to become a dad. I read that in so many comments. In fact, I received such a comment from a man this week. "Ezz" is 49, his wife, 33. When they got married five years ago, they agreed they didn't want kids. Now she has had a change of heart and wants to have a baby. He's still not into it and feels that he's too old. Sound familiar? Sure did to me since my husband and I were almost exactly the same ages when we got married. I hear it a lot. The guy says, "Nah, I'm too old."

Is he? We know that while women's time to procreate is limited, men can keep producing sperm all their lives. We know that some celebrities, like Paul McCartney, Rod Stewart, and Michael Douglas, fathered children when they were in their 60s, and they claim to be very happy. But what about your average guy?

My husband had three children from his first marriage and didn't want to do it again. The thought of going through all the stages with new children just made him tired. As it was, he was the oldest dad in every setting with his youngest son, who arrived as a surprise when Fred was 39.

As I write this, I realize that if Fred and I had had a child in 1986, the year after we got married, that child would have been 14 when his dad was diagnosed with Alzheimer's, would have spent his teen years watching him deteriorate and would have been 21 when he died. But nobody could have predicted that. Fred might have stayed healthy and full of energy into his 80s or 90s. Would it matter that people mistook him for his child's grandfather?

There are practical considerations. An article from *Time Magazine*, "Too Old to Be a Dad?"[66] by Jeffrey Kluger, certainly raises some concerns. It suggests that babies conceived with older men's sperm might be born with autism, schizophrenia and various physical problems. We don't hear much about that, but it's certainly something to talk to the doctor about.

Another concern is that the father may die, like Fred did, when the child is still relatively young. He might not live to be a grandparent. And the child's grandparents might already be gone when they're born. I was blessed to have my mother till I was 50. My dad lived to 97. And I had all four grandparents for a big chunk of my life. Two of my great-grandmothers were still alive when I was little. Are we cheating these children out of important life experiences by starting our families late in life?

Think about that older man. Just when he's looking forward to retirement, to having time and money to travel or pursue new interests, there's a kid needing to be taken care of and educated. If he has a baby at 50, the child will be a teenager when he's ready to retire. When you look at it that way, it's hard to blame the guy for being reluctant to start a family.

But what about this younger woman who wants to be a mom, who is and will be an appropriate age? Is it fair for the husband to deprive her of children because he's older?

I don't know the answers to these questions. I would love to hear what you think about this, especially if you're in this situation now.

Check out this article that offers a response to the *Time Magazine* doom and gloom piece: "What My Son has Taught Me in the First 100 Days"[67] by Robert Manni.

Nicole: I think one thing that's important is not comparing ourselves (or our husbands/mates) to extremely wealthy celebrities, who no doubt have full armies of nannies, housekeepers, personal assistants and private chefs to take care of them and their offspring. Sure, for them it might be easy to be a dad at 60+, or a mother in her mid/late 40s, but what about a typical run-of-the-mill average Joe working nine-to-five (or later) just struggling to still pay basic household expenses?

At 44 now myself, I know there is no way I'd want to be trying to take care of an infant or toddler while struggling with the very real issues of growing older and just struggling to keep my own health and energy up—while also having to spend increasing amounts of time taking care of my aging mother. I spend so much time helping her I don't know how I could do it while managing an infant. I understand now why my partner, who is nine years older than me, was hesitant to want to take on the burden of parenthood when I was pressing for it and agonizing over the issue in my late 30s some time ago and had to make my choice to stay or leave. I've seen a few of my high school girlfriends who finally got pregnant (through assisted technology) in their 40s now regretting their decision and/or talking about how difficult it is to rework their lives at this stage when many of their friends have their kids now out of the house in college or in their own jobs.

So no, I don't blame a guy for being hesitant at 50, even if the biology may still be functional. And I think we should be aware it's not easy on women either, at even 40+, if they've spent their lifetime childless whether by choice or circumstance. We can have a lot of dreams of what might have been, but the reality of aging is still there and not something to just ignore, no matter what the baby-crazed celebrity media might espouse.

Tony: Sue, this post was very thought-generating. In my opinion, 49 isn't too old for fatherhood, although many men think it is. The way I see it, if an older man has children in a prior marriage, then remarries a younger woman and doesn't want kids with her, it is patently unfair. Excellent post.

Brigitte: Disagree, Tony. If he made it clear from the start of relating to the younger woman, it was then up to the younger woman to accept the deal.

Or to clarify whether she would independently adopt or use artificial insemination to have a child, established as solely her responsibility, all established while living separately—would need to be if adopting. Would he be still interested in having a relationship with her as a single parent, and if so to what extent and what way? Many men are too old at 50 to take on the full extent of fatherhood yet don't mind a child's presence if not their shared lifelong responsibility practically/financially/emotionally.

Some may even balk at the presence of any little kids, and such an older guy means just him and no kids. It's unfair and pointless with the no-kids steadfast older guy who was honest in the first place to resent him for his authentic life choice position.

Younger women need to grasp that an older man who has raised his kids and doesn't want to go there again won't change his mind, so don't waste time with him.

Anyway, unless you are dateless and desperate, why does a younger woman without her own kids want stepkids in the background to start with, plus an aging "had enough of breeding" older man? Maybe this woman is just lucky to find such an older chap as a good partner and be grateful for that. She may have otherwise still ended up childless and single anyway.

Erica: Whether 49 is too old depends on the person, but I could certainly understand someone not wanting to have a new baby at that age. They may have plans on the horizon for retirement and a certain kind of lifestyle, and having a child will delay that, possibly forever.

On the other hand, if that's the way the guy feels, is it really right for him to marry a 20-something woman who is in a completely different stage in her life and then insist that she adjust for him and instantly fast forward to a late 40s pre-retirement sort of lifestyle and mindset? I realize that people can't help who they fall for. I wouldn't be a reader of this blog if I didn't understand that all too well. Still, I think a 40-something-year-old man who feels he is too old to have children should be dating a 40-something woman who is also past the age of wanting or being able to have children. If they want the younger woman, I think they should be more prepared to take on everything else that comes with that.

Candy: My husband wavered on his decision in his mid-40s, so I started seeing a doctor for artificial insemination. But as time went on, I could see he just wasn't into it at all, and he admitted he regretted telling me yes. So I stopped seeing the doctor. Fast forward 15 years, he has been diagnosed with an incurable and untreatable degenerative brain disease and I am now slowly watching him slip away. I could not imagine taking care of him and a teenager with raging hormones right now. I know that would be beyond anything I could manage gracefully. I'm struggling just to hang on as it is.

I so love him. He is my world, and watching him slowly deteriorate is breaking my heart. It scares me to think my time with him is being cut short. Although I am saddened by not having children, I wouldn't have traded him in for anything. He is a good man and loves me to the ends of the earth. I am very blessed.

ttlizzy: I have stumbled on this brilliant blog just today, and this post could not be more relevant to my life right now.

I am 32, madly in love with a 53-year-old man who treats me better than I could ever have imagined. We haven't been together long (only six months) and we aren't yet ring shopping or anything like that. But it's clear this is a long-haul situation in the making.

I have never wanted kids, probably in part because I hadn't found anyone worth partnering up with. But also probably because I have a very busy, undefined professional life. And, the way things are going, it will be that way for a while. So, when Mr. 53 told me at the VERY beginning of this relationship that he'd had his children (they're grown now) and would not have any more, I was okay with it; they weren't anywhere near the radar.

But now, as I've found myself in a good, healthy relationship with a wonderful person, and have begun to trust my own judgment again, I have realized that I don't feel comfortable shutting the door. I am in no way ready for a child. But I am not comfortable with the idea that it's already off the table before I have really had a chance to consider it.

Mr. 53 said that if I felt motherhood was something I needed to take on, he and I would have to break up because he couldn't be responsible for holding me back from experiencing something so wonderful. He also told me that he didn't want to reproduce again because he'd done it, he doesn't make very much money (we're both freelance, artsy types), but mostly because, when he was 17, his father died of a heart attack and it devastated him. He refuses to put a child (or me) in that kind of situation.

It's sound reasoning, and I wouldn't dare ask him to reconsider. But the idea of this relationship, which I treasure, already having a big, fat caveat stuck onto it is heartbreaking.

We've only recently had this discussion. Neither of us wants this to end. We've left it at "take it a day at a time," but I can't help but feel like I'm never going to get any further. I mean, yes, this is a very new relationship. But if the question of whether or not I'm going to suddenly come down with Baby Rabies is always looming, do I have to give up the idea of being married to this guy? I love him. I just don't love that I'd have to decide about kids right away in order to move forward with our relationship.

Do I leave now and find someone I love with this much of my heart and soul who doesn't have any restrictions? Or wait it out, enjoy what we have, and see what happens down the road?

The Book Studio: Hi ttlizzy, I was in your situation and feel like I can give some insight after eight years of marriage. I never really wanted kids until I met the right guy for me (when I was 36), who happened to be ten years older and a divorced dad of one son. We were both ambivalent about kids during our (too brief) conversation about it before we were married. I just told myself that I wanted to be married to this guy and kids would be icing on the cake. And it was true.

But after we were married about three years, I got bit by the bug BIG TIME. My husband said he enjoyed our lifestyle too much and did not want kids after all. I hated that he used the word "lifestyle" because it sounded so shallow and selfish to me. It was the biggest fight we have had. Our only fight. He graciously and through tears said that if I needed to go do this, he understood. I had to ask myself, do I stay or do I go? I stayed, but it was a very difficult time for me. I questioned everything. But now I don't regret a thing.

That isn't to say that I'm not sad. I'm still very sad. And my husband is, too. We talk about how we wish we had met years ago. We joke about his young nephew who is so like us, he "should" have been our son. It's that shared camaraderie that is of great comfort to me now. It cuts through "I should have's!" and "Why didn't we?" and "Why life whys?"

I have developed my own personal Plan B. Because while I love being married to my husband, I'm still a person. We all are. So I have developed relationships with my nieces and nephews. I travel with my husband. And without (with friends and through work). I volunteer and became a Big Sister. So my pieces of insight for you are:

- Allow space for questions and sadness, because that will never go away (that's just life).

- Even though the decision is made and is non-negotiable, talk with your boyfriend in a way that you both are very clear on each other's feelings and you can both (HIM included) come to an acceptance of them. This leads to a mutual peace and love from which you can support each other in times of sadness (counseling was helpful for us) and even enjoy the shared camaraderie of it and laughter (through sadness).

- Enjoy your own Plan B activities to help fulfill your other dreams.

I hope that makes sense! It's taken me a while to be able to even articulate these feelings. Reading blogs like yours, Sue, has been a big part of my healing.

ttlizzy: Wow. Thank you very much for taking so much time to reply.

It is so encouraging to hear that your life was made full by yourself, by your love of your chosen activities, and by the love you have for someone who really seems to be a partner to you.

Considering I have a very full life, a happy and healthy relationship, and a dog who could win World's Most Spoiled Animal, it is nice to hear from people who use these as their life purpose, instead of motherhood.

I have always been of the mind that motherhood should not ever be something I do just because it seems like the next culturally acceptable step. Even though my fear of regret is a big one, I know in my heart that doing something because that's what I think I am supposed to do is not going to go well for me and could end up hurting my other relationships in a big way (it's happened before, in other areas of my life).

I also appreciate knowing that, just because it was the right choice, doesn't mean it wasn't hard. That is the kind of realistic thing I need to hear, so I know what is in store for me, should my decision be to remain childless. I guess a lot of this depends on having a true partner in everything.

Really, really thank you from the bottom of my heart. Expressing my feelings on this blog was something I was doing with the very small sliver of hope that I might find some insight, but I sure didn't expect all of this.

Anonymous: Thank you so much for this reply. So helpful for me. I love especially the "Plan B" piece. I realize after reading your writing that I have done this myself and not even realized I'm doing it, and that's okay. It's an okay thing to do!

My fiancé is 15 years older than me, doesn't want kids, and I used to feel like I didn't but am reconsidering now. I have since been involved in a mentor program where I'm matched with an at-risk child. My fiancé is completely open to being involved in that with me. He's even okay with the child coming over, staying the night, camping with us, etc. He just doesn't want the financial commitment of a child at this stage in his life.

Am I "settling" because I decide that I'm okay with that? I don't think so. I think other people in my life tell me that I am settling, but I don't think they get it. I'm also so in love with my fiancé and I want to marry him! And this still feels hard off and on, and it probably will continue to. We need to ride this wave together.

Bringing him into riding the wave with me would be helpful. I want to take him to see my therapist with me. Right now he's pretty unsure about how to do this and what it will look like. He knows what he wants. He loves me too much to talk me into anything, so how can he be of help in therapy with me when he's not willing to change his mind? But having his support there and being able to talk about the sadness without him feeling like he needs to fix anything, that's important to me.

Love the Plan B. It's okay to have one! It's not settling. It's finding a balance within the gray area. Life is never black or white.

Thank you so much for sharing this. I feel as though a weight has been lifted for me!

Colleen: Anonymous, I'm so glad my comments helped you! Plan B is totally an okay thing to do! In fact, Plan B is going to happen anyway. It's life. We might as well have a say in it.

The funny thing is, the older my stepson gets, the more I'm seeing my husband having to figure out his own Plan B, i.e., who he is when he doesn't have to be a hands-on parent every day. Maybe this kind of thing happens to everyone, even parents, at some point. That's a new idea to me.

That's great about the mentor program! And as far as therapy, just getting my husband and myself in a room with a therapist we agreed on went a long way. Having a third party present and able to guide us through our blind spots and encourage us and support our talking about hard stuff made a lot of difference. We wouldn't have been able to go that far at home.

FATHER'S DAY TORTURES CHILDLESS MEN

Sunday was Father's Day. We tend to kind of forget about it, getting all obsessed about Mother's Day and then a month later, oh yeah, we have to send Dad a card. Right? There's a lot more hoop-tee-doo about Mother's Day. Remember all those commercials? All those people wanting to wish you Happy Mother's Day when you're not a mother, so it just makes you feel worse? The gatherings where everybody has kids but you? It's brutal. But as Tony, a frequent commenter here, reminded me on Sunday, it's just as bad for the men.

Tony and I had a brief e-conversation on Sunday as he tried to survive church. People kept wishing him Happy Father's Day, and he felt like "chopped liver." His stepchildren sent their obligatory wishes, but it didn't ease the emptiness of not having kids of his own. I reminded him that in less than 24 hours, Father's Day would be over and life would return to normal. He gritted his teeth and got through it.

At my church, we had a visiting priest who had just been ordained. He threw out an offhand "Happy Father's Day," and that was it. No making the dads stand for special blessings like our regular priest did for moms on Mother's Day. Maybe the fathers felt ripped off, but I was relieved. Afterward, I went to lunch with a friend and didn't realize at first why the restaurant was packed. Of course. People taking their fathers out to brunch. And the servers assuming any man over 30 was a father.

I told Tony it would all be over in less than 24 hours. Technically, it was. But when I opened up Facebook on Monday, it was loaded with pictures of fathers and posts about Father's Day celebrations. Among them were pictures of first-time fathers and grandfathers, including my nephew, my brother and my cousin. It was all very nice, but I had to stop looking. All that happy family business was too much. Let's get back to dog pictures and trashing the presidential candidates.

Next year, I recommend running away. Go fishing, take a hike, watch a movie. And do not look at Facebook until at least Tuesday.

Tony's a little concerned that we don't hear from many guys here. Men, if you're out there, tell us how you deal with Father's Day.

Candy: I have to admit I admire Tony for showing up to church. I stopped going to church on Mother's Day 27 years ago. I figured if God wanted me to be in church on Mother's Day, then he could make me a mother. Both these days are good days to just stay home. My dad has since passed, so it's just another day. I don't do anything for my husband that day. I don't even acknowledge it. I figure if my husband wanted something from me for Father's Day, he could make me a mother. Still resentful?? Yep, just a wee bit.

Tony: Candy, I'm not going to attend church on Father's Day anymore. Seeing all the young families on that day is more than I can take. I guess until I leave for my younger girlfriend and have my own little family, I'll feel this way.

sdelmonte: Just discovered this blog. So late to the party.

Father's Day doesn't really bother me. But then, I grew up without a father (he died when I was 3 and my brother was a newborn), so I long ago I shoved the day aside. It was a lot more difficult to be a kid without a dad who was forced to make a Father's Day card for his grandfather (who lived with us and who did help to take care of us) than to be an adult coping with the day from a different direction. Honestly, since my family makes a bigger deal of Mother's Day, I feel worse for my wife —not able to have kids and still missing her mom—than I feel for myself on Father's Day.

But thank you for asking. Really. In the years since my wife and I stopped trying to have kids, in the years since the miscarriage, I have struggled mightily with being childless and male, and have found that men just aren't supposed to talk about it. That someone out there asked "How are you doing?" helps. It might not cure the blues I get sometimes, but it's good to know that my wife and I are not entirely alone.

james h: I wish every day that my wife could have children. All of my friends have kids. My brothers have large families. It is every day I feel pain from this.

When I see a father and son having fun together, or a little girl holding on to her daddy as if life itself was at stake . . . some days it drives me to tears. It is every day, not just Father's Day. I will have no legacy. And it hurts my heart.

MAN WHO DOESN'T WANT KIDS DRAWS REACTION

Sometimes I get comments on posts that appeared here months or even years ago. You may or may not remember what I wrote last August[68] about a friend's daughter finding herself in a pickle shortly before her wedding when her fiancé declared he did not want children. Not fair, I said. What a horrible thing to do to her. The young woman subsequently broke off the engagement and took herself on a tour of Asia instead. Now she's back home with her new dog. She has gone back to school to finish the education she interrupted to be with this man.

This week, Aaron responded. His words are harsh but include a lot of truth. So I offer his comment in full and encourage you to respond.

I know it's a little old now, but this post is completely ridiculous.
"What is she supposed to do now?"
Leave him. It's not complicated. They disagree on a fundamental life decision. The timing is far from ideal but better to end it now than getting divorced later, or him having children he doesn't want.
"I want to throttle the guy."
Really? You want to throttle someone you seemingly have never met, over an issue you know almost nothing about? You have no idea what was actually said. For all you (and your friend) know, he made it clear from the start and his fiancée chose to ignore it. I see it all the time on forums; someone posts all weepy about "never getting to have a family" but admits that their partner told them they didn't want children before they ever got married. They'll add in some rationalization like "we had a miscommunication" or "I didn't know he meant never," but we all know what really happens in most cases: He told her upfront that he never wanted children, she heard it loud and clear, and she thought she could change him. That is 100 percent on her, no sympathy.
"What right does he have to take motherhood away from her?"
Thankfully he doesn't, and that isn't what's happening. She can choose to leave him if she wants to be a mom that badly. Not sure why so many people infantilize women in relationships like this; that's something else I see all the time. The woman wants marriage, children, etc. and her man is "dragging his feet" or whatever. Every-

one talks about how he needs to step up, s*** or get off the pot, let her go, when all they should really be doing is telling her to leave him. Women are adults with their own agency. They shouldn't be waiting for or depending on a man's actions. It's pretty misogynistic really, and that's coming from someone who is disgusted by much of modern-day feminism.

"He's not old, does not have kids from another marriage. So what's the deal?"

Maybe . . . he just doesn't want kids? Like, you know that's a thing, right? Some people just don't ever want to have children. I'm one of them. You aren't, and I respect that. And you should similarly respect the choices of others.

I hope I haven't offended any of you, and I can appreciate that you and many here have been through terrible emotional pain regarding having your own children, but that isn't an excuse for posting nonsense like this.

Thank you, Aaron, for giving it to us straight. Readers, what do you think?

Aaron: Thanks a lot for this. I appreciate your kind words. I also apologize if mine were a bit too harsh at times. I'm actually really happy to hear how that situation turned out. The young lady sounds like she has a good head on her shoulders.

Mali: I 100 percent agree with Aaron, except his rather harsh last phrase! I do feel that it is completely hypocritical when women insist that their wishes be taken into account but refuse to respect their partner's views.

SilverShil0h: The bride was grieving the loss of a life with a man she loved plus the loss of raising their kids. I don't fault her for needing support in that situation. It's fine for people to have a differing opinion, but why so harsh? It's possible to differ with someone and not be condescending and critical about it. Take a look in the mirror. Who hasn't made a mistake? Lighten up, folks.

Anon S: I remember reading that post and thinking, "Well, it's good that she knows now and not later." Obviously not ideal, but as imperfect human beings, I assume the man was "trying" to imagine himself with children but ultimately could not follow through. He did honor your friend's daughter by ending something he knew to be wrong.

Your comments, Sue, I felt were appropriate. We see our loved ones hurting and we want to feel that pain for them. Your history as a childless woman gave you a unique perspective on her situation. Of course you wanted to throttle him!

I like that Aaron's words were empowering to women. It's true that certain people (as men also fall into this mistake) "assume" that everything will work out. The assumption, of course, is that "our" agenda will be fulfilled by the person who will ultimately disappoint us.

Too many times in my past, I've "assumed." How I wish someone in my life would have said, "Really? You want to put up with that? Really? You don't see how terrible this person is for you? Move on. You deserve better. Don't be a victim. Travel, learn, work, do anything except follow this man."

A great deal of my 40ish years of life, I've been a victim. But I'm different now. Life is overwhelming because I'm finally seeing all that I missed and I'm mourning all that will not be. I'm also seeing all the potential that still exists, and I know I cannot do it all. How am I going to cram 40 years of missed joy and opportunities into the remaining life I have (however many years it may be). I regret all that I will not experience while reminding myself that I am exactly where I'm supposed to be. Like your friend's daughter, I've been given a gift by the universe. I just don't know yet how much beauty is there.

C: Aaron was dead on . . . 100 percent.

IF YOU DON'T WANT KIDS, JUST SAY IT

This morning, I found a card in my files that I wrote 13 years ago: "We are biologically programmed to reproduce. Like every childbearing creature on earth, our whole beings are set up to make babies, to continue the species in an unending chain. If we don't, we wander, lost, trying to find our way home. It's as basic as eating, sleeping, and excreting." Ironically, I woke up thinking the same thing this morning as I wondered what to write this week. Maybe it was seeing the pregnant women on TV's "Bachelor in Paradise"[69] last night.

Before you get mad, think about it. We have all these parts designed to make, carry, deliver, and feed our offspring. Why would we choose not to use them? Why would some people go so far as to surgically disable the baby-making parts? What other animal does that? It seems unnatural. What do you think? I really want to know.

My recent post about my friend's daughter's fiancé suddenly announcing that he doesn't want kids sparked a barrage of comments both at the blog and at the Childless by Marriage Facebook page. Some were sympathetic, some quite angry. How dare I suggest that that guy or anybody has to want children? He has a right to change his mind. He might have good reasons for feeling the way he does. I know. It's all true. And it still sucks. In every situation like this, somebody is going to wind up brokenhearted.

Consider this: For most couples, having children is the default position. Children are assumed until someone challenges that assumption. Four out of five women give birth. The number of childless couples is growing, but those of us without children are still the minority.

When you're dating someone, I think it's natural to assume you're both planning to have children someday—unless someone says something. And that's the thing. It's an awkward conversation, could be a date-stopper or a relationship-killer, but someone has to ask the questions. Do you want children? Are you able to have children? How will you feel if I get pregnant? How will you feel if I never do? You both need to honestly say how you feel about it: I really don't want children. Or I want children so badly that I don't want to live without them.

If you're not going with the default position of having children, someone has to say it. And not after the wedding flowers have already been ordered. People can feel the way they want to feel. That's fine. Just say it before it's too late. Please.

Yes, folks change their minds. But—and this is the old Catholic lady talking—if you agreed to children before you got married, you can't break that contract later. That's just selfish and you shouldn't hurt someone you love that way.

Brandi Lytle: This is a difficult subject, but I appreciate that you are willing to open up a conversation about it. After struggling with infertility for 10 years, my husband told me that he didn't want to keep trying. It was really difficult because I always thought we would have biological kids of our own. Even though he "changed his mind," we got through it—by talking, by yelling, by crying . . . But it was unforeseen circumstances that caused his change of heart, and our marriage was 13 years strong at the time. I'm not sure we would have made it if we hadn't been willing to talk to each other, though. You have to be willing to have those tough conversations with your partner.

Susie: My partner of eight years never said he didn't want children. His standard line was, "Yes, but not right now." This went on for years until at age 40 I broke up with him. At 41, after a year apart, he won me back over with promises of "we will try for a family." And then his actions continued to be in the way. Obviously, me being "old" made things harder. At the same time, he did not participate in the process 100 percent (I mean he did not alter his habits of drinking, smoking, and putting off sex because he was too tired/stressed/maybe later). He resisted seeing a specialist and dragged his feet about tests and medical appointments. He postponed plans for IVF. So it never happened for us. And four years on from when we got back together, I am torn between the grief and sadness of childlessness and anger and resentment towards him. I am angry because he was not honest with me, and I feel he kept me there whilst not really having the same view of what the future should hold for us. I was always honest about what I dreamt to achieve in this world (parenthood being a big part of who I want to be in this life). I feel manipulated into a life I did not want. Sometimes I take full responsibility for this outcome and see it as a result of my choices. And sometimes I feel I was cheated. I don't know how to reconcile this. I love my husband. He is the best thing that ever happened to me. He is also the worst thing that ever happened to me. I don't know how to go on from this.

Brandi Lytle: Susie, I'm really sorry to hear about your struggles. My story is a bit different, but ten years into our infertility journey, my husband told me that he didn't want to keep trying. It was shocking, to say the least. I had to figure out where to go from there. I'm writing about my journey (both infertility, accepting infertility, and "recovering" from childlessness) on my blog, http://notsomommy.com,[70] I really want to help others because I remember the loneliness, sadness, and just not knowing where to go or how to continue. I hope you'll read some of my story. Maybe it will help you discover how to move forward with your husband.

SFL: Susie, I am so sorry this happened to you. For most women, 41 is late to try to get pregnant. And if your partner is reluctant to have children in the usual way, he surely won't be up for IVF, which is difficult and expensive. You have a right to all of those feelings, but you both need to share the blame. He kept putting it off, and you let him. Somehow you need to find a way to accept your life the way it is and go on. You can have a full life without children, I promise.

Linda: Thanks for this post, Sue. I think honesty is the key. I have to take responsibility for the fact that in the early days of my relationship with my husband, I didn't know how much having a family was going to mean to me, and I didn't want to seem pushy. I always thought we would have kids or at least adopt. I should have stood up for myself and he should have been clear too.

Jennifer: Thank you for this post. My husband and I had been together for several years before we got married. We talked about and named our children. We were married in Oct 2013. I was in my late 30s and he was in his late 40s. You can imagine my surprise and heartbreak in January 2016 when I asked why we never spoke about it anymore or he changed the subject when it came up, and he confessed that he had changed his mind. Not only had he changed his mind and hadn't told me, he told his boss first (she's a mutual friend). I know I took vows for better or worse, and I'm 40, so the odds of even getting pregnant are slim but I am having such a hard time "getting over it." The worst part is that he won't acknowledge my sadness. He says that "he doesn't know what to say." Any suggestions to get through this would be helpful, I'm failing on my own.

Susie: Jennifer, I am so sorry to read of your struggles. I feel I can relate to what you have described in that my partner is exactly the same. I have felt very alone in this grief. Some days it is absolutely unbearable. All I can say is that some days are a bit better than others and that finding and reading blogs on the subject helps me not feel alone, or like a strange beast from another planet.

10

I CAN'T BELIEVE THEY SAID THAT

Is your home perfectly clean because you don't have children? Do you dare to buy white sofas? Is your schedule wide open? Do you have lots of money to spend?

Somehow parent-type people seem to think those of us without children luxuriate in quiet, neatness, freedom, and money. Ha. Not me. How about you?

I just spent a few minutes standing in front of the pellet stove looking around my living room. What a mess. Dirty clothes waiting to be carried to the laundry room. Grocery bags I didn't put away last week. Books and sheet music everywhere. The carpet is stained, the old green furniture is coated with dog fur, and this pellet stove I depend on for heat needs cleaning and servicing. Ashes fall out when I open the door.

I do display pieces of my antique glass collection where a child might be able to reach it, but there are many things I don't dare leave lying around because my dog will eat them: eyeglasses, Kleenex, pencils, paper, food, paper clips, anything small and plastic.

Lots of spare time? Nope. Why do you think my house is such a mess? Work takes priority over cleaning.

I'm rich, so I can afford a maid, right? Well, way back in San Jose when my husband was alive and working, we paid someone to clean, but we weren't childless then. His son lived with us full-time. So what am I saying? I'm trying to say that people assume things about childless folks, most of which are not true.

Have you heard that people who decide not to have children are selfish, career driven, strange, or immature? That they're no good with kids, so you wouldn't dare let them babysit? That they don't want to be around children? Otherwise they'd have them or they'd adopt some kids.

That if there's a fertility problem, it's always the woman whose parts don't work.

Here's a good one: If you really wanted children, you would have tried harder and made it happen, so you must not have wanted them that bad.

What about you? What do people assume about you that makes you nuts?

For more ideas about the annoying things people assume, check out these articles. You might find a few things you identify with.

Melanie Notkin: "4 Unfair Assumptions About Childless Women"[71]

Ruth Sunderland: "Childless is Not a Synonym for Weird"[72]

Tony: I've heard all these things. And then some. Let's see, I waited until I was 42 before I married. I was accused of being gay. Never mind the fact that I was a rounder. Didn't want women with kids, although I married one. For that, I wasn't a "real man." Yeah right. The moon shots were fake and 'rasslin is real. But stepchildren to me aren't the same as bio kids. Sue, I empathize with you about these assumptions. They are wrong.

SFL: Thanks, Tony. I forgot the gay one. I think men get a few extra assumptions tacked onto them. And no, stepkids are not the same, not at all.

SilverShil0h: This is such a sore subject. My stepdaughter assumes I don't want kids and don't like kids. So painful. I refuse to attempt to control what other people think, so I go on with my life, but the occasional jabs she sends my way further the gap between us.

I'm not sure what others think. Those closest to me know that I long for kids of my own, and are quite generous with their love in that area.

Ourmaybebaby: I always hated that people assume you have tons of money, especially since both my husband and I are working professionals. Given that we didn't have children, I could afford to take a lower paying job that I enjoyed. But with a mortgage, car payments, student loan payments, etc., you really have to make TONS these days to have a large disposable income. Also when we had difficulty getting pregnant, we got a Corgi. Nothing was the same in our house ever again!

k2k9dogs: My all-time favorite: "Well, if you had KIDS, you'd understand."

MJ: A colleague's favorite expression is "you must not have kids!" in response to any lifestyles that might differ from her own family's. It makes me feel guilty that I can go shopping late to avoid crowds and have time to engage in hobbies. Why do I feel that I need to defend my lifestyle?

Candy: Yep. Heard them all and gagged on them all.

The comment that I would always hear the most though is, "Be glad you don't have kids, because . . . blah blah blah"

Sure. Whatever.

Mrspolyglot: Yeah, I get the assumption that I didn't want children, or that I'm the one with the fertility problem. (Nope. DH had a low sperm count with low motility.)

And then DH had the damned nerve to tell me that I should have insisted on the fertility treatment that he refused and—even worse—told me that if I'd wanted children, I should have made sure that I carried them! (I had two very early miscarriages—possibly because of the wonky sperm, possibly because of my age. I was checked out, and everything was in order, but I was in my forties by then.)

Yes, I also get the assumption that I have plenty of leisure time and am rich. In actual fact, I've spent the past few years caring for my parents (now both gone) and now my husband—whilst working.

I've turned into a cantankerous old so-and-so, I'm afraid.

12 THINGS CHILDLESS PEOPLE DON'T SAY OUT LOUD

Political correctness touches all areas of life, including childlessness. Friends and relatives who know we're touchy about not having kids may struggle to say the "right thing" or avoid the subject altogether. Some just say stupid things that make us want to strike them. "Guess you don't like kids, huh?" "Lucky you, free to do whatever you want." "You can always adopt." "Dump the bum and marry someone else." "You don't know; you never had a baby." Know what I mean?

But there are some things we childless folks also avoid saying, things that we think and feel but don't dare say out loud because then it would look like we're selfish, we don't *really* want kids, or we're just nasty, trivial people. Have you ever felt like saying any of these?

1. I hate you for having children and grandchildren when I don't get to have them.

2. I hate my husband (wife) for not giving me kids.

3. My body looks better than yours, ha ha.

4. Good thing we didn't pass on his nose or my butt.

5. I'm glad I don't have to worry about having a child with a birth defect.

6. I hate being around whiny kids.

7. I have no idea how to take care of a baby.

8. Thank God I didn't have children with HIM.

9. My mom had no life; I don't want that.

10. I'm terrified of pregnancy and childbirth.

11. Sometimes I'm glad I don't have children.

12. My God, that baby is ugly.

I'm sure I will think of more. Can you add some unexpressed thoughts of your own to the list? Please don't anyone take offense. We can be honest here, right? Has anyone not thought some of these things?

Charmaine: Ha Ha! I don't have anything to add. I just wanted to let you know I appreciate your humor! We (meaning I) need to laugh about this stuff once in a while!

Dana: I continue to have thoughts like these. Such horrible people having kids and I'm unable to (hysterectomy). Feels like I've been robbed, and undeserving people can pop out a baby whenever they please. I know it's unhealthy and extremely bitter of me to think that, but it's automatic in some situations.

Anonymous: I love this list!
I recently read a blog post by a woman who was talking about, well, peeing a little when she sneezed, jumped, etc. after having three kids. Now every time

I encounter a woman with children, especially more than one, all I can think about is whether or not she too has issues with her bladder control. It makes me feel better (and happy not to have that problem).

Anonymous: "I could raise those kids so much better than you."
  "How come any irresponsible and reckless teenager can be a parent, and I can't?!"

Tired: "Please stop flooding my Facebook feed with yet another picture of your 'adorable' baby/grandbaby."
  Adding that if I did have little ones, I wouldn't join in on the overposting pictures of them. There is a movement, I think out of New York, to raise awareness that it's a) not safe for the child and b) when the child is older, they could easily resent their parents/grandparents for violating their privacy by oversharing information and pictures of them.

Anonymous: My husband has caught me with my nonverbal comments: 1) Rolling of the eyes when I see a mother doting on her baby. 2) The wrinkled, snarled look when I have to look at a pregnant woman.

Anonymous: What I think but don't say: "Why is your ex-wife special enough to have children with, but not me?"

Anonymous: OMGosh!!! Yes, I've said that one a few (well, okay . . . more like 100 million) times!!

Anonymous: Yes! I am so bitter about that! "You bred with that crazy manipulative woman but won't with me?!"

Anonymous: Here is my list of things I think but don't say: 1) Wow, you have aged since having those kids. 2) I look so much better than you. 3) Your husband is going to have an affair if you continue to talk to him like he's one of the kids. 4) Your house smells like a nursing home from all these diapers. 5) Your kids are out-of-control because you don't know how to be a good parent.

Bought At a Price: What kills me is when I hear moms COMPLAIN about the pains of childrearing. If it's really that bad, let me have them. Also recently I had a woman tell me to put things in perspective. At least I didn't have my sister diagnosed with cancer (as hers was, and of course both ladies are mothers). That is supposed to help my heart how??? Did I mention my mom has been fighting cancer for eight years? There are also the mothers who tell me about how much their children love me or how good I am with kids. Seriously, that's going to fill one heck of a void in my life!!! When people want to tell me they know how I feel because they tried for three years to have a child before they got pregnant, I just want to punch their teeth out. I'm well past the three-year mark, ten years past it, to be exact, and the desire is stronger than ever.

Anonymous: Exactly this. Sadly what crosses my mind are: "How on earth did you get to be a mother and I didn't????" "They don't deserve their children." "Honestly God, you gave them a child, but not me?????" Also, "I get all the hassle of periods, and I don't even get to have kids?" "Whoa! I've got to cover classes for someone who's getting her annual holiday entitlement because she was on maternity leave? Seriously? But I've got to beg for a day off to visit the doctor with my mother or my husband?" I'm afraid I actually said this one out loud: "Your first wife runs off with another man, but I'm hopeless because I'm slow to organize the dinner? You adopted with that, but you wouldn't with me?"

CHILDLESS AND KEEPING MY SECRET

So, we're at this restaurant, sitting outside, a big happy group of writers attending a workshop at the University of Arizona. Each of us submitted a prize-winning essay to get here. All day, we have been discussing the craft of writing and the writing life. We feel like equals despite varying ages and the fact that we come from all over the U.S. But now, the workshop on break, cocktails in hand, I realize that everyone is talking about their children. They're talking schools, toddlers vs. teens, funny and frustrating things their kids do. They're showing pictures on their phones. Suddenly I don't fit in.

Seated in the corner, I smile and nod as if I too left a house full of kids at home. I do not want to confess that I am different, so I eat my salmon and cornbread and pretend I'm not. I also don't admit that I do not struggle to find time to write. I struggle to fill the bottomless well of time I have at home when it's just me and the dog. They know my husband died because that's what my essay is about. Bad enough that I'm a widow and I'm one of the oldest people here. I am not going to tell them I don't have children.

After dinner, I volunteer to walk the two miles back to the campus with the young, fast-walking group. I struggle to keep up, but I'll be damned if I'll say it. I can do this. I can fit in.

Are you ever embarrassed because you don't have kids? Do you ever pretend you do? It's easy when you're among relative strangers. Everyone assumes people of a certain age are parents until you tell them otherwise.

I'm not proud of being childless. I feel like I messed up. Truly. I didn't make motherhood happen. No matter how successful I might be otherwise, there's this moment when a colleague asks, "How old are your kids (or grandkids)" and I have to admit that I never had any. I'm not one of the childless-by-choice people who boast about not having children, who say, "I never wanted any, and I'm happy with my life." With the implied *if you don't approve, that's your problem.*

To be honest, most people don't react much when I tell them. They go back to their own conversations, and I go back to smiling and nodding. I can share a little bit in the conversation. I helped raise my stepchildren, I do have a niece and nephew, and hey, I was a kid once. But it's not the same.

As I was getting on the plane to come home to Oregon, I overheard a conversation in which two strangers discovered they were both going to Portland to welcome new grandchildren.

Do you ever feel like you need to hide the fact that you don't have children? When does this happen? Have you ever pretended to be a mom or dad and gotten caught? Please share in the comments. Let me know I'm not alone.

LMS: Whenever I'm at a party and people start talking about their kids, I chime in with stories about my nieces and nephews, but I always feel like a fake, like I'm appropriating other people's stories. I also notice that a lot of people will ask about my nieces and nephews in the blank space of conversation where they would normally ask about my kids. And unless it's another animal lover, I always feel like anyone asking about my dog is trying a bit too hard to fill that blank space where they would ask about kids.

I don't think I could ever pretend that I have kids. I think that would hurt too much.

SFL: LMS, I know exactly what you mean. I don't exactly pretend I have kids; I just don't mention that I don't. It hurts either way.

Tony: LMS, I feel your angst. I too have been in that situation. I come right out and say that I never had kids of my own. Invariably they ask why and I tell them it just didn't happen. Or I say something obnoxious or funny, but God, it does hurt.

Candy: My favorite comeback that usually gets people to stop asking such personal questions quickly when I tell them that I wasn't able to have children is that I don't feel that moment is the time or place to discuss our reproductive organs, and then I stare at them. It works every time. Hahahahahaha!!!!

Laura: I'm so glad I finally found someone who has said exactly the same as how I've been feeling lately, like a fraud, because the only thing I can contribute to a social situation when people talk about their kids is a funny story about my niece/nephews, but it's not really my story to tell. And I can't figure out whether I tell the stories to make up for the fact that I otherwise have nothing to contribute and hence, will be a complete outsider until someone decides they've had enough talking about their kids and changes the conversation, or because I'm so proud of my niece/nephew that I want to share their stories. I just wonder if it will ever get better, because one day these same people will be grandparents and then what?

SFL: Laura, these same people will be grandparents and then you'll feel doubly out of it because they'll be showing the grandkid pix and you're not telling them you don't have grandchildren OR children.

Debbie: Yes, I sometimes "pretend" I have children either by not saying anything or trying to blow it off with the "they are grown," as my three stepchildren, whom I did not help raise, are grown. Most recently, as I was leaving yoga class, an acquaintance there, whom I have previously told I didn't have children of my own, asked in a rush, "Do you have kids?" I was caught off guard and responded "no." He then said what seemed very loud to me: "You don't have kids?" (in a small lobby packed with people) so I responded, "Well, three stepchildren, but they are grown." Turns out he was filming a commercial and the kids cancelled at the last minute so he was looking for some other kids to fill in. Because I was in my mid-40s, I guess he assumed I must be a mom.

I also find myself in situations at work where I choose to smile and act as if I understand when the all-female department goes into their childbirth stories or goes on and on about their grandchildren. Of all the environments I have worked in during the past several years, this is definitely the most baby obsessed, but I am finally to the point where I am used to it and expect it. Some days it hurts more than others. I love when I meet older women who have other things to discuss besides their offspring. I started volunteering at an animal shelter a couple of years ago and have met such a diverse group of animal lovers, some with kids, some without, and that, combined with aging, I imagine, has helped me get to a point of peace with my childlessness.

Mrspolyglot: I've lied by omission—you know these conversations where a complete stranger just assumes you've been through shared experiences, because you're about the same age?

I've also laid claim to my step-granddaughter, just to fit in, even though I've never been allowed to be her step-gran.

Last month we were staying in Aberdeen (Scotland) for a couple of days. While I was shopping, a friendly shop assistant asked whether I had grandchildren. I replied, "I'm afraid not." To my horror, she started to weep. The poor woman kept apologizing for upsetting me. I tried to laugh it off and blamed it on the menopause.

BEWARE OF THOSE EASY ANSWERS

I was reading a question put online by a woman who is 40, childless and married to a man who doesn't want kids. She says it's too late for her to get pregnant. What should she do? She sounded really heart-broken. I'm betting none of the answers given will ease her pain much. It's so simple for people not in this situation to tell us what to do. It's very likely this woman already thought of all the possibilities suggested and knows why they might not work for her.

Commenters offered this advice:

1. *You're not too old to get pregnant.* Maybe yes, maybe no. It is harder when you're over 40, and the problem with the husband remains.

2. *Adopt.* First, a husband who doesn't want to father his own child probably doesn't want to adopt someone else's. Second, many adoption agencies have age limits.

3. *Get a dog or cat.* Well, that helps some, but it's not the same.

4. *Get counseling. Maybe you're depressed.* Perhaps, but not having children (when you want them) is a loss and she should be allowed to grieve. It can help to talk about it with a therapist, but it doesn't solve the underlying problem.

5. *Talk to your husband.* Maybe she has, and he is not going to change his mind. If she hasn't told him exactly how she feels, she should tell him and see if they can work out a solution that makes both of them happy.

6. *Leave the bum.* Maybe she loves him and wants to spend the rest of her life with him. She just wants to have children, too.

Judging by the comments we get here, I suspect many of you already understand the dilemma. There are no easy answers. Someone has to sacrifice, and it's going to hurt. The best hope is to make a decision and try to find peace with that decision.

Anonymous: I have heard each and every one of these answers. I can add one more: "Stop taking your birth control and 'accidentally' get pregnant." Have these friends of mine who dole out this kind of advice lost their minds? Trick him? Are you kidding? What kind of a person would I be to trick my husband?? You BOTH need to want to have children. It simply doesn't work if you both are not on the same page. To those of you who have said "trick him," I say you need examine your own scruples.

Anonymous: I was told that too. Along with "You are still young," "Plenty of time," "You should just be happy," "He'll change his mind," "You can share my child" and "Why don't you just travel?"

Anonymous: You are soooooo right. Many people don't consider either what it means to "leave the bum" or "talk to him and give him a deadline" and so on: Losing your partner. They don't consider what that MEANS. You have to choose between a person you love—and having together another little person you love . . . AND do they ever consider how hard it is to find a new partner? How much time it will take, that it might well be too late to have a child when you've found a partner? Do they ever remember how many years it took them to find their partner for life, and how many attempts they had to make which didn't turn out . . . ??? No, they think we are still 25 years old and willing to simply find a new boyfriend to have some fun with . . . when we were on the verge of founding a family.

HAVE YOU HAD 'THE TALK' WITH YOUR PARENTS?

I often write here about the need to have THE TALK with one's partner about whether or not you're going to have children. But after that talk, we'll probably find ourselves having another talk—with our parents—about how they're not going to be getting any grandchildren from us.

If they're like most parents of adult children, they're going to start hinting for grandchildren shortly after the wedding. As time passes and you're not pregnant, they're likely to start dropping hints, asking questions, noting that you're not getting any younger, and laying guilt trips about how their friends are all welcoming grandchildren.

How do you respond? Do you put them off with "not yet," tell them it's not going to happen, or change the subject?

In my own case, although I remember many conversations about marriage while we did dishes together, I don't remember telling my mother I wasn't going to have kids with Fred. I know we talked about it, a lot, when I was with my first husband. Children were still a possibility then. After the divorce, I remember talking about whether or not I was too old—I wasn't.

But when I hooked up with Fred, did we have the talk about his vasectomy and reluctance to have more children? I don't think we did. I do remember that my mother took my side when other family members bugged me about kids. When I moped about not being a mother, she insisted I was a mother because I had stepchildren, even though she didn't have much of a relationship with them.

As for my father, we didn't talk about that kind of thing. I'd talk to Mom, and she'd talk to him. I know he would have enjoyed the children I might have had. But we've never spoken about it directly.

How about you? How did you break the news to your parents? How did they react? Or have you put off that conversation indefinitely?

Professor: My mother was a baby freak—when she married my stepdad, she was desperate to have more kids. Turns out, he wasn't able to because his diabetes had inhibited him in that area (he never, actually, had any kids—just a stepkid in me). She was devastated, but looked at me as her next hope. When I told her that John and I wouldn't be having babies, I was afraid of crushing her. But to my surprise, I got the complete opposite reaction. She was super supportive and insisted, like your mom did, that "giving birth" was the least important part of mothering, and as long as I mothered my stepkids, neither she nor I would be missing out.

My dad, on the other hand, thought I was ruining my life by being in an unconventional marriage, and he and I haven't talked for many years now. Not just because of the baby thing, but that was a factor.

My solution is that I catch myself every time I talk with my stepkids about their futures, and I am careful to use words like "If you choose to get married . . ." and "If you have children . . ." instead of "when you get married" and "when you have children."

Anonymous: When my mother asked me when I was going to have kids, I jokingly answered, "You used to say that 'someday you'll have a kid just like yourself,' and I just couldn't take the chance." Of course I desperately wanted a child, but never felt that I could talk with my mother about it, so I made jokes instead.

Kathleen T: When I was married to my first husband, my mother-in-law kept asking when we were going to have kids and I laughingly said, "When pigs fly." Joke was on me when every birthday and Christmas brought a new flying pig picture, garden ornament, or figurine.

Circumstance and timing did not work out for me in the children department, crushing my mom's hopes for a grandchild from me. (I decided when I turned 35 and was still single after being divorced for five years, that I should not have children. I reconsidered when I married my husband at age 38, but he said he definitely did not want more children.) My mom has two granddaughters from my older brother, but their relationship is strained and she has not had much contact with them.

Last year, at age 44, I had an unplanned pregnancy after being told by my doctor I could not get pregnant (PCOS), and I didn't have to take birth control anymore. At the end of the first trimester, I had a miscarriage, one of the most difficult and painful periods of my life. My mom took it so hard, to come so close and then have it taken away. I know it comes from a place of hurt when she makes little digs at me about not having children. I have had to limit my conversations with her during the last several months while I recovered emotionally. It must seem so strange to her, seeing me live a life completely alien to her. She tells me I don't know what I'm missing but I'm pretty sure I have at least a sense of the loss.

On the other hand, parents might not know what they are missing out on by having a life with children. We don't get to live two lives and then compare them. We live the life we are given, and somehow find the blessings that each day has to offer.

SFL: Kathleen, what a story. Thank you for sharing this with us. At least your mother-in-law had a sense of humor with all those pig gifts.

When I got to the part where you lost the baby, I gasped. I suspect everyone will. How hard that must have been and probably still is. But we do have to live the life we're given. I wish you all the best.

Doubleme: My parents thought [and think] it is unfair that my husband would not give me a child when he had one. It still makes them mad even now. They feel he is totally selfish on that subject.

DUCK! MOTHER'S DAY IS COMING AGAIN

If we're to believe the images we see in the TV commercials, Mother's Day is a joy to all women. Their children shower them with gifts, cards, and breakfast in bed, and the whole family gathers to honor the grandmothers and great-grandmothers. Picture little girls in frilly dresses hugging their moms and grandmoms. Picture picnics, feasts at a family dining room table, or gatherings at a favorite restaurant. Picture flowers and cards, and the whole world wishing you a happy Mother's Day because you, the mother, deserve it.

Yeah. Now picture what it's really like for many of us. First, our mothers may be dead or terminally ill or we don't get along. The holiday emphasizes the fact that we don't have a mother to honor. Second, we don't all have children. We go to church and feel left out when special prayers are said for the mothers. We go out to eat, and the waiter assumes we're mothers, but we're not. We go to a family gathering and feel left out because we're the only ones without kids. We wait all day for some kind of acknowledgement from our stepchildren, and it doesn't happen. Everywhere we look, people are talking about Mother's Day, and it makes us feel like crap.

For those who are mothers, congratulations. Enjoy your day. For the rest of us, if we can focus on the moms in our lives, that's a great thing to do. If you just can't, run away until it's over. It's a good day to turn off the TV, stay away from Facebook, and avoid going to restaurants. How about a hike, a walk on the beach, or a movie instead?

If you have stepchildren, don't expect them to show up bearing gifts. They're busy with their biological mother and probably won't even think about you. Don't take it personally.

Why not buy yourself a gift? You know you deserve it.

I'll be playing music for two Masses at church and then going to my monthly song circle. In between, I'll probably have lunch with a friend who hates Mother's Day as much as I do. Her mother, like mine, has died. She has adult children, but their relationship is rocky. So I'll pretty much do what I usually do on Sundays, and I'll enjoy it.

Over the years, Mother's Day has gotten easier for me. It will for you, too, I promise. Try not to get yourself all upset about it. If you need a good cry, go ahead and cry. Then move on. It's just one day.

Anonymous: Mother's Day has been difficult for me over the past few years. I have been married almost seven years and still have no children. I am also 30. It's really hard because people have expectations about married women in my culture. I have gotten harassed a lot about not having children, as if that is a decision entirely up to *me* and me alone. My husband and I haven't tried because he's too scared due to the things we've had to deal with--health issues, job loss, family issues. I sometimes think others see what they want to see, and they dole out their opinions without thinking about what they say. I have prayed so much about this, and I am very close to giving up. I try not to be bitter whenever people share that they are parents and have their families and just remind myself that life will go the way it needs to for me and that is the way it is. I can't write the chapters for other people's lives, and they can't do that for me either.

Anonymous: I wish I had come across your blog sooner because this Mother's Day was especially hard for me. I just found out that my husband isn't open to the idea of adoption or fostering after almost five years of marriage, when we had previously discussed that this would be our natural next step. What a bomb! I guess I've been okay on past Mother's Days because I still had a modicum of hope left that one of these days I could be actually celebrating a Mother's Day as a mom. But now I'm thinking future years will be hard, too. Definitely need to stay away from Facebook on that day. And now I can't sleep because the thoughts occurring are whether I stay with the love of my life in a forced childless situation or leave him and try to be a single parent, which was my original plan before I even met him. I don't want to resent him for the rest of our lives.

The main reason we are still childless is we got married later in life, but also, he has some morphology issues with his sperm. When I was tested for EVERYTHING three years ago, the RE, who expected my results to be horrible because of my age, was actually shocked at how good all my tests were. We were told that to ever get pregnant with our own eggs and sperm, we HAD to do IVF with ICSI (intracytoplasmic sperm injection). You know, we would make it work financially if we got pregnant on our own, but paying for IVF with such a low chance seems like throwing money away. He is also not open to the idea of donor eggs, which I would actually prefer for the chances of it taking would be far greater and I am not tied to my DNA anyway. But he can't see how we would raise a child by telling that child from the start that he/she is not biologically mine. Today was just horrible. Sorry for such a long post.

Ruthie: Just posting to add two other scenarios where Mother's Day is excruciating, besides the ones that have been brought up. First, I had a friend who was forced by her father to give up her baby for adoption. She got pregnant while living at home. I met her when she was around 45, and the grief was almost unbearable for her. Second, I do women's prison ministry. Mother's Day is heartbreaking for the mothers inside as well. Some of them have kids who won't speak to them, which adds to the pain. Of course, I have my own story. Mother's Day and baby showers were like icicles in my heart for many years, but no more. Jesus has slowly softened this blow over the decades.

Anonymous: I thought I would throttle the next person to wish me a happy Mother's Day. My stock answer is always, "Thanks, but I'm not a Mom." I even gave that response to my stepson when he wished me a happy Mother's Day. He replied "Yes, you are." He's 12, and that made me cry. I ruined the moment by stating "No, I am not." I hurt his feelings, and for that, I am sorry. I guess sometimes it's not always about me.

CHILDLESS? HERE'S WHAT YOU SHOULD DO

Lots of people offer solutions for our childlessness.

Who hasn't heard, "Why don't you just adopt?" Or "You could become a foster parent." We all have. Of course, that totally ignores the fact that if your partner doesn't want your own children, why would he want someone else's? Also, adoption and fostering are not easy, and not everyone can meet the requirements. Sure, we have all heard beautiful adoption stories where everything worked well, but we have also known people who waited years through one disappointment after another or who got turned down flat for some reason.

"You should look into IVF, donor eggs or sperm, or fertility treatments of some sort." As if you never thought of that. Maybe you're already doing it and prefer not to talk about it. Unfortunately, all the science in the world cannot guarantee a baby, and it costs a fortune. Think one Mercedes for each procedure.

"Oh, he can just get that vasectomy reversed." Well, sometimes. It doesn't always work, especially if the original surgery was performed years earlier, and if he doesn't want to get the vasectomy reversed, you're stuck.

"Just relax. God will send you a baby in due time. Look at Abraham and Sarah in the Bible." Yeah, they were a bazillion years old, and there was an angel involved.

"Volunteer to work with kids. Become a Big Brother or Big Sister. Tutor, mentor, babysit." Not the same. Sometimes it makes you feel worse.

"Just enjoy your stepchildren. That's all the kids you need." Um, no.

That's what I have come up with so far. I welcome you to add to the list of "Why don't you?" comments you have gotten from friends, family, and well-meaning strangers.

SilverShil0h: In the "you should look into . . ." department, I was told, "Why don't you use a surrogate mother?"

I rarely get that angry, but I allowed myself to feel it and gave her a piece of my mind.

I've also been told that I don't like kids. Very false.

My naïve younger self even said, "Since I don't have kids, my pet is like my child"—ha! Nooooo.

Off the top of my head, Sue, that is all I can think of for now.

Jo: "You want to get married and have a family, but your partner doesn't want to? You should leave your partner."

Easier said than done.

Anon S: "Volunteer to be a 'Big Sister.'" I've heard that one.

The thing for me is—a Big Brother/Big Sister[73] situation is unique on its own. Usually it's an adult who feels the desire to selflessly give of themselves to a child who is disadvantaged in some way. It's a wonderful unique friendship that many people consider to be very rewarding. And usually temporary.

It's a great situation for people with time on their hands, a calling in their heart, or someone who wants to build their resume. It's not a proper substitution for someone who wants to build a family. It's just not.

It's like telling a person whose dream in life is to own a restaurant, "Oh, you don't have the money or skills to have a restaurant? You know what you should do? You should volunteer at a soup kitchen."

It's not fair to compare a soup kitchen gig to a real human relationship. Many good things come from Big Brothers/Big Sisters. Many good things come from devoting time to a soup kitchen. But they do not fill a real burning void in a person's life and, as such, are stupid suggestions.

Singlechildlessover40: Become a single mother (as if it's so easy). You get to make all the parenting decisions on your own! No one to fight with! (And no one to help either—financially, emotionally, physically, etc.)

Try this "new" dating app! I know someone who met their partner on it and now they have kids! (As if the last 20 years of dating just never happened. Of course, yes, it's always the NEXT guy who could be The One.)

Just go out to a bar and have a one night stand.

And my least favorite: "Take mine!"

Jenny: Just go on holiday and relax; that will help (to conceive).

And, long after we had been trying to conceive, but just after our fostering of siblings for four years had come to an abrupt and unplanned end and I was broken-hearted: "Go on holiday for a week to get over it." Took me years to even begin to get over it!

IS ADOPTION AN OPTION? WHY NOT?

We haven't spoken much about adoption here. Perhaps it's irrelevant in cases where one partner doesn't want to have children for whatever reason. A baby is a baby, a child is a child, and they don't want one. But for couples who don't have children because of infertility or a health problem, adoption would seem to be an option. I'm betting many of us have been asked: "Why don't you adopt?"

Fred and I considered it before he decided he didn't want to do kids with me at all. He and his first wife adopted his two older children as infants through government agencies in the 1960s. They were given only the most basic information about nationality and health, with no names or background. An effort was made in those days to match parents to children in terms of looks and ethnicity. Overall, it worked pretty well. When Michael came along in the 70s, his siblings were jealous. He looked just like his dad, and they felt that his parents gave him more attention and spent more money on him. Of course by then, their parents were older and better off financially.

When we got together, the older kids were in their teens and Michael was turning 7. We looked into adopting the way Fred and Annette had done before. We discovered that Fred, in his late 40s, was too old. Although we had friends who were adopting from other countries or through private agencies, we didn't pursue it any further.

Fred wasn't anxious to start over with a new baby. But for me, it was something else. I wanted children who were biologically connected to me and my family through all the generations. I wanted them to share my ethnicity and my physical characteristics combined with Fred's. I wanted people to look at us and see the connection. I wanted a child who was part of me. If I couldn't have that, well, never mind. I didn't want just any babies; I wanted my babies.

Selfish? Perhaps. I know there are children who need parents, and I'm glad there are people willing to take them into their homes.

Adoption is not easy or inexpensive. Couples who have spent years trying to get pregnant may already be drained of hope and cash. Prospective parents have to jump through a lot of hoops to be approved. Adoptions fall through, sometimes several times before parents get to bring home a child. Adopted children always have that other family out there somewhere, and they come with a big set of unknowns about their physical and mental background that may surface later. They're yours but not quite.

And yet, it can be wonderful. I have seen beautiful adoptive families in which biology doesn't make a bit of difference. But it would for me.

What about you? Have you thought about adoption? Would you do it? Why or why not? Does it matter if they're not biologically yours?

Additional reading:

This post from loribeth, who blogs at The Road Less Traveled, got me thinking about adoption: "The A Word: Why We Didn't Adopt"[74]

General information about adoption: National Adoption Center (promotes adoption from foster)[75]

Adoption Fact Sheet[76] offers lots of good into. Adopting from China costs $20,000 or more!

Statistics:https://www.americanadoptions.com/pregnant/adoption_stats[77]

"What Does It Take to Adopt a Child in Britain?" Telegraph, Nov. 5, 2012.[78] Stories of three adoptive families in the UK

Anon S: I think I COULD be the sort to adopt. I have neighborhood kids who visit with me, and I love it. A few have mothers who seem to not really care. These kids are running around town at 8:00 at night (on a school night). I feed them often. One day, one of the girls sat and visited while I was doing dishes and she said, "Sometimes I wonder what it would be like to live here." I cried after she left because I too wondered what it would be like to have her live in my home, tucking her into bed or throwing her a birthday party. Those tugs on my heartstrings make me feel that I could be a good mother.

However, I have neither the proper home nor the finances to be entrusted with a child. My husband and I are a happy couple these days, but we, especially he, do NOT look good on paper. Still you hear of all these terrible people who are somehow allowed to be foster parents or even adopt and they end up chaining the kids to the kitchen table or locking them in a closet as punishment. I could certainly do better than that.

I would worry about the unknowns of a brand new baby. An older child would help you to know what you are getting into, but then you might have to deal with fixing the bad things that the child has already experienced, and I don't know how seamlessly a half-grown child would fit into our extended family. That could be stressful.

If I adopted, it would probably have to be a child that was another nationality or background than me. Then I wouldn't look at them and try to find myself in them. They'd be their own person and I'd just be the person giving them a nice life. It would be wonderful to do that for someone. I daydream about adoption more than birth, now that I think about it.

mary eileen pat jane elizabeth insert random name: There you go again, Sue. Hitting a sensitive spot. I love it though. It helps me flesh out the thoughts swirling in my brain, and if thoughts can swirl in my heart, they have done so. I have recently been asked by two people why I never adopted. Funny how people think that is their business, but I digress. My reason is the same as yours. Call me selfish (I can handle it; besides, it's the truth), but I want the full package deal: pregnancy, childbirth and raising my own wee one with my own genes and quirks. Of course with hubby's genes and quirks, too. That doesn't happen with adoption. Also my cousin adopted a baby and it didn't turn out so well for her. In the 90s, I sat through two adoption spiels through various adoption agencies. A healthy white American baby started at $20K. A possibly healthy Russian baby started at around $4K. Any child with a disability or that was not a baby was significantly cheaper. I know, I know. Buying and selling of babies is illegal. Guess what. Adoption sure does come close to it, especially with those price tags.

The other factor is my faith. I have really strong faith. 1) If the Lord wanted me to have a baby, He would make it happen. 2) If the Lord wanted me to adopt, He would have put a much stronger burden on my heart about adoption. Neither has happened, so I go on with my very active and fulfilling life childfree until He turns that boat around. From a faith angle, why force a situation that God has not called me to? At least not yet; at my age, likely not ever.

Candy: I have been asked that question more times than I could have dreamed of. So tired of it!! Over the years, I have just developed a short snappy response and say, "It's not like I can just run down to the five and dime and pick one up on sale." But in my heart, I would adopt one in a second. I wouldn't care about the race or color. I would call the little bundle of joy all my own and love them to the ends of the earth.

Erica: It's not an option for me because I fit into the "married someone who won't have kids with me" camp, but even if it were infertility, I don't think I would adopt either. I think to adopt you have to be the kind of person who really just loves children. I never particularly enjoyed being around kids in general, but despite that I always wanted my own. I think, like you, Sue, I wanted to have a child that was an extension of my own family line, a continuation of my grandmother's and great-grandmother's story. I assumed that even though I wasn't crazy about kids I would instantly love and bond with my own, that it would somehow be different. Since I never got to experience it, I can't say for sure that it would work that way, but that was always how I thought it would be. If I adopted a child, there might be a part of me that would still feel "less than," just the way I do now, that I am missing the full experience of what it means to be a woman and a mother.

I do sometimes think that maybe I might find myself in a situation where I would be free to open up my home to an older child who needs help. It certainly isn't going to happen while my husband is still living with me, but I guess you can never tell where life will take you.

HAVE YOU CONSIDERED ADOPTING A FOSTER CHILD?

People often suggest adoption as an option for those of us who can't have children for whatever reason. They don't realize that it's a long hard process, that some of us don't want somebody else's child, and that partners opposed to biological parenthood aren't likely to want to adopt children either.

One option to consider is becoming a foster parent with the possibility of adoption down the road. Fostering is not an easy way to go. In many cases, the hope is that the child will eventually be able to go home to his biological parents. But many never go home, which makes them available for adoption. Whether it's temporary or forever, becoming a foster parent is a way to use your parenting energy to help a child, a way to become a mom or dad. Not the same as raising your own? No, but it can come close.

Yesterday, my niece's adoption of a little boy she named Bobby became official. It has been a long process. Single, working full time, she waited a long time to become a foster parent, with the hope of eventually adopting a child. Bobby's biological mother had to give up her rights. But it finally happened. My brother and his wife have a new grandchild. I have a great-nephew.

My father doesn't understand why my niece didn't just get married and have children in the usual way. Well, she didn't have a man, and she wanted to be a mother. Bobby needed a mother. Like any single parent, she's making it work. I'm proud of her.

Could I have done it alone like she has? Probably not. I'm a workaholic. I have trouble taking care of my dog. I would only want a biological child. But for others, fostering and/or adopting can be a wonderful thing.

The articles below offer information and debunk some of the myths about foster adoptions. Did you know that you do not have to married, it does not cost a fortune, and almost half of foster kids wind up becoming available for adoption?

I welcome your comments as always.

"About Adoption from Foster Care"[79]

"Curious About Adopting from Foster Care? Here's What It's Really Like?"[80]

"Adopting from Foster Care"[81]

"5 Reasons Why You Won't Adopt from Foster Care, and Why They're Wrong"[82]

Candy: Absolutely never wanted to be a foster parent. I was a stepparent, and to me that was pretty much the same thing. It was a child who wouldn't be truly mine. It would be a child that already had a mother, whether present or potentially present. Plus it would be a third person in the house with baggage. It all just seemed way too much. I sincerely admire those people who have that gift. I just wasn't one of them.

Anon S: I've always been fearful of the idea of fostering. In our small town, I think it would be a nightmare for a foster kid to be shuffled in and out of our school system, having to explain that the people he lives with aren't "Mom and Dad." Not to mention plopping a school-aged kid into a home where the husband and wife wouldn't have a clue how to do anything child-related. I mean, we'd figure it out, but could we do it successfully before this kid is shipped back to their own family?

And then mixing a kid into our extended family. My family would certainly find it uncomfortable. My dad would likely be worried about not wanting to adjust his will. Not in a mean way, just because he worries about things like this. My husband's family has tons of small children and a few who are suspicious of others. I sense that a foster kid would be watched like a hawk and blamed for any drama that might happen.

Ah, but my husband's cousin adopted children. And they are welcomed warmly. Babies always win over the masses. I held their latest addition this past weekend. He didn't look like the rest of the clan, but he was so sweet and perfect. I hated to hand him back.

We're in our 40s. We're just not up to these challenges. We can't see the reward in our current lives. We haven't been spending years preparing. Our church had an informational meeting recently, and I mentioned it reluctantly. My husband didn't jump on the idea, and for him that means something. We didn't go.

I feel God nudging me to explore this avenue. I told my husband once, "I could see us in a foster/adoption situation, but I think it would have to be an incredibly special child and situation." I'm confident that God will do His will. It's just a bit sad sometimes to be a square peg in a round hole.

Sharilee: When I was teaching, and single, I looked into fostering a child who was in my classroom, but it didn't work out. I had a friend from England who took kids into her home for years, and she said it was a very rewarding experience, but you had to always support their mom and dad and go in remembering that they are not yours. A foster parent can't get too attached because until they are legally yours, they are someone else's.

My husband and I also talked about fostering a former student of mine that was always being shifted between homes, but we decided against it, and she ended up getting into the best home for her.

YOU MAY CALL ME 'ANNIE'S MOM'

I had just left my dog at the vet's office for surgery. I was walking down the aisle at the Fred Meyer store looking for chocolate chips when a familiar-looking woman saw me and yelled, "It's Annie's mom!"

I smiled. "Yes, it is." Let the other people shopping around us think what they would. Does it matter that our "kids" are dogs?

Dog moms connect wherever they are. This woman had joined the crowd in the waiting room at Grove Veterinary Clinic while Annie and I were waiting to check in. Annie raced over to greet her. She just knew this was another dog mom, and ooh, she smelled good. As the dog mom waited for $200 worth of dog meds, she told me about her three pups, including a big Lab a lot like Annie. I never learned the woman's name, but her Lab's name is Walker.

Like Annie, I love dog moms. I don't have much experience as a mother to people, but dogs I understand. I admit I can get a little obsessed. Catch Annie and me alone together and you're likely to hear me tell her she's the best dog in the world, that I love her soooo much. I'll rub my face against her fur because it feels so good. This week, she has a cone-shaped collar blocking her movements and keeping her away from her stitches. Luckily, the tumor she had removed was benign.

When a friend was visiting the other day, I realized that I was being just as distracted and disgusting as human baby moms can be. I kept watching the dog, interrupting the people-talk to ask Annie, "Does it hurt? Are you thirsty? Want to go out? Did you fart?" Call it mothering. Call it taking care of a friend recovering from surgery, but my first thought these days is always "Where's Annie? Is she okay?"

Friends who have watched her when I've been away report that she worries every minute until she sees me again. What if I never come back?

Although the typical household contains at least two humans, there are a lot of single women whose life partners are big dogs. I think of Episcopal priest-friend Susan, who is rarely seen without her two big hounds; my late friend Jill, whose dogs were her constant companions; and my friend Orpha, who for years traveled with a massive Akita named Sgt. Pepper.

It's different with little dogs, which remain like babies. I met a friend with her four-pound pom-poodle mix at the vet's office yesterday. She obsesses about that dog, talks baby talk, and buys it tiny clothes. That's fine, but I prefer big dogs you can hug hard without hurting them or spoon on the sofa when you're both weary.

Big dogs provide protection as well as wonderful companionship. With their superior hearing, they detect invaders before you do, and with their big teeth, they scare them off. Annie would probably invite a burglar in and give him big kisses, but a criminal can't tell that by looking through the window at her 75-pound hulk while she's barking and growling.

Annie, 11, is considered old. People keep telling me she won't be around much longer. I'm trying to enjoy every minute with her. Annie follows three other big dogs I loved, Heidi, Belle, and Sadie. When she goes, I'm planning to get a smaller dog. My aging body can no longer handle such a large creature.

I'm drawn to stories about women with dog partners. A few suggestions: *A Three Dog Life*[83] by Abigail Thomas, *Part Wild*[84] by Ceiridwen Terrill, and *Woodswoman: Living Alone in the Adirondack Wilderness*[85] by Anne LaBastille.

Also try *Dogs and the Women Who Love Them*[86] by Allen and Linda Anderson. I haven't read it, but it sounds good.

If you know of other good books—or movies—about women and their big dogs, please share in the comments. Are you a dog mom with fur clinging to your clothes and saliva smears on your car windows? Tell us about it.

Men, don't feel left out. You can tell us about your dog bond, too.

Mary: I'd love to be dog-piled by a heap of dachshund puppies. I can't shake the desire to have a baby though. I've wanted one of my own since I was 4. My mom had just had my baby brother, and I asked for a real live baby for Christmas that year. They gave me a baby doll I named Cynthia. I had opportunities to have children several times, even had someone offer to father my babies even if they weren't his, but I declined. I was forced into several abortions and wish now that I was still running in fear. At least I wouldn't be childless.

I have a dog instead. I even found someone to marry me. He told me he wanted more kids, as he has a daughter from a previous marriage who wants less and less to do with him. But two weeks after our wedding, he came clean and told me he actually doesn't want them. He hates babies apparently. I feel tricked, and it's eroding away at the love I feel for him. During the five years of our courtship, this was never an issue. But then I also didn't know about his addiction to erotica. Sigh. I've just turned 37. I feel there are a good 10 years still left in me. I wish I had found your blog 10 years ago.

Marigladys: Definitely! Last night my stepdaughter called my Lucca ugly because of his haircut. I was so offended! I shared it with a FB group of step-moms, and some of them said I was being ridiculous. I don't think so! I would not call someone else's child ugly as I know it would hurt their feelings. Same with us dog moms! Right?

SFL: Oh yeah. Don't call my dog ugly. Or old either.

lifeANZ: Our Rachel girl is a Lab, too! We hope Annie will be just fine. I find it funny how quickly I can learn and remember a dog's name. We moved to our neighborhood about six months ago and I know more of the dogs' names and where they live than the people.

11

DO THE CHILDLESS GET RIPPED OFF AT WORK?

Childless employees, especially women, get the shaft in the workplace. Right? How many times have you watched a co-worker run off to watch a soccer game or take her child to the dentist while you had to cover her hours or finish her work because hey, you don't have any kids to worry about?

Jody Day[87], speaking at the 2017 NotMom Summit,[88] described five areas of dissension:

1. The dominance of mom talk and mom activities. People who just want to do their jobs are subjected to baby showers, mothers bringing their babies to work, baby pictures, and co-workers conversing about subjects the childless don't feel comfortable joining in.

2. Unfair holiday allocations. Who gets to work on Christmas? Not the moms and dads.

3. Lack of consideration for any real-life needs besides children.

4. Caring for parents, pets, spouses, etc., does not get the same consideration as caring for children.

5. Unfair work load distribution. Give it to her; she doesn't have kids.

Does any of this sound familiar? I have certainly felt left out when the moms at work all gathered to talk about their children. But I haven't experienced discrimination in the same ways that others have. During my years in the newspaper business, we all worked nights, weekends, and holidays, lucky if we got time for lunch. I suspect my co-workers' kids were fending for themselves.

I think we have to understand that it's not easy balancing work and family. Children require a lot of maintenance. Somebody has to take them to doctor and dentist appointments, pick them up when the school calls, or accompany them to sports activities or lessons. Somebody has to take care of them when they're not in school. Parents would tell you that's more important than any job.

But how is that our problem, you might ask? It's bad enough that we don't get to have kids, and now we get extra work dumped on us because of it. It's definitely not fair. Employers need to understand that we have lives, too, and that includes taking care of our homes, spouses, pets, and aging parents. And ourselves. We need time for doctor and dentist appointments, too.

Have you experienced discrimination in the workplace because you are the one without children? Are you constantly forced to deal with baby pictures, baby showers, and baby talk that just makes you feel worse about your own situation? Let 'er rip. I want to know.

Here are just a few of many articles on the subject of workplace discrimination against employees without kids.

"Discrimination Against Childfree Adults" by Ellen Walker, *Psychology Today*[89]

"Family-Friendly Workplaces are Great, Unless You Don't Have Kids" by Amanda Marcotte, *Slate*[90]

"Do Childless Employees Get the Shaft at Work?" by Aaron Guerrero, *U.S. News & World Report*[91]

Crystal: Maybe I'm too young to know, but I don't see the childless getting ripped off, unless you live in Canada, where moms get one year 50 percent paid salary for maternity leave. Of course, I am saying this when I just came back from maternity leave (Not ready to give up my not-mom card yet!). At my job, we had no fewer than three people having children within four months of each other. So I went on maternity leave, as well as my coworker who became a father, and he took six weeks off, too. We work shifts at my job, and the other workers did have to work overtime to cover our shifts. But they have the option to refuse a shift, and they did some other rearranging so as to have minimum staffing for summer hours. There are a couple of people who want to take as much overtime as possible because the money is so good.

In other jobs I have had, where I was the childless one, I didn't feel taken advantage of at all. The vast majority of working parents I knew were very hard workers, and I didn't notice them ever skipping out of work because of children's activities. I mean, we all take vacations, not just the parents. I would also like to point something else out. More than a couple of people my age chose to leave the workforce when they became moms. Of course, a lot of this happened prior to the 2008 financial crisis. However, there are a lot of millennials that are choosing to raise their children much the same way as our grandparents did, with one parent staying home.

SFL: Crystal, it sounds like some people are starting to understand and try to be fair to everyone. And yes, maybe millennials have learned from my try-to-do-everything generation that it doesn't work very well. Now, did you have a baby? It's okay to share the good news, if you did.

Crystal: Yes, I did have a baby! Thank you. Everything is great! I had this whole thing written out, but then the internet went down. Okay, and now the place I had it written down, I can't get to. Stay tuned.

ANOTHER KIND OF WORKPLACE HARASSMENT

I just completed a long, irritating online class on sexual harassment in the workplace. Our local Catholic leaders require all workers and volunteers to take these courses every year. "John has a photo of his wife in lingerie on his desk. Is this harassment? What type of harassment is it?" I click "visual," and they tell me what a genius I am. "Steve tells Sally she needs to loosen up and insists on giving her a back rub, even though she says she doesn't want it. Is this harassment?" Yes. Right! Again, I'm a genius.

I'm at church only a few hours a week, mostly playing music and leading the choir. Our staff consists of four women and a priest whom we rarely see outside of Mass. I work mostly with kids and old people. I have experienced plenty of sexual harassment in past lives, but not here. Oh wait, there is that one parishioner who touches me all the time . . .

Preventing sexual harassment is important. God knows the Catholic Church needs to clean up its act. We have all heard too much about priests molesting little boys. And I suspect most women in all types of work have been harassed in some way by unwanted touches, comments, or suggestions that they need to cooperate if they want raises, promotions or simply to stay employed. It's awful. I applaud the "me too" movement, but in my case they are literally preaching to the choir.

One section of the course sparked thoughts that we can apply here at Childless by Marriage. A group of men were seen as harassing a male co-worker when they started making comments about his manliness and his fertility. There's a related kind of harassment for those of us without children.

For example:

1. Someone makes casual jokes about slow sperm, spoiled eggs, or menopause.

2. A group of women in the break room share stories about their children. When you come in, they either stop talking or ignore you.

3. A mom tells you, "You wouldn't understand. You don't have children."

4. A co-worker casually asks, "When are you gonna get knocked up? You're not getting any younger."

5. Someone has to work overtime, and you're elected because you don't have to rush home to your kids (although you might have something just as important to get home for)

6. You and another man are up for a promotion, but the boss stresses that they prefer a "family man."

7. Co-workers throw a surprise baby shower at the office. Not only do you have to attend, but you're expected to buy a gift.

I'm sure you can come up with more examples.

Unlike sexual harassment, none of this is illegal. In most cases, people don't realize they may be causing you pain—or that not having children doesn't mean you don't have something equally important going on outside of work.

Have you experienced these things or other instances of mommy-daddy harassment? Tell us about it.

Tony: Sue, I've experienced many of those things you mentioned. I agree, it's harassment. When I finished college, I had a hard time finding a job. The most discriminated-against groups were white single males between 25 and 40. Some man sued Proctor & Gamble for this and won $5 million.

Anon S: I work for myself (and by myself) so not a lot of room for error here. Lol. Although I've had clients make insensitive remarks.

"Let's make the appointment for 7:00. That way you can get home to your little ones and spend some time with them before meeting me."

Umm? This was suggested by a client who was a real "take charge" mama bear. This mostly annoyed me because she was so assuming and controlling. Her first assumption that I have children and her second assumption that she knew best how to arrange my day. Imagine! Trying to control an appointment with a professional woman by dictating how and when she should take care of her children. Children that didn't even exist!

My response was, "Actually I do NOT have any children, but I DO have evening plans so, if you are able to make it, a 4:00 appointment would suit me better."

Turned out that 7:00 worked better for HER schedule with HER children. She just wanted to put it on me.

Other times when clients have asked if I have children, they reply with things like, "Oh, no wonder you are able to make so many nice things." The implication that my talents exist in place of children.

When I've been caught working late, "Oh, it must be nice to not have to rush home to kids. No wonder you are able to work so hard." Well, actually it's NOT nice that I work 16-hour days. I don't do it because I have no life outside this office. I do it to pay my damn bills and to reach a few of my goals. Yes, I do have a nice work environment and I'm glad I get to call my own shots. But this isn't an "easy" life because I don't have children.

Other comments are either backhanded or bittersweet. It sort of depends on who utters the words. "Oh, you have so many lovely ideas. You would have been a wonderful mother." This time the compliment was said with a sweet and honest heart. I did appreciate that recognition, even if it hurt a little.

I recently joined a committee of women, and I'm reminded of why I prefer working alone. They all have children. Those comments like, "Do you want my kids? They kept me up half the night," or when one joked with another one about getting pregnant and the other said, "Good Lord, I don't think any of us here would want that." And the recent development of one leaving the rest of the group high and dry. She returned to us (and her responsibilities) and all is well, but the rest of them clucked, "Well, she does have two little ones. I can see why she needed a breather."

I am a bit sensitive where these women are concerned. And probably a little judgmental. But it grates me that this woman was given an easy pass simply because of her children. And of course I could NEVER say that out loud because "Well, you don't have kids, you wouldn't understand."

Right?

SilverShil0h: I know someone who says to every difficult challenge, "I completely understand! I have six kids!"

It's an only-mommies-have-a-clue about-difficulties-in-life club.

Anonymous A: For me, it was experiencing different attitudes and discrimination because as a divorced single woman I was doing more of the caring for my parents. I was a director in a team of seven others. The colleague with children got every school holiday off, no question. He got to leave at 4 p.m. every Wednesday in term time to take the children to football matches, no question. The only time I got was the legal minimum time off for emergency events. The assumption was that I was single and without kids and therefore didn't "need" flexibility. Caring for elders doesn't enjoy the same legal protections and entitlements as maternity and parental leave. Pro-natal discrimination comes in all shapes and sizes.

Loribeth61: I never would have thought of it as "harassment" before reading this, but yeah, you're right. In some cases, it really can be harassment! Thank you for giving me something to think about, Sue!

Lorraine: I have often thought of this as harassment and find it refreshing that this is finally being addressed. I have experienced this in not only the workplace but also church and in social circles among other women. The worst case of this happened while I was working as a salaried manager for a large retailer. There was another manager, (who was male) who was harassed like me (i.e., we were called in on scheduled days off, expected to stay long hours beyond our schedule and even called in on vacation time). The common denominator was that neither of us was married and neither had children. After addressing the store manager, who felt her actions were okay because, after all, our time out of work isn't important because we aren't tending to the care of kids like the other managers, we both went to our district HR rep and reported harassment. The problem was corrected and never brought up again, but we were treated differently and more harshly afterward for our actions to report this.

Heaven Austin: Thank you SO much for sharing this! Coworkers have no idea how much their comments (not all are intentional, but still) hurt.

SilverShil0h: Hi Sue, gotta love those mandatory baby showers. I actually don't mind forking over money for a group gift, whether it's work or church; I just don't want to sit for an hour ooohing and aaaahing over baby clothes and toys because it is a painful reminder of what I wanted but wasn't able to achieve. One thing I didn't see mentioned is the visiting mom (co-worker's wife or co-worker visiting the office to show off the baby) breast-feeding in the bathroom which has happened to me. When I heard the noises, I turned and went to a different bathroom. I know this may sound wimpy for some but when it invokes such deep pain, you do what you have to do to stay sane.

Mali: My husband was told by his brothers to "prove he was a man" and get me pregnant. That sort of comment is not uncommon! I was told by a colleague I should go and have babies. As if that would solve the discrimination I already felt at our company.

Fortunately, in New Zealand no boss with any brains would actually admit to preferring a "family man," as it would be completely illegal.

A sister-in-law told me that no one ever wished on their death bed that they had travelled more. The implication being that family was the most important thing, and I didn't have it. (Interestingly, my elderly father-in-law just admitted he regretted not travelling more.) (And yes, we use two Ls in travelling/ed in NZ! lol)

I could go on. All the subtle put-downs, the omissions, the assumptions everyone has kids, the implication that those of us without kids don't have any investment in the future, etc., etc. If it isn't harassment, it is definitely bullying, or at best, insensitive.

Juli A.: I called my boss out on her pronatalism. I've never experienced so much anger and hostility. In the past, a co-worker had brought her kids in when they were sick or had days off school. Luckily, they have grown up. As part of a tour for a potential new employee, my boss was excitedly explaining how we used to set up a sick kids section of the office. I said, "Well, we're more friendly to all fertility levels now." Later, while I was trying to explain how it sounded like she was inviting the new employee to bring children to work and what a distraction that would be, she got livid. Now, she treats me as if I hate all children, makes snide comments on how I must find them "so distasteful." I honestly wish I had never said anything.

Lisa G.: I've had people stop into my office and, without the conversation even remotely leading in this direction, ask me if I have kids. When I say that I don't have children, they get this sad look on their face—you know the concerned look with the head cocked to the side. I sometimes even get, "Oh, I'm sorry" as the response, as if I have said that I have some incurable disease. It's crazy. I second the post above about the visiting moms and how everyone stops everything that they are doing to run out and stare at the babies. One of them tried to hand me her baby (another assumption—because you are a woman you will want to hold her baby). I politely declined. I usually cooo at them for five minutes and then sneak back into my office.

Aspadistra: Nearly six years ago, my husband had a stroke. He was in hospital for four months, learning how to walk again. The hospital decided to discharge him the same weekend I was moving my mother in with me. I should explain that Mum had severe mobility problems because of osteoporosis, and she had dementia. Also, I was in full-time employment.

Mum moved in. Husband was discharged. I tried to cope with the fact that there was still work being done on our home to make it invalid-ready. Two nurses came out to check that I didn't need help. (They decided I didn't. Apparently I could manage fine on my own.)

When I said that I didn't know how I was going to manage, working full-time and looking after two disabled adults, one nurse looked at me scornfully and said, "Oh, I'm just the same. I work, and I have two children."

CHILDLESS WOMEN IN POWER FACE SCRUTINY

Today's post is sparked by an article at The Australian news site which discusses the rise in power of several childless women, including British Prime Minister Theresa May,[92] German Chancellor Angela Merkel,[93] New South Wales Premier Gladys Berejiklian,[94] former Australia Prime Minister Julia Gillard,[95] and the first woman premier in Tasmania, Lara Giddings.[96] None of them have children.

In her article "Berejiklian, Gillard, May, Merkel: Power to Childless Women?"[97] author Caroline Overington[98] notes that these women in power are always asked about their motherhood status. They are rarely mentioned without that word, childless, attached. Is it really relevant? When Merkel was running for chancellor, she got lots of flak for not having children. People asked: How can she understand the needs of parents and families if she has never given birth?

Do people judge the males in power by their parenting prowess? Sure, most of the men trot out their families on special occasions, but does it have any connection to their ability to govern? Still, can you think of any male world leader who does not have children?

All of these women have been publicly asked why they don't have children.

May has struggled with infertility, so it's like *that's okay, she tried; it wasn't her fault*. In Australia, a former male senator commented that Gillard had kept herself "deliberately barren" while she pursued her career. Ouch.

Things don't always turn out the way you plan, Berejiklian says, refusing to get more specific. "I hope that people judge me on my merits and what I can do."

Women are still rare in high office. Overington contends that most women are occupied with childcare while the men, despite whatever moves toward equality have occurred, are freer to work their way to the top because they've got wives to deal with the kids.

You have to admit there's some truth to that. Although we may not have done it, we can all see that childcare is and should be an intense round-the-clock occupation that doesn't leave much time or energy for anything else, unless you can afford to pay someone to take care of the kids. It is easier to work at any career without having to worry about children. Most of us here would be willing to take on the challenge, and some of us are already dealing with the responsibilities of parenthood through our stepchildren, but it's hard.

To me, it seems like women in power will be criticized from both directions. If they have children, then they must be neglecting them. If they don't, something must be wrong with them. Right?

If Hillary Clinton had won the U.S. presidency, she could please the pro-parenting crowd because she's a mother and grandmother, but she was also free to do the job because her only child, daughter Chelsea, is a grown woman who not only can take care of herself but can campaign for her mom. Clinton did not become president, but it had nothing to do with whether or not she had children.

In the U.S., we have seen many pictures of politicians on stage with their spouses and their children. If I were running for office, I might be standing on that stage alone. What would people say about that? Does it matter?

What do you think? Does a woman need to be childless to rise to the top? Will she be forever disrespected if she doesn't have children? Why is it so different for men? Or is it?

Jenny: I think there are examples of many women at the top (or trying to get to the top) both with and without children. Was it Sarah Palin[99] in the U.S. who had a large family, including a child with Downs I think, who in part tried to play the "I'm just a regular mum" card? I can't recall other names, but certainly I remember a high flying mum in the banking sector with a large family in the UK a few years back.

I think you are right that women in power can be judged either way, as neglectful mothers or something wrong with them for not having children.

Maybe mums at the top can afford to buy in lots of childcare and domestic help, so they don't have to be at home in time to cook dinner every night.

Turning it around, do others, or we ourselves, expect childless women to replace being a mum with something else of notable achievement? I don't think I have done anything special that I couldn't have done with children.

12

IF YOU DON'T HAVE CHILDREN, YOU WILL NEVER . . .

GOT YOUR ATTENTION WITH THAT TITLE, HUH? Well, good. At 4 a.m., I started making this list, and I encourage you to continue it in the comments. Before you say it, I will note that some of these can become *you WILL* via step-children, nieces, nephews, friends' children, jobs and volunteer gigs.

If you don't have children, you will never . . .

1. Have to worry about the school schedule (unless you're a teacher).

2. Have to find a babysitter in order to go out to dinner, a movie, a party, or a trip around the world (You might need a dog sitter).

3. Have to share your cookies with a child.

4. Add any names to your Christmas card signature.

5. Have anyone come after you on your family tree.

6. Show off pictures of your own children on your cell phone or post them on Facebook.

7. Have grandchildren or great-grandchildren.

8. Have sons- or daughters-in-law.

9. Have to worry about paying your children's college tuition.

10. Have children to list as your next of kin.

11. Have to attend Little League or soccer games.

12. Learn the latest kid songs (unless you work at a preschool).

13. Be required to hang out in a roomful of sugar-crazed children.

14. Have to be careful about cussing in your own house.

15. Have an episiotomy (Thank God!).

16. Have to watch cartoons before breakfast.

17. Share your pregnancy story at a baby shower.

18. Be a full-fledged member of the Mom or Dad Club.

19. Have someone who looks like you call you Mom or Dad.

20. Stop answering questions about why you don't have children.

That's my list for now. I know you can add some more. And yes, I know you can do all this stuff with other people's kids or with adopted children, but it's not the same, is it?

Mali: Okay, I had to laugh at #15. There are lots of "nevers" that are very beneficial. I'd add:

Never have to travel only on school holidays (unless you're a teacher). And also that we never have to attend a baby shower (I'm so lucky it's not a big thing here).

There are plenty of childless women who can share pregnancy stories. Just not ones that resulted in a child. And lots of people's children don't look like them, but still call them Mum and Dad.

Jenny: I could add a few you will nevers, such as "breastfeed," "hold a crying baby for hours during the night," "tuck a child into bed with a loving heart," and similar.

I did also think it is worth highlighting that there are a few on your list that aren't givens for parents. Such as many of today's parents will never be grandparents, due to greater numbers of people not having children or because they had children so late in life they may well die before their children get around to reproducing. Surely that's parents missing out on one of the greater joys of life, children who you are related to and (probably) love but for whom you are not 100 percent responsible.

Anon S: If you don't have children, you will never . . .

1. have to pretend to like another adult because your kids are friends.

2. get to help pick out a prom dress.

3. know the heartache of losing a child.

4. have the opportunity to save your child's first PJs, the hair bow from her first day of school or her Girl Scout patches.

5. have the pleasure of receiving handfuls of weeds that you are expected to pretend are flowers.

6. have the obligation of feeding a child a healthy meal at least 50 percent of the time.

7. have bathtubs full of tub toys.

8. be able to connect to certain people who walk this world and simply can't imagine a life without children.

I could go on and on. Many good and bad things about not having children. Many.

mdoe37: I'll add:

1. No projectile vomiting.

2. No nuclear diaper blowout.

Thank you. I needed a little "pick me up" after having all the small people saying twick er tweet tonight.

Maribeth: Worry about them taking the car out for the first time by themselves.

1. Worry about them drinking and driving.

2. Make cookies with grandchildren.

3. Get a call saying, "Hi, Mom, how are you?"

loribeth61: Some of these "nevers" are heartbreaking, while others are a relief, lol.

ARE CHILDLESS WOMEN IMMATURE?

Does not having children cause a woman to miss an important stage in becoming a mature adult? Does she remain the perpetual daughter and never learn to put others' needs before her own?

I have asked these questions of many women. The answers vary. Some admit that yes, the childless woman misses some of the critical lessons that come with motherhood. In fact, a recent New Zealand study maintains that mothers have been proven to be smarter than non-mothers, possibly due to the hormonal changes that come with pregnancy or to the demands of motherhood.

Other childless women claim that that's ridiculous, that in fact some mothers are less mature than they are because they have had less time to work on their own development. And many say that childless women learn the same lessons in other ways, perhaps by caring for other children, their own aging parents, a spouse or people they nurture in their jobs. I'll add taking care of animals to the mix. Of course it's not the same, but sometimes their needs do outweigh yours.

I don't have the answers to my questions, only opinions. I'm sure that no one answer fits all. What have you seen or experienced? Does one need to have kids to fully grow up?

LFHalleck: In response to "Does she remain the perpetual daughter and never learn to put others' needs before her own?" I guess my initial reaction is: Are women defined by putting others' needs before their own? Is that a requirement for us to be considered "real" women? Are we not allowed to put ourselves first? Do we define men in our society in that manner? I don't think so. I'm 35, childless by marriage but have also come to the decision that I do not want children at this point. I'm intelligent, successful, dedicated and far more mature and responsible than the majority of people I know, with or without children. And of course I know how to take care of other people or put their needs before mine when that is needed. I think it is absolutely ridiculous to assume that just having a baby all of a sudden makes you a "more worthy" mature individual. I disagree with that wholeheartedly.

SFL: It doesn't seem fair that in some ways men get to be perpetual little boys while women are expected to take care of everyone. As for maturity, a lot of people have told me the ones who don't have children are actually more mature because they made a conscious decision not to have children and because they continue growing as individuals out in the adult world.

Anonymous: I am outraged at this question. Where is a study on whether or not having children makes men more or less smart? As a childless woman, I never hear my husband asked about "why" he doesn't have children. In fact, he is rarely asked whether or not he is a father. However, even in business situations, I am almost always asked about my status as a mother and almost always isolated from elements of the subsequent conversations that arise. Really, really, really, I don't think talking about the heft of my baby's dirty diaper over lunch would make me smarter than someone else!

Anonymous: Yes, yes, yes. Women without children are lacking . . . in basic experience, in putting others first, in sacrificing, in empathizing. They seem less human because having and nurturing children is essential to the human/mammalian experience. They are hopelessly one dimensional, victims of their own one dimension. They simply don't know what it's like on the planet of mothers and think they are having a rich life experience when in fact they are tragically stuck in their own broken record.

SFL: Whew. Anonymous Yes Yes Yes, I think you're going to ruffle some feathers with that comment. I suspect you are a mother yourself. "Less human" is a little harsh, don't you think? Is it not possible that women who haven't had their own children gain experience in other ways, taking care of stepchildren or caring for loved ones who are sick, for example?

Anonymous: Can I rephrase the question? "Are childless *people* immature?" or even better, "Are people who do not have dependents immature?" To that I say, yes.

My wife and I are childless because I am sterile. I, however, was the one to really want children. She really didn't care either way, but prefers not having them.

My mother is in need of more care these days, so we live at her house. I believe it is my duty to care for my parents. I didn't always think this, but now I do. My father has been dead for 24 years; therefore I must take care of my mother.

In our household, I am the only cook, day-to-day caregiver, and driver; I am the only homemaker, gardener, and maintenance contractor. As much as possible, I try to meet the needs of my mother, my wife, my job, my family, the house, and myself (not always in that order). In order to have a smoothly running household, there are times when your needs are less important than the needs of your animate and inanimate dependents. If you cannot understand that—whether you are a man or a woman, whether you are with or without child, whether you are with or without dependents—then you are immature.

It is true that many men have immature behaviors. It is also true that many women have immature behaviors.

SFL: Mr. Anonymous, you are so right, and yes, let's change it to "childless people." Thank you.

SOMETIMES CHILDLESSNESS PHYSICALLY HURTS

When you have children, you won't have cramps anymore. That's what my mother used to tell me as I sat bent over double, sharp pains slicing through my lower abdomen. Every 28 days, waves of hurt would leave me gasping. Gynecologists never found anything wrong; it was just "cramps." They'd get better when I grew up and had a family. Except I didn't.

From age 13 to menopause at age 53, I suffered horrible cramps. My best friend stayed home when she got her period, but my mom did not believe in babying me. I took those cramps to school and work. I suffered through algebra tests and physical education classes, through interviews and deadlines.

You might say, "Why didn't you just take something for it?" I took what was available at the time. Aspirin did nothing. We took the 70s version of Midol, really just aspirin with caffeine, which wasn't much help either. I tried getting drunk, which left me bombed and still hurting. I didn't just need a pain reliever; I needed an "anti-inflammatory" drug. Ibuprofen was not available until near the end of my first marriage. I needed a prescription to get it. The first time I felt the relief from that miracle drug, I couldn't believe it. I wanted to hug my doctor. And when it became available over-the-counter, oh my God. I still experienced cramps, but at least I could do something to mute them a little.

What I'm saying is my cramps were horrible, and I never experienced the permanent relief that childbirth might bring. Toward the end of her life, my mother confessed that she had never had cramps, so she didn't know what I had been feeling or whether giving birth to me had made any difference for her.

Dysmenorrhea is the formal medical term for painful periods. The sharp pains are caused by the uterine muscle constricting and tightening. Most experts say that the stretching of childbirth eases the cramps. An article at Parents.com[100] suggests that childbirth eliminates some of the prostaglandin receptor sites in the uterus. Prostaglandins are the hormones which direct the uterus to contract during labor and may also be involved in monthly menstrual pain.

If there's something wrong, such as endometriosis, periods can become absolute agony. It's important to get medical treatment, but for plain old cramps, the only hope seems to be medication and motherhood.

I'm no medical expert. I have read comments online from women whose periods have gotten worse after pregnancy, but in general it seems to offer relief—relief we will not experience if we never have children.

Doesn't seem fair, does it? Have you experienced killer cramps? Have you seen relief via childbirth? I would love to hear your experiences in this area.

BTW, menopause was a picnic compared to my monthly periods, and now my cramps are gone, so that's something to look forward to.

Male readers, I know this is one of the girl subjects you don't want to hear about, but maybe someone you love is having cramps right now. Give her some love. They hurt like hell.

mrsp: When I was 20, a GP told me that my cramps would go away when I had a baby.

When I finally hit menopause, I remember thinking, 'What? I went through all that for *nothing?*'

Crystal: Thanks for talking about this! Yes, I had horrible cramps too as a childless woman. My cycle was even shorter than 28 days, too. Nobody ever gave a crap when I specifically pointed out that a pregnancy would bring relief. They all said pregnancy is bad for your body, pregnancy brings more pain. Umm, BS! I just had a baby four weeks ago and it was a breeze. The delivery was made easier due to medical help, and I'm nearly back to feeling normal. It's too soon to tell with the cramps, but I don't care. Everyone was wrong!

Chap: I also had severe cramps growing up. My mother always said they would get better after I had a baby. About 10 years ago, my doctor retired and his replacement noticed fresh chemical burns on my abdomen. Heat helps relieve cramps, and monthly I burned myself with those hand-warmer things by using too many for too long, but oh they felt so good when the heat soaked in. The doctor was shocked by how much ibuprofen I was using and put me on a continuous pill. I have not had a period in 10ish years. Yes, it's weird, but surviving the cramps was wrecking my body. I never did have a baby. Now my husband is disabled, I'm 40, and the time will never be right. Anyway, talk to your doctor. They can help with severe cramps.

SFL: Chap, thank you for sharing this. I made myself sick with ibuprofen trying to conquer the cramps. The doctor suggested way too high a dose, and my stomach couldn't take it. One should definitely see a doctor for problems with cramps, and if their advice seems wrong, seek another opinion. One of the great things about menopause: no more cramps.

ghj: Use birth control. That will solve the problem. In fact, some forms of birth control cause you to NOT have periods (Depo Provera, birth control pills taken continuously without the sugar pills). This is known to be completely safe. Do it! You'll love it.

YOU DON'T HAVE CHILDREN, SO YOU GO

As the daughter with no children, I seem to be the one expected to drop everything to take care of her parents. It really came home recently when I was sitting in my father's hospital room talking to the social worker about his future. Dad and I had both told her that I lived in Oregon and couldn't stay in San Jose forever.

"Of course you have to get back to your family," the social worker said.

"No family," I corrected. "Just me."

Which seemed to mean that I had no excuses, nothing to hurry back for. If I didn't have a husband, children and grandchildren, how dare I claim that I was not available for as long as I was needed? It's hard to argue that even with myself.

"Stay here and I'll pay you," my father said. But it was not about the money I was losing by not being at my job. I love my work. I've spent 50 years building up to this place in my writing and music careers. "People are counting on me," I said, even as I knew that another woman had stepped in to do my church music job.

There's a certain amount of sexism to this. My brother, who has children and grandchildren, has a job that my father brags about to everyone. "Don't bother him," he tells medical personnel. "He's working." In my brother's defense, he has been driving six hours round-trip every weekend to be with our father and do what he can to take care of his bills and his house. He's doing more than his share, and he does understand what it's like for me. But I'm the one who gets the phone calls from the hospital and the nursing home, the one who in theory does not have to be in Oregon when her father needs her in California.

Am I a bad daughter because I wanted to limit how much of myself I sacrificed? Part of me wanted to stay with him. I had his house to sleep in, food to eat, family to be with. It was sunny and warm while it kept raining back in Oregon. I was writing all the time. No wi-fi, no TV, no distractions, except for Dad. Shoot, it was like a vacation, except for all the worry, caregiving, and lack of sleep.

I was gone for a month that time. Back in Oregon, everything fell apart. The heater died, the washing machine quit, my debit card got stolen, the dog was limping, and the church choir seemed to like my substitute better than me. As for the business part of my writing, I couldn't begin to catch up. When are you coming back, my family asked. Two weeks, I said. Just give me two weeks.

For the last years of his life, I yo-yoed back and forth between Dad's house and mine. I'm glad I was able to do it, but frustrated that nothing else in my life mattered as much as the children I didn't have.

If I said, "I miss my kids," no one would expect me to stay. That's just the truth of it. In some situations, motherhood seems to be the only acceptable excuse.

What do you think? Are you expected to babysit, take care of ailing relatives, run the errands, etc., because you don't have kids? How do you react to that?

Tony: I've been through this as well. I took care of my elderly mother for years. My brother, who's on marriage number three, has two daughters and was MIA for years. One weekend, I was going deer hunting in Georgia, and he was horrified that I wouldn't give up my hobby to take care of Momma. I told him, she's your mother as well and I'm not giving up my life to take care of old people. I guilt tripped him into helping. Anyway, it reached a point where I couldn't do it anymore. And I dumped it all on him. I mean 13 years with no help. He would always hold his daughters up as a preclusion. Sue, too many siblings will use their kids to emotionally blackmail you. That I resent.

lifeANZ: I think some of it is that usually parents rely more on their daughters to take care of them. I am the childless one in my family, but my parents are still doing fine. My mother, however, is having to take care of her parents. She has a childless brother who is rarely around. I wonder if it has something to do with women being "more nurturing," and I also wonder if when my parents are older more will be expected of me as the daughter without children.

Mali: Yes, I've been through this as well. Just because you don't have children doesn't mean that you don't have a life. And it's that life that you're being expected to give up. Which, considering what else you've also had to give up, is a huge thing. I understand you asking those questions (I've asked myself too), but it doesn't mean that doing something you don't want to do is the right answer. Good luck.

IS IT HARDER FOR US TO LOSE OUR PARENTS?

My father, Clarence "Ed" Fagalde, died last week. He was 97. I have written often about needing to travel to San Jose to take care of him. It's hard to believe I won't be doing that anymore.

When your last remaining parent dies, it leads to all kinds of thoughts. We're orphans, my brother noted that morning. Can siblings old enough to collect Social Security be orphans? Can adults with their own children be orphans? There's a connotation of helplessness in the word. But then I think about "widows." We hear about "widows and orphans" a lot in the Bible. By definition, they are poor and need help.

The only help I need is in dealing with my grief, with the pictures in my mind of those last hard days, and with feeling more alone than ever.

I told the hospice chaplain through my tears that I was afraid I was going to feel terribly alone. My brother has his wife, kids, and a huge group of in-laws. I live all the way up in Oregon with my dog. It hasn't sunk in yet, but I know it's going to hit me.

I was more attached to my father than I think most people with children are. My sister-in-law's first thoughts when Dad died were about the effect on her grown children. She said my Facebook posts had upset them. I feel bad about that. Perhaps if I had children, they would have been my first priority, too.

I don't feel as guilty for an earlier post when Dad was suffering and I really needed someone in the family to sit with him for a while. One cousin-in-law said she would come if she weren't out of town taking care of her grandchild. From the rest, no response.

I can understand those with young children not wanting to expose them to the nursing home or to the way Dad looked toward the end. My brother and I still bear the scars of visiting our great-grandmother in the nursing home. It was terrifying for little kids. But what about the adults?

My friends called and texted often. *How are you? How is your dad?* After I complained that I couldn't sleep because it was almost as hot inside my father's house (95 degrees) as it was outside (102 degrees!), a Facebook friend I had never met said I could stay at her house. She was in the middle of moving, but she would make it work. I declined, but was deeply touched.

I'm so grateful for my friends, people like Pat W., Pat S., Fran, and Bill, who have been taking care of Annie, watering my plants, doing my church job without pay, and calling often to check on me. Now that I won't be talking to my father on the phone every night, I want to use those times to reach out to others, both friends and family. Too often we say, "Let's keep in touch," and then we don't.

If I had children, would we be having heart to heart talks, helping each other through our grief? Maybe, maybe not. They would be young, busy, involved in their own lives, just as I was when my grandparents passed away. I felt bad, but not the guts-ripped-out bad that I feel this time.

I may have held on tighter than most people to my parents because I didn't have children. When my mother died in 2002, I still had my husband, and that made it easier. After Fred died in 2011, my father became the man in my life again. Now, well, it's hard. I keep waiting for the phone to ring. I'd like to think if I had kids, they'd step in to help me and my brother take care of things and distract us with the concerns of youth so we don't dwell on aging, illness, and death. Surely it's a comfort to my brother when his granddaughter climbs into his lap now for a little "Papa" time.

So what am I saying? I've got grief brain, a little PTSD, and a runny nose. I'm still having trouble believing this really happened. I'm saying treasure your family. Reach out to them if they don't reach out to you. But also hold on to your friends because you're going to need them, especially if you don't have children and grandchildren.

How are you with your parents? Do you think your relationship is different because you don't have children? If you never have children, how will you feel when your parents are gone? Let's talk about it in the comments.

Mali: I'm so sorry you lost your father. But I'm glad that you had time with him in the end, even though I know how hard those vigils can be (I lost my father 14 years ago and my mother three years ago). I'm with you in your grief. My husband and I are now spending a lot of time caring for his father (though that was shared briefly with another of his siblings).

Both my parents suffered in the end, so when they went, there was a sense of relief that that was over for them. Though I wish my father had had at least ten more (healthy) years.

The sadness I have experienced since losing my parents has been that there has been no one to ring and tell about our lives. Yes, I tell my friends and sisters. But there have been times (not always, but just sometimes) I have wished I could call my mother, or that my father would have loved to have heard about our travels to, for example, South Africa. (He would have adored it—I'm so sad he never got to go.) I don't know if that's because I have no children, or if it is just because I know they would have loved to have learned certain things. I do know that I'm grateful not to be one of the sandwich generation, as caring for the elderly (which perhaps is left to those of us without children) is stressful enough.

When the grief goes, I will confess to feeling a certain freedom. We can realistically do whatever we want, completely without responsibilities. I know my parents felt that too, when we were grown and self-sufficient, so I don't think it's unique to the No Kidding amongst us.

Bamberlamb: Sue, I'm so sorry to hear of your loss. I've blogged about feeling cut adrift when you have no parents and no children; I was close to both of my parents and by the time I was 35, they had both passed away. Friends of mine who have children but have lost parents have told me they don't have the disconnected feeling I get when there are family-oriented holidays. That's one of the occasions I really yearn for that special connection that I just don't have with anyone else.

Don't get me wrong. Both my parents suffered before they died, and I was grateful when their suffering ended. My parents had me in their mid-40s, so I was doing the caring from a very young age. Like Mali says, there is a release when you aren't tied down with the weight of responsibility.

What I also found though was I had all this excess time with no purpose, and it took a while for me to channel all of the energy into other things.

I think it's harder to lose your parents when you don't have your own kids or kids whom you're close to, in answer to your question. Some kids aren't capable of supporting their parents—my eldest brother has Asperger's, amongst other issues, and isn't capable of being there emotionally for anyone.

Thinking of you whilst you navigate this newfound path. My heart goes out to you.

SFL: Thank you, Bamberlamb. I agree with all of this. This morning at church an older man not known for tact, and who has 12 kids, said of my news, "Well, that's the evolutionary process." Sure, but what if you don't have children? I didn't challenge him, but that's what I was thinking.

13

WHERE DOES GOD FIT?

BIRTH CONTROL PILLS BECAME LEGAL for unmarried women in 1972, the year I lost my virginity. I realized this last night as I was reading a new book called *The Baby Matrix*,[101] written by Laura Carroll, who also wrote *Families of Two*.[102] I'll write more about this book when I finish reading it, but the section on birth control is the most complete I've ever seen. I was shocked when I suddenly understood the chronology. In the 1960s, birth control became legal for married couples, but it wasn't until I was in college that women who were not married had an effective means, aside from abstinence, to prevent unwanted pregnancies. This blows my mind.

I was a late bloomer when it comes to dating and sex. My mother said "don't" and I didn't until I was 20. It was only when I met the man who became my first husband that I finally learned how much fun sex could be. The first few months that we dated, he kept pressuring me to "do it." I knew that he'd dump me pretty soon if I kept saying no. After I finally gave in, he hustled me to the San Jose State University health center, where I got my first birth control prescription. The pills made me sick and fat, but they kept me from getting pregnant. After we got married, I switched to a diaphragm, a rubber disk that I filled with spermicidal cream and inserted just before intercourse. That's what I used until I met Fred, who had had a vasectomy.

I got those first pills in 1972, hiding them so my parents would never know. A year earlier, the pills would not have been available. Nor would the diaphragm. We might have used condoms, but the chances were good that I would have joined the many women who are pregnant on their wedding day. In the old days, lots of women got married to men they might not otherwise have married if they weren't pregnant. To have a child outside of marriage was a scandal to be avoided.

Today, according to the Centers for Disease Control and Prevention,[103] 40.8 percent of babies born in the U.S. are born to unmarried women. Today they have a choice, and they choose to become single mothers while their sisters may decide not to become mothers at all. But before I was 20 years old, we didn't have these choices. Even then, it took a while for attitudes to catch up with legalities.

Without birth control, it would be a lot harder to choose a life without children unless you also chose a life without intercourse. It would also be considerably more difficult for a spouse who didn't want children to keep from having them anyway. Many of us who are childless by marriage would not be if this were 1963 instead of 2013.[104]

Makes you think, doesn't it?

Olga: I had been using pills and rubbers since I married my husband. Then after three years, we acknowledged he is infertile—so it may seem that we used birth control for nothing. But as I have skin, ovary and period problems, I was advised by a doctor to use them anyway. So I kept on taking the pills even though I knew I wouldn't conceive. But a couple of months ago, the doctor announced I have a fibroid—and the reason is the pills. He advised me to stop taking them. I had to choose between skin and period problems and a growing fibroid. So, I agree with Sue. Pills do have both sides. As for women who think they control childbirth by means of pills, in my opinion, the one who is really controlling is God. It's not in your hands to change His plan for yours. I know girls who missed only one pill and conceived immediately and other girls who have been trying all means to conceive and failed. Don't think that it's you who decides whether to have babies or not.

Anonymous: Without rights to birth control, it would also be considerably more difficult for women to choose to have a career. There are a lot of single moms out there, but there are also a lot of dual income households. I vaguely recall reading that there are now more female heads of household (primary breadwinners) than male. This could be due to single-parent situations, but there is no doubt that birth control has changed the economic landscape. Without it, I think the level of poverty, and the number of children living in poverty in this country would be devastating.

BIRTH CONTROL DECISION NOT SO SIMPLE

As most of you know, I'm Catholic. I'm not only a parishioner but an employee, so what I'm about to write might get me in trouble, but I woke up this morning knowing I needed to say something.

Basically what I want to say is that too many people and too many institutions, especially churches, don't even try to understand that some people who would like to have children do not have them, for various reasons, and that our lives do not fit into their neat little boxes. And that it hurts.

Tucked into last week's church bulletin was a handout about the evils and dangers of birth control. It discusses the physical risks of oral contraceptives, contraceptive patches and IUDs: cancer, blood clots, heart attacks, septic shock . . . scary stuff. Plus, the handout, produced by the U.S. Conference of Bishops (all men), says these methods are actually forms of abortion because they kill the embryo before implantation in the uterus. It doesn't mention "barrier methods," such as condoms and diaphragms, but those are also forbidden.

The bishops blame "the pill" for women having sex outside of marriage, out-of-wedlock births, and single mothers living in poverty.

In contrast to these horrors, they offer the "fertility awareness"[105] method, whereby couples abstain from sex when the woman is most fertile. This, of course, takes total cooperation by two horny people and assumes the woman has regular, predictable cycles. One of my friends named her "surprise" son after the priest who prescribed this method for her and her husband.

All of this assumes that we can avoid sex outside of marriage and that within marriage we have husbands or wives who will follow the rules. I don't know about you, but my partners inside and outside of marriage, including the Catholic ones, would not have gone along with either abstaining or having a bunch of babies. I used birth control—pills, condoms, diaphragms—right up until I married a man who'd had a vasectomy. A vasectomy is also considered a sin.

Despite the church's mandate, a majority of Catholics use artificial birth control. Numbers vary, with sources saying it's from 72 to 98 percent of American women. Honestly, the church puts us between a rock and a hard place. How many of us are lucky enough to marry someone who will agree to take a chance on the "natural" method? How many people here at Childless by Marriage are with partners who do not want any children, period? How many are not sure about it, so they aren't willing to take any chances? How many of us would be delighted to throw away our birth control and have a baby, but we fear we'd lose the man or woman we love if we did?

Being alone and past menopause, I no longer have to worry about this, but I know most of you do. I'm not going to preach for or against. Just be aware of the risks and make your own decision.

I worry about the lack of understanding shown in documents such as this. For some of us, life cannot be boiled down to being alone and chaste or being married and happily making babies. It's just not that simple.

For more on the Catholic viewpoint, visit www.usccb.org/respectlife.[106]

It's not just the Catholic Church that doesn't seem to understand the variables in our life situations. We see it in our government, in our society, and around the dinner table.

What do you think? Have I ruffled some feathers? How do you feel about this? Please share (and don't tell my pastor).

YariGarciaWrites: You said, "The bishops blame 'the pill' for women having sex outside of marriage, out-of-wedlock births, and single mothers living in poverty."

That says it all. They're not thinking of family planning (even within a marriage), prevented abortions, or the health benefits of oral contraceptives outside of birth control. Yes, a lot of people take the pill to deal with other health issues.

They think that a woman's morals are based on the availability of birth control.

As if women would sink to their baser instincts just because birth control is at hand. As if contraceptives would turn us all into promiscuous beings! Like we're just wanting the pill to become harlots!

And I say "women" because of the quote written above. I believe men AND women are both capable of making sound moral decisions, whether they have contraceptives or not.

I am not a Catholic. From an outsider's point of view, the Catholic Church should prioritize its child molestation issues before speaking about sexual morality (feathers ruffled).

Tony: Sue, as usual you're the voice of reason and intelligence. I've been through three abortions when I was young. It kicked my ass! Emotionally, mentally and spiritually. That said, I'm absolutely pro-choice. It's none of any religion's business how people conduct their sexual practices. They need to stay out of the bedroom. Your comments were very thought-provoking. Bravo! Well done.

Jenny: The Catholic Church (and other religions, too, maybe to a lesser degree) is out of touch and unrealistic on birth control. And they should butt out of women's business while they are mostly run by men. They know most faith followers cannot, and do not want to, go without birth control and that in private, people ignore their silly advice.

Also, technically, surely they are wrong about the pill causing abortions. It prevents ovulation, so therefore the egg cannot be fertilized, so there is no fetus. I stand to be corrected, if I am wrong.

You should not be nervous about your post. They have to be challenged.

SFL: I agree. And you are absolutely right about birth control not causing abortion. It prevents conception. Oh and btw, in vitro fertilization is a sin, too.

X: Ha ha, if birth control pills are causing abortions, I wouldn't be a mom right now. I took the Plan B, and it didn't do anything.

AND THEN THERE'S THE QUESTION OF ABORTION

Today is the 40th anniversary of the Roe v. Wade Supreme Court decision that legalized abortion in the United States. Before 1973, women seeking abortions were forced to find illegal practitioners who were not necessarily trained or licensed to perform the procedure. In many cases, they suffered from illnesses or injuries as a result. Whether or not one favors abortion, at least now one can hope for a procedure that is done properly in sterile conditions with minimal danger to their health.

How many people have abortions? More than you would think. In interviewing childless women for my *Childless by Marriage* book, I was surprised at the number of women who told me they had had abortions, legal or not. Some had more than one. And that turned out to be their only chance to have children. Some admitted they didn't really want an abortion but did it because their husband or boyfriend insisted. If anyone is in that situation now, I hope they can find the courage to say no and have the baby despite their partner's objections. A man who insists you abort a baby you want is not worth keeping.

I'm having trouble finding consistent figures on just how many American women have abortions. A fact sheet from the National Abortion Federation[107] offers some interesting facts about who has abortions and why. They maintain that "at the current rate, 35 percent of all women of reproductive age in America today will have had an abortion by the time they reach the age of 45." That's a lot. As has always been the case, most are young, and most are unmarried. A substantial number are older and belong to religions that say abortion is a sin.

What drives women to abort? It's the feeling that "I just can't have a baby right now in this situation." They see no other way out.

As a Catholic, I truly believe that abortion is murder, that it's ending a life. I would not have an abortion or encourage anyone else to do it. But do I have a right to impose my religious beliefs on other people who believe differently? To force pregnant women who see no other choice but to seek dangerous and illegal means to end their pregnancies? I don't think so. I know others will disagree.

Tell me what you think about it.

Anon S: I have the exact feelings as you on abortion. It's murder and it's wrong, but a majority of our nation feels it's "okay." For them, there is a gray area where they do not feel they are killing anything. I could never feel that abortion is a medical procedure to remove unwanted material. You can remove tumors because they are dangerous. You can remove a mole that is unsightly because it might turn into something cancerous (even if it is only for cosmetic reasons). But to remove a growing child—no way. Of course, people will argue that abortion is "okay" when it threatens a mother's life or has genetic issues that will make it die soon after birth anyway. Or rape victims who shouldn't have to deal with an unwanted child. These, I suppose, are the gray areas. In this instance, I do not see a gray area. I see a life being taken. Still, this is MY faith and my morals talking. I will never get an abortion and most people I know wouldn't either—regardless of whether it's legal or not. Others will, regardless of legality. So I guess the answer is to make that option safe.

The one thing I can't explain is my lack of passion on the subject. I don't vote according to what the political leader feels because I feel abortion is one issue of many, many issues and I must look at everything the politician stands for. Most people I know vote ONLY according to the abortion issue. The issue of abortion is so large. My answer is to never have an abortion, and I would do everything in my power to stop another person in my life from having one. I suppose it's like domestic violence. I would never put up with domestic violence and would help anyone I know who is in danger. But do I speak out about deaths resulting from domestic violence or vote according to what politicians feel? No, it's not something I have experience with, and it's only one issue of many. Where do you start?

SFL: Thanks, Anon S. We do seem to think alike. I don't vote based on a candidate's abortion stance either. There are so many other issues to consider. And I don't really do anything about abortion beyond believing that it's wrong. People I love have had abortions. Do I shun them as sinners? I can't.

Anon S: I certainly wouldn't shun them either. Which is weird because I DO believe that it's killing. If someone I loved murdered another person (like a husband flipped out and killed his wife's lover), I suppose I could come to terms with their behavior and still love them as a person who made a grave mistake. I'd see them differently, and that might alter the relationship. Yet when a woman panics and kills her fetus, it just doesn't seem to be as "shocking." Even though she made a "pre-meditative" decision to have it done. For me, I think I could handle a friend having an abortion if it had happened in her past, especially if she was remorseful over it. If I had a current friend who chose to have an abortion, I'm not sure how I would deal with it.

Anonymous: Thanks for bringing up such a delicate subject. I respect the religious beliefs of others, and I am also grateful that as a woman, the law allows me to make my own choice if I were in a situation in which abortion was an option. Personally, I could never go through with it, except in a situation where I knew the fetus was not going to survive anyway or was a threat to my own life. I have NO respect for politicians who attempt to impose their religious beliefs into federal law, and find it offensive, especially with respect to rights and decisions about very personal and private matters. You may be aware of a recent wrongful death lawsuit against a Catholic hospital in the case of the death of a young woman pregnant with twins.[108] Defense is arguing that the fetus is NOT A PERSON, and so they are not at fault. It seems the Catholic Church recognizes a fetus as a person, except in cases where it costs them money. I cannot get behind an organization that will not uphold its own policies in difficult situations. And they expect young women with no support to do so?

RELIGION AND CHILDLESSNESS

I don't usually get into religion here. Everyone has different beliefs, and I don't want to offend anyone. In my interviews with childless women, most insisted that religion played absolutely no role in their decisions about having children. This surprised me. But I didn't consult God in the matter either.

I'm Catholic. Catholics have a reputation for reproducing, but I didn't know until I started researching my book that using birth control was a sin and that abortion was grounds for excommunication. I had no idea. My formal religious education ended at age 13, when the nuns probably assumed we were too young to even think about sex. In my case, they were right.

I had fallen away from the church by the time I started dating the man who became my first husband. When he escorted me to the student health center for birth control pills, I didn't think, "Oh no, this is a sin." I took the pills. Later, I switched to a diaphragm, and later still, after a divorce and several boyfriends, I married a man who had had a vasectomy. Sin, sin, sin. But I didn't think of it that way. I was just trying not to get pregnant when conditions were wrong and then wishing I could get pregnant when conditions were right. A strict Catholic would say I was trying to manage a part of life that is supposed to be up to God. Furthermore, they would say that my lack of children now is my punishment for being a big old sinner.

I believe in a kinder God who believes we screw up and forgives us. He may even have planned for me to be childless so that I could do other things. Still, when I'm around my Catholic friends, I don't say much about how I came to be childless. I just look sad and change the subject.

How about you? Does religion have anything to do with your thinking about whether or not to have children? In what way?

I welcome your comments. I know religion is a dangerous topic. Please be kind to one another.

Anonymous: Yes it did. We decided not to do IVF because of our belief that life begins at conception. It is possible to do IVF where only one or two embryos are created and implanted at a time, but it was too expensive for us to pursue.

Anonymous: I was raised Catholic, too and also was just trying to not get pregnant at the wrong time and pregnant at the right time, but as you said, I didn't know it was a sin. Looking back, I did sort of control the future. My first husband wanted kids with me. When he decided I was waiting for the perfect time, he met someone with a child, and he had an affair. We divorced and I married my current husband, who, like your husband, was divorced. He said he wanted children, but his kids came first, and he made decisions that caused too much financial hardship and (he gave too much for his kids in child support while I worked two jobs).

We couldn't afford to have children, and time went by without him realizing it, and now I am 45. He says now we could adopt, and I remember a time he said, "Do you have to go through that whole 'birth' thing?" Clearly not the special experience I wished I could create for us. I told him the "time has passed." I am 45. Where has he been? I spent many days crying in the bathroom to God: *Why is this happening?*

On bad days, I would think I was being punished because I didn't have children with my first husband and now I must suffer. I longed for my present husband to want kids with me and choose this as a priority. He never did. I feel overlooked and not cherished, and being a stepmom makes me a threat to everyone, so even though I would have been a great mom, I am the spare wheel whenever my husband puts me in that role. Otherwise, he defers to his ex, and I am left alone to grieve and not feel accepted. I have prayed and do not get comfort. I believe God loves me, but maybe I did do something wrong and this is my punishment.

SFL: Anonymous, I am so sorry for your pain. I don't think this is your punishment. I truly believe God forgives us for our failures. Of course, I want to give your husband a good swift kick in the nuts, but that wouldn't do any good. Now I guess it's time to figure out how to make the best of the way things are.

doubleme: When people ask me why I don't have children, I just say, "God said no." And I believe that. It wasn't in God's plans for me to have a child or it would have happened. My husband used withdrawal, but I knew that was not foolproof and wished it would have just happened. It was God's choice in the matter as well.

Anonymous: I'm Catholic and have used birth control at various times in life with no qualms. The last several years we've used the "pull and pray" method, knowing that if we get pregnant it will be okay. Of course lately there hasn't been much of anything going on. My issues are marital—not medical—and I lean heavily on my faith. On good days, I believe that when/if the time is right, God will help me be a mother. Sometimes I feel like a mother already—to my husband who seems to be lacking in some of the teachings that he should have learned as a child. After two rollercoaster years, I find I love him unconditionally, much like a mother loves her child. We're on the path to healing and sometimes it feels like we'll never get there, but I (try) to remind myself that as long as we are working, God will make it happen.

Elena: I'm a bit the other way round. I'm not religious anymore, but when I was in my late teens and early twenties, I participated in some evangelical youth groups and churches. Of course there the main dogma was no sex before marriage. I really do believe that because of that I have missed out on developing my sexuality through experience during the crucial years for that step in personal development. I don't know, but sometimes I think that it also has an indirect but hidden influence on my ability to 1) find a partner in the first place (not fun to be dating someone at age 26 and still be a virgin) and 2) make the right decisions about my partner/relationship.

SHOULD NUNS TAKE THE PILL?

Did you hear the one about how doctors in Australia are recommending that nuns take contraceptive pills to reduce their death rates from cancer? It's true. Dr. Kara Britt from Monash University, Melbourne, and Professor Roger Short from the University of Melbourne published an article in the medical journal the Lancet[109] recommending that nuns be allowed to take the pill.

Why? It has been common knowledge for a while that women who never bear children have a higher risk of breast, ovarian and uterine cancer. Apparently, pregnancy and breastfeeding offer protection by reducing the number of ovulatory cycles a woman has in her lifetime.

Studies in the 20th century showed a higher death rate from these cancers among nuns. The Australian researchers suggest that putting them on the pill would help. Using oral contraceptives has been shown to reduce the cancer death rates by 12 percent. Using the pill for this purpose shouldn't violate the rules of the church because it's being used for health, not for contraception, Britt and Short argue. No response from the Vatican yet.

Assuming most of us aren't nuns, have you ever had a doctor suggest you take the pill for health reasons even when you weren't worried about contraception? My doctors have suggested the pill to regulate my periods and to even out my moods but never for cancer protection. If we've never given birth, we're in the same boat as the nuns.

Mali: I've never had it suggested I take the pill as cancer protection. But you're making me think about it. And I perhaps wish it had been suggested if it is a significant difference. It was recently suggested I use the Mirena Coil[110] for health reasons—not as a contraceptive (I don't need one)—and I'm considering it.

If you're taking the pill for health reasons, it's no different from any other medication. I can't see why nuns couldn't take it. It seems logical. I will watch this with interest.

Professor: This is a very interesting post! I was put on the pill when I was 18 to combat the PMDD (premenstrual dysphoric disorder) that came along with my inability to naturally ovulate. When I began attending a Catholic university, I was first blocked from receiving the progesterone pills, but the health center later got around it because I was taking it for regulation and not contraceptive purposes. I later decided (with the urging of my husband) to take myself off of the pill and deal with the PMDD spiritually. I'm glad I did; even if I am at a higher risk of certain cancers, I don't think hormonal regulation for the rest of my life is the way I'd want to deal with it. I have a very different understanding of contraceptives now that I'm both Catholic and childless-by-marriage. I regret having supported the contraceptive industry for as long as I did, and I am willing to take whatever the Lord gives me. I'm not in favor of medicating women who have not borne children because I don't believe there is something fundamentally wrong with us. Maybe the good Lord wants us by his side sooner?

Professionally childless: I know the pill is used to control endometriosis, and I've known women who absolutely needed that therapy to survive. Generally, birth control pills are safe, and any health risks from taking them are low, but I wonder if taking them as a preventative measure for cancer is enough to outweigh any risk (however low) of taking them at all. That said, it's hard to know whether the incidence of cancer in nuns is because of being childless or because of some other predisposition or circumstance (such as less attention to gynecological care). I've read that the incidence of Alzheimer's disease in nuns is considerably lower than that in the general population. Do you think it's because they never had kids? Hmmm? Interesting post.

DO THE CHILDLESS FEEL WELCOME AT CHURCH?

My last post about religion and childlessness has brought in so many comments I think we should keep talking about it.

Let's talk about another aspect of the religion question. I wonder how many childless people stay away from organized religion because most churches are so family-oriented. The pews seem to be filled with couples and their children. The older folks bring their grandchildren. And here you are, sans offspring. If you're like me, widowed, divorced, single, or married to someone who doesn't share your faith, you also come sans spouse. It's lonely. You feel left out of all the "family" activities. Perhaps you stop going to church.

On the other hand, the people at church can become your family. They have for me. I sing for the children, sing with the choir at Mass, share lunches, dinners and picnics with the other parishioners, and spend holidays with my church friends and their kids. On my last birthday, it was the church ladies who surprised me with a big party and a pile of presents.

I suppose it's a question of attitude. Organized religion, with its "go forth and multiply" philosophy, can make us feel worse about not having children, reminding us that we are different. But if we can get past the fact that we aren't like the other parishioners (or members of the temple or mosque), if we can join in the activities and trust that God knows what he's doing, religion can be a great comfort. When I really look around, I realize I'm not the only childless woman or widow there, and it's good to not be alone.

What do you think about this? Again, be kind in your comments. No religion-bashing, okay?

Melanie: You're right. Although I may feel alone in my childlessness at church, I'm not. Others are without children. Those who are not married may have the same left-out feeling.

So many of the anecdotes told during the homily involve parents and children, so it would be nice if more pastors occasionally "thought" about those who are childfree or single, for whatever reason.

I tend to feel more left out on Mother's Day, when typically all the mothers are asked to stand for a special blessing. This must be a tough moment for others, too, though, so once again I'm not alone.

I'm learning not to let it get to me or drive me away from church services.

Certainlydifferent: Being one of Jehovah's Witnesses, it's not as focused on having kids now. In fact, many view the best goal to remain single to focus on preaching or work, or just remain a married couple to do same. So it's not that hard, but all the same this year at convention, there was the release of a children's video. I cried when they announced it. It's such a great provision, but it cut deep that it wasn't something I would be able to really use to the full.

Anonymous: I also feel a little bit out of place with all the families. Our town is very religious (Baptist), and everyone has a family. It seems as if people who don't have families move away because of the pressure. I did move here with my husband with the intent to start a family. We bought our house with four bedrooms. I thought one would be a nursery. My husband was mostly focused on bedrooms for each of his sons and an office. I should have said something, but I didn't. I thought he would change his focus. I don't want to move and leave many friends and a wonderful business I have built. I have been asked to work with the youth groups, etc. I have done this, but on some days, it is too painful, holidays especially. I haven't really found a church that I feel comfortable in. I can still be in a huge room full of people holding my husband's hand and feel totally alone.

TeacherJillK: I just can't go to church right now. The happy families make me feel left out. There are no couples classes for the childfree variety that I've found. I was involved in choir and that helps, but I found myself crying through the services, and being on display in the choir loft doesn't help! Ten years after stopping infertility treatments, I keep waiting for it to stop hurting. Church makes it hurt.

14

THE JOYS OF STEPPARENTING

I'M JOKING WITH THAT TITLE. Stepparenting is often a thankless job in which you get responsibilities you never asked for, with no authority, no respect, and not much love, all because you fell for someone who already had children. Being childless yourself means you may not know much about raising kids, and the steps' very existence may be the reason you'll never have a baby of your own. It's not always bad. I know blended families where everybody loves and supports each other, but I wouldn't expect that to be the norm.

When the stepchildren start having children of their own, you become this oddity called a step-grandmother or grandfather. Little kids not knowing any different may come running to hug you and call you Grandma or Nana or Papa, but there are those other grandparents out there with stronger claims, so where do you fit in?

Some of my posts on stepparenting brought only a few comments, but others . . . wow, watch out. I don't know whether it was my words or the timing, but I hit a nerve.

In the "childfree" community, there's a lot of talk about how having children can mess up a marriage. Check out the anthology *Being Fruitful without Multiplying*[111] or any "childfree" website for testimony from writers who cite that as one of the reasons they didn't want to have children. There's no question that having a baby can lead to sleepless nights, attention going to the child instead of each other, endless expenses, and physical and emotional changes.

But what happens when a child from a previous relationship is thrown into a childless marriage, especially when the other biological parent is still involved in their lives?

1. You find yourself helping to raise a child who has been formed by someone else. Not only do they have the ex's genes, but they spent their critical early years learning how to walk, talk and think from someone whose values may be very different from yours.

2. You find yourself responsible for a child you barely know without any experience in being a parent.

3. When conflicts arise, your partner's loyalties are divided between the two of you, and sometimes you lose.

4. A serious amount of your money is being used to raise somebody else's child.

5. The children know you are not the "real" mom or dad and may decide they don't need to do what you say or worry about your feelings. You and your partner may, no, *probably will*, quarrel over discipline.

6. On major occasions, such as graduations, weddings and court dates, both biological parents are likely to be there, making you feel left out and barren.

These are just a few of the things that happen. I'll bet you can add to the list. But I can make another list of the good things about marrying someone who comes with children from a previous relationship.

1. You go from being single to feeling like part of a real family.

2. You have someone to complain about and brag about when everybody's talking about their children.

3. Coming in without the baggage of their early years, sometimes you can become a special friend and confidant, a mother without so many rules.

4. You might get to be a grandmother without ever giving birth.

5. You have an opportunity to love and be part of the life of a young person who shares many of the qualities you love about your partner.

6. They might even friend you and send you baby pictures on Facebook.

If for some reason, their biological parent is not in the picture, having died or gotten sick or abandoned them, you may find yourself taking care of these kids full-time and loving them every bit as if they were your own.

I know this is a big issue for a lot of us. We don't have children mostly because our partners already have these other children. I'd love to hear what's on your list.

Anonymous: This might be easy for me to say as I am not in your situation, Sue, but I do not consider stepparents to be childless. It's different with my husband and me, who have no kids. At least you are acceptable to society while we are not. Also, people don't accuse you of hating kids.

SFL: Anon, you are so right. Having stepchildren does make you fit into society better. You become an associate member of the mom club. It doesn't matter how well you get along with the stepkids; they do get you the motherhood badge. But they don't make up for not having your own biological children.

STEPPARENTS CAUGHT BETWEEN TWO WORLDS

Evil SM commented last week:

In thinking about my biggest concerns as a childless woman that I'd love to discuss with other women who "get it," I'd say it's definitely the tension between feeling 100 percent childless and still having to reconcile the relationship with my stepkids. I'm not going to lie. I'm very resentful, and I am trying to make my peace with it all. Sometimes I want to embrace having no children, and then there are my husband's kids. I feel stuck between two worlds, and no matter how much I have given to them, tried to feel something parental towards them, I just don't. But, I can't say that. I have to put on a mask and pretend I feel a certain way about them and my role, or lack of, in their lives. Some days it eats me alive. I have most, if not all, the responsibility of a parent, and none of the warm feelings. Like you, Sue, we are custodial. My husband expects that if/when the kids have kids, I will feel like, or want to feel like, a grandparent, and that's just not my truth. In the beginning of our relationship, I thought I wanted a baby, but for some reason that changed and now I'm almost completely on the other side of the fence, though I still have some of those baby blues days. I feel more childless with my husband and his kids than I would otherwise. It's constantly in my face. Anyone else feel this way?

I do, Evil SM. My stepchildren are all grown now, and with my husband gone, I rarely see them, except on Facebook. But I remember those feelings. To be accurate, only the youngest of Fred's three lived with us. Sometimes I felt like his mother. Sometimes I felt like I was co-parenting with Fred's ex. More often, I felt like a babysitter who had no idea what she was doing. I loved him, but I'm not sure how he felt about me. I was always aware that he had a "real mom" who had first dibs on him.

As for the other two, we tried, but that warm fuzzy feeling proved elusive. Now that Fred is gone, I'm out here by myself. I'm watching my words because I don't want to hurt anybody's feelings or start a war. I wish we could have made it one big happy family. I wanted that so bad. But they weren't mine. So now I "like" their Facebook posts, send Christmas and birthday greetings, and pray for them every day.

So, readers, it's your turn. Many of us have stepped into relationships that include children from previous partners. Does the presence of these offspring make you feel worse about not having your own children or does it ease the pain? How do you get along? Can you love them like your own? What gets in the way of that?

Let's open up this can of worms and see what's inside. You can be as anonymous as you need to be. Me, not so much.

Thank you for being here and sharing with me.

CaliStepM: Evil SM's comments do resonate with me, although my situation is slightly different. I kind of liken my situation to Lisa Manterfield's.[112] When I married, my stepkids were already out of the house (early 20s, late teens). One already had kids, and I embraced being a grandparent eagerly, too eagerly, as it later came to bite me. I never attempted to fill the mom role with my stepkids because (thankfully) they are both super close to their own mom, and besides, even if they weren't, I don't believe in 'forcing' a relationship. My infertility challenges have caused much grief and angst each time they have another baby, but that is a pain that I own and work towards healing that has nothing to do with their building their own families.

My stepdaughter once rubbed it in that I don't/can't have my own children in a taunting, condescending tone; I certainly placed some extra distance between us after that conversation.

Although I don't believe in forcing a relationship, and even told my stepson that when I married his dad, oddly enough, he and his wife are trying to force one on me.

Evil SM writes: "In the beginning of our relationship, I thought I wanted a baby, but for some reason that changed, and now I'm almost completely on the other side of the fence, though I still have some of those baby blues days."

I'm kind of the reverse. I went into the marriage thinking I could not have children and had mostly made peace with my situation. Then surprisingly I got pregnant (x3) and miscarried (x3). Only once I got pregnant did my longings to have a baby of my own resurface. It's been an awful rollercoaster ride. Any time a grandbaby is born, I am genuinely happy for them, yet I am also crushed to pieces on the inside. My last miscarriage, I was pregnant at the same time as my daughter-in-law. Thankfully she went on to have a gorgeous healthy baby, but, as you can imagine, on that day I wanted to crawl under a rock and die. So many emotions, some good and some bad. The important thing I've learned (coming from a military family where feelings are not encouraged) is to allow my feelings of grief and sadness to happen naturally, to feel them, embrace them and honor them as a natural part of being human . . . .

I have many, many times loved my stepkids as my own, and at other times I've really had to work toward having a positive attitude toward them. Even in those moments, I never stopped loving them, just not at the "as my own" level of love. I only lived with my stepson a few months (it didn't go well). I think *living* with a child is far different, so I don't feel experienced enough to speak to your situation or Evil SM's because you guys shared a home for a far longer time period with them.

Their presence doesn't make me feel worse; it might even ease the pain, but only slightly. Of course, I hate Mother's Day, but it's gotten better over the years. Stepson's wife insists on recognizing me; before she came, there were several years with no recognition on Mother's Day. Then around the tenth year, my stepkids went in together and bought me jewelry for Mother's Day. I was utterly floored; I cherish that necklace. My stepdaughter no longer recognizes me on Mother's Day; I've just made peace with it. I would never want her to fake anything, and—far more importantly—my husband honors me on that day in his own way. I've learned to stay home though; the kids used to invite both me and their bio mom over to celebrate Mother's Day together (one big happy!) and after a few years I said thanks but no thanks. If we do anything on Mother's Day, it will be apart from her and, frankly, it will be on my husband's and my terms.

A stepmom has to constantly put herself last and be okay with little to zero recognition for her efforts. Many don't make it. A supporting spouse can make or break the situation.

I hope that Evil SM's heart gets healing. I feel the angst in her words and I pray for her to find peace.

It doesn't speak to the question of whether or not to have children, but the book "Stepmonster"[113] was helpful to me in establishing healthy boundaries with my stepkids.

Colleen: I'm a stepmom to a 20-year-old college junior. He was 3 when his parents divorced and 11 when his father introduced us to each other. My stepson has a very close relationship with his mom, with whom I get along, but I don't see her very often.

So those are the facts. Oh, the feelings!

In retrospect, I probably pushed the stepmom role early in our relationship (trying to engage with him a lot when he stayed over, making a lot of meals, etc.), but he and I are different people and we were introduced when he was just starting to be a tween. The awkwardness! In a couple of years, I got a clue and decided 1) not to take anything personally because I realized I was a person in a role in his life, but he and I didn't really know each other yet; 2) let time take care of how close we'd become; 3) accept that his mom and dad would make decisions and his dad as my husband would let me know what they were, but I didn't really have input; 4) I'd be a consistent presence because that's what kids really need, and to demonstrate that I really loved his dad.

As needed, I cried and pouted to myself and vented to my therapist and shared my feelings with my husband.

Now, nine years later, we have a nice relationship. It turns out we have the same taste in a lot of sitcoms and comedian podcasts and so we share these things with each other. He finally returns my periodic texts. His hugs seem genuine now and honestly the low-pressure approach feels like a relief.

That being said, I have a lot of feelings about the future. I hope he turns into a young man who enjoys his relationship with me and, if something happens to his dad, lets me still be involved somehow in his life. I hope, if he marries, that his wife likes me and doesn't compare me (too much) to bio-mom. I hope, if he has kids, that I'm allowed to get close to the kids. If none of that happens, I will be very sad, but at the same time, I'm intentionally developing a relationship with the same ideas in mind with my nephews and nieces, and I have the same hopes for them as I do my stepson.

Most of the time when asked, I say I don't have kids. Because I feel that I don't; I have a stepson. But if my husband or a friend is with me and I say I don't have kids, sometimes they'll correct me. Which doesn't embarrass me. The subject is so complicated that I can barely keep myself clear on it, let alone others. But sometimes others seem surprised or a little embarrassed for me if I'm corrected like that. It's one of the few things that I don't take personally because only other non-bio stepmoms will EVER understand what this is like.

It's a role I didn't ask for, was unprepared for, and have no idea how it will pan out. It's one of the biggest challenges of my life. Thank you for bringing this subject up.

Evil SM: "It's a role I didn't ask for, was unprepared for, and have no idea how it will pan out. It's one of the biggest challenges of my life."

This . . . exactly! I think I thought at some point I would figure out how it would pan out, but I still have no clue. I feel like I will always have a polite relationship with the kids, but it seems clear that this is all they and I are capable of. It is disappointing, and sometimes I wonder if the neutrality is worse than flat-out rejection. To some extent, what they say about love is true. The opposite of love isn't hate; it's indifference. I've never been a big enough presence in their lives to accept or reject. I am just here, existing on some parallel plane.

M2L: OMG, this is so true. "It is disappointing, and sometimes I wonder if the neutrality is worse than flat out rejection. To some extent what they say about love is true; the opposite of love isn't hate, it's indifference." I've really been struggling to put my finger on it, but this is exactly my experience. Thank you for sharing. At least we know we're not alone in what we're experiencing! Hugs.

I am so, so grateful for this blog!! Thank you, Sue!! Completely understand how Evil SM feels. Even though my husband's children were grown up and living independently by the time we got together, I find it incredibly difficult to be with a man who has children, and now a grandchild, when I don't have children. It definitely doesn't help that he didn't want children with me. I try to understand that he had "been there and done that" and didn't want to start again at his age and in his financial situation, but it doesn't make it any easier to bear.

Just like Evil SM, I feel that I'm not able to move forward, to embrace and accept my childlessness. This may sound ridiculous to others who have not been in a similar situation. I am extremely reluctant to voice how I feel anywhere other than places like this blog for fear of the kind of negative responses I might get. Deep down, I feel like I am a "bad" person for not being able to embrace these people in my husband's life. Surely if I was "nicer," I would be able to separate my childlessness from them. But it is a visceral feeling. Whenever he is in contact with them, it hurts me and it feels like he is rubbing it in my face that he wanted these children, with those women, and not our children, with me. Ugh. How is this my life!?!?

Matt: I'm a stepfather. 35. Been with my SO (significant other) for five years now. I met my stepdaughter when she was 5 years old. So she's just entering her teen/tween years right now.

My SO has always been very supportive in easing me into the stepfather role. She's always included me as an integral part of our family. My stepdaughter spends 90 percent of the time with us, only a few days per month with her dad. The latter has never been a source of friction or anything. My SO and I have a cordial relationship with him in the interest of my stepdaughter. I never felt resentment or the need to force myself as a "replacement parent" towards her. I've always accepted the situation for what it is.

As such, I can only say that right now I have an outstanding relationship with my stepkid. I do all the things a regular father does: we play together, I tuck her in bed, we share secrets, I take care of her, she talks to me about what troubles her, we have family trips. When she was younger, we were more distant, but right now, our bond is strengthening as I am also opening up to her while I age. I can see it in the small things like her drawings of our family, how she acts around me, demands my attention to her daily activities, how she includes me in our family. She is a real joy to have in my life. And my SO reminds me of how important I am to her and her daughter each and every day. So, I don't feel like a "mere" babysitter or an "uncle once removed." I'm the most important person to her after her dad and mom, and she's becoming the second most important person, after my SO, in my own life, as I slowly let myself open up to her, too.

My SO doesn't want any more children. I'm very ambivalent about the matter. Always have been. During my 20s, I didn't have children on my mind at any time, and the idea always elicited a big red no on my part. Having a child of my own felt like something that really wasn't the thing for me.

However, only recently, after five years with my SO, I realized what it means to have no children of my own. That there is a difference. You see, while I do all the dad things, she doesn't call me "Dad." And I can feel that her love isn't unconditional. So, only a few months ago, I started feeling this incredible sadness about what hasn't been and will never become. And yes, as a man, I cried about this. I don't hold my tears back when I feel a bout of sadness because I feel so relieved when it passes.

However, I don't feel longing or burning, wishing that I had a child of my own (at least not right now). I also don't feel regrets about my choice. I'm happy with how I am doing right now. I'm happy to be a stepdad and a godfather to my two godchildren, and an uncle to the nieces of my SO. I do feel some guilt towards my parents, though, that I won't grant them grandchildren. They don't resent me for taking this path though; they are very understanding and caring.

On a side note, my nan isn't my "real" nan. My granddad remarried before I was born. But to me, she's always been my nan. No questions asked. The knowledge that we don't share genes has never bothered me one bit. And it is something that I reflect upon quite a bit when you ask me to define (grand) parenthood. So, my own experience speaks volumes to me when I ask myself, "How important are those genes really?"

IS A STEPMOTHER A REAL MOTHER?

In a previous post, I asked whether having stepchildren made you a mother. For me, it's part yes, part no. Fred's kids have been in my life for more than 30 years, but their biological mother is the one they think of as Mom. And that makes sense. If my father remarried, his new wife might be the most wonderful woman in the world, and we might love her very much, but she could never take the place of our birth mother. That's just biology, plus family history.

If your partner has children from a previous marriage, he will always have a connection to them that you can never have. They are his kids, not yours. When a conflict arises between you and the kids, who is he going to side with? The new wife may find herself competing for her husband's time and attention, as well as his money. This can put a real damper on a marriage.

When he (or she) has kids and you don't, that can add to the stress. As several readers have commented here, it gets even worse when his children grow up and have babies of their own. Now he gets to be a grandparent, and you don't.

Some couples have no problem with any of this. They and the kids become one happy family, and they don't even think the word "step." They're all "our kids." They are blessed. I hear from plenty of people for whom having stepchildren makes a painful situation even more difficult.

Does your partner have kids from a previous marriage? Let's talk about it.

Anonymous: I can't thank you enough for this post. I am a childless stepmum. My husband had a vasectomy after having two children with his ex and just before they broke up. We tried for a reversal, but it wasn't successful. I am almost 39, and every day without a child of our own is a painful and lonely journey. I am lucky in that my stepchildren are lovely. They accept me and I get on well with them, but at the end of the day, I am just the wife of their father. I will never be equal to their parents, and every weekend that they are here, I have to see everything that I want but know that I can no longer hope for. Struggling to come to terms with life without a child is so much harder when stepchildren are involved. There is the fact that your partner already has children and doesn't share the desperate need or disappointment that you do. There is also the terrible sadness that sharing in their wonderful experiences brings. The fact that they love me but don't need me, I will never be called on when they are sick or afraid, they will never make me anything at school, I can see them rehearse, but I will never see a school play, I can help them with their homework, but I will never meet their teacher . . . the list is endless.

The special and beautiful bond is the one that they have with their mum and dad. It is an impossible task for a biological parent to see a situation or to understand an issue without feeling protective of their children. I understand this, but I long for a conversation with my husband about what infertility means to me and our future that doesn't get translated into criticism of his children. It's such an emotional subject, but wanting a child of your own and feeling sad because I can't be as integral to his children's lives as I want to be isn't the same as rejecting them. I just want more.

I am afraid of what it will be like when we get old and they have children of their own, and that adds terrible sadness to thoughts of growing old and gray with my husband that really should be happy and wistful. The thought of it doesn't fill me with warm feelings. It makes me sad because my stepdaughter will experience pregnancy and being a mother, but I can't. I know that I will be a grandparent of sorts, but it just isn't the same, and this just isn't something that my husband can understand. He feels that I am cutting myself out and not that the experience really will be different for me than it will be for him. This isn't the dream that we grew up with. Having stepchildren doesn't sate the terrible burning and all-consuming hormones that the biological clock brings. It amplifies them. It's all terribly selfish stuff. It hasn't been long since I found out that I can't have children and that my stepchildren are all that I can hope for. I want more from them and our relationship than I can have or that they can give me.

Maybe it will get easier in 10 or 20 years' time. At the moment, it is heartbreaking and bleak—for both my husband and me. He wants me to be happy and love the experience and joy that his children bring us every day. I can't do this though. I'm not sure what future I have anymore, and it is hard to enjoy the present when it is such a reminder of what I want, and the primary reason why we'll never share the experience ourselves is due to the decisions that he made with his ex. It all boils down to utter complicated confusion. I wish that I was the infertile one and then I could see his children as such an added bonus. Life in stepfamilies never seems to be simple, but this one is an absolute doozy.

Anonymous: Anonymous [Stepmum], I'm in basically the same boat, but, as my husband has been married twice before, I became a step-grandparent this same year that I'm also somewhere between the bargaining and depression stages of grief and existential crisis I've been managing, while also the stepmother of his three teenagers from his second marriage. I think I've moved beyond most of the anger, most, not all. I haven't been included in his grandparenting experience thus far. I've been kind of detached and doing my own thing when his kids visit, joining in on a meal or an outing when I feel like it.

It was a real gift to read what you wrote this day, knowing that right now I'm not so different from an another woman right now. I've finally accepted that I should probably see a psychiatrist. I don't even want to talk about any of this stuff, but you know it's hard, so if you haven't, I suggest you reach out to a mental health professional. Take care of yourself. Don't be so miserable. My husband is just beginning to realize the support I need from him as I keep myself away from the verge of a nervous breakdown. A good husband can make all the difference. I'm hoping I can continue to count on him. Talk with your husband about what you need from him as your friend right now, setting the "whys" aside for the conversation. Try to reconnect with him to help you through your current angst.

Anonymous: Thank you for posting this! I am a 35-year-old soon-to-be first-time mom, and my stepmother does not have children of her own. I know she is really excited to be a "grandma," but it brings up a lot of confusing feelings for me, especially since my mother died 13 years ago. My stepmom means well, but I guess I just feel like I constantly have to set boundaries with her because I know she envisions some kind of "mother-daughter" relationship (she's been with my dad since I was 9) that I do not want. I have finally accepted that she is here and in my life, and all that I can do is continue to be kind but also keep setting boundaries. It is working, but I guess what I really wish is for her to just go away. But that's not going to happen, and she makes my dad happy, and I know that all she wants is to be loved and included. Her deep desire to express her love (she used to send me lots of "I love you" text messages but has stopped since I stopped replying to them) comes off as not genuine and I often think she only wants to be close to me so that she can talk to all her friends about "being a mom" and "mom stuff." To put it simply, she annoys me, and I know that I judge her because she has no idea what it means to be a parent.

Ms. Jones: Wow, Anonymous [stepdaughter], that is heartbreaking and downright cruel.

The reason I am responding is because I am currently in the position your stepmother was. I am about to get engaged to a man who has a 9-year-old daughter, and I do not have any children.

I spend hours studying my butt off trying to do the right thing: understand my role, show the right support and the right respect. I am also trying to understand the viewpoint of someone who has a stepparent. I talk to as many people in similar situations as I can because I can't think of anything more AWFUL than a post like this.

The line I take issue with is that you judge her so harshly for trying to be a good parent to you. It sounds like her heart was in the right place and she did the best she could—what she was EXPECTED to do. But I have the feeling if she was detached instead, you would complain about that too because you are taking out frustrations you have in life on someone who doesn't deserve it.

She may have no idea what it means to be a parent (she does—you selfishly withhold giving her credit), but YOU have no idea what it means to be a stepmother.

Whatever trauma you are dealing with is not HER fault. Do you honestly think she wanted to come in and ruin your life and take over as a mom? You yourself said she just wants to be liked and included, yet you kick dirt in her face. Why doesn't she deserve your respect? Why doesn't your FATHER? Can you imagine how heartbroken the man would be to hear you say such mean and nasty things?

A person who accepts the role of stepmotherhood is a SAINT. She is a person who knows she will be expected to love the children as her own, to care for them as a mother would, and for her finances to be affected by people she has no obligation to, to feel marginalized and excluded and accused of doing things she hasn't. After a lifetime of sacrifice, THIS is the thanks they get. What the hell is wrong with you?

After reading comments like this, I am seriously doubting that marrying a man with a young daughter is a good idea. I can only hope you learn some things about life you have missed before you pass on this pattern of hatred to your future child.

Anonymous: I have been in a relationship for five years, for most of which I thought he wanted children with me also. The youngest stepchild was a baby, in a crib, in my room. There is a bond that grows—a sugar cookie smell—when they are babies and cry in the night for you to care for and love them. And the second oldest called me "Mommy" straight away. I didn't dissuade it, because I never wanted to have a difference between my own kids and these beautiful, loving children. But, truth be told, they are not my kids. I can list 18,000 examples here of how externalities make that so. And he told me first that he "would never take motherhood away from me." Should have been a red flag. That was five years ago. Then he told me that motherhood would ruin my body. That was years three and four. Then he said that kids were nothing but work. They are not good, only work (nice). Last year. Now the newest one, since we have reduced ourselves to hate apparently, is that I am not fit to be a mother of my own. But I looked after his kids for five years, paid all of the bills for almost two, did everything possible, and now everything has just disintegrated into nothing. I love these children, and I love him despite the shitty, selfish behavior. I don't know what to do.

SFL: Oh rats, Anonymous. What is his problem?

I'm sure you know the choices. Leave him. Keep taking care of his children without having your own. Or find some way to insist on having your own babies. If the relationship is dead, there is no real choice, is there? I'm so sorry this is happening to you.

Anonymous: I do love him, and we have talked about this. We have concerns about how long ago the procedure [vasectomy] was done. I'm generally okay. However, when his children visit, I can count on being in a funk all weekend. It makes it harder for me. Almost makes me feel like I'm cheating myself. Guess I'm on my own here. Thanks.

Anonymous: You are not alone. I feel a little funky when his child comes every week, too. It is hard when you are used to doing your own thing and then a kid comes and takes everything over. Sometimes I am not in the mood or not feeling well. I am 38 and a homebody and feel forced to my room so I am not being a grouch. I feel like I have to be someone else just because there is a child around. Sometimes I miss my own place and privacy.

SFL: Boy, Anonymouses, you expressed what I often felt when the stepkids came around. It sounds selfish, but it's so true, isn't it? It's just not easy. Thanks for your comments.

WHAT AM I TO MY STEPCHILDREN NOW?

You marry the man who doesn't want to have children with you; he already has children from a previous marriage. Sometimes his children live with you; sometimes you have partial custody or visitation, but they are definitely part of your life now.

Maybe it's a close and wonderful relationship in which the word "step" disappears. Or maybe it's a mess, and you can barely be in the same room with each other. For most of us, it's somewhere in-between. You inevitably connect because you have their father in common. They grow up, they marry, they have children, and you become a step-parent-in-law and step-grandmother. Again, you may be close or distant, but there is a connection.

Then the worst happens, and your husband, their father, dies. Regular readers know that I'm living this reality right now, but let's stay hypothetical for a minute. Your husband, the link to those children, is gone. Or your wife, if you're a stepfather. You all grieve the loss, but now the question arises and sits out there like a hippopotamus in the front yard. What is your relationship now?

A web search turns up lots of legalities, mostly concerns about custody and inheritance. In both cases, let's hope you've got something in writing. If you and your husband had custody of his children, and somebody wants to take the kids away from you, that's a big issue that I'm not going to address here. Better find a good attorney.

When it comes to his estate, what happens if his wishes are not stated in his will depends on where you live. In some states, his kids are entitled to half of what he owned, and you get the other half. I don't know about you, but giving up 50 percent would leave me homeless and bankrupt. In some places, as his spouse, you get it all, but it varies and you should know what the law says. You should also both have wills, even if you're young and healthy.

You should also know that in most states, stepchildren are not your legal heirs. When you die, they will not automatically receive anything from your estate unless you specifically leave it to them in your will.

So, if they're not your legal heirs, we come back to what is your relationship now? I'm reminded of an aunt by marriage who has been widowed for several years. No one ever considered that she was no longer a member of the family when my uncle died. Of course, her kids are blood relatives . . .

It's different with childless stepparents. We don't share one drop of blood. Our only familial link is our spouse, and when he's gone, then what? I guess it depends on what kind of relationship you've established over the years. If you have developed a close-knit family, you will remain in each other's lives. If not, you may drift apart. In my case, we'll see, but I fear it's going to be the latter.

I'd love to hear your ideas and suggestions on the subject. And of course, if you're a childless stepfather, just reverse the genders and the same questions apply to you, too.

Anonymous: I am going through a heart-wrenching time because my stepdaughters told me I would still be Nana to the grandchildren, but no one cared to ask me if I had plans for Easter and today I find the oldest grandchild is graduating high school today and I have not been invited. Very hurtful. I will send my granddaughter a graduation card and gift card, but I will no longer expect or even hope for an invitation to anything.

Anonymous: For me, the problems started as soon as my wife died. She was older than me, and I was widowed at 55. That leaves her two sons that we had supported since we married in 1983. As of today 6/17/14, I have not spoken to one boy since August of 2013. I have given him money, helped them every time they needed help but still only get grief in return. The oldest boy will hit his kids if they mention my name or desire to come see me. For me, I am at a point in my life if they don't want me in their lives, so be it.

Marilynn: One of my deceased husband's sons is so selfish now that they own the house. He's threatened law enforcement because I told him I had guests and he wouldn't be able to start inventory. But thank God, my life is not contingent on him being understanding.

Anonymous: Let go and let GOD. When you know you have treated people kindly, you can sleep at night. They are the ones with the issue.

15

NOT THE LIFE I EXPECTED

I'M A CHILD OF THE 50S. Born in 1952, I came of age at the peak of the women's movement, devouring every issue of *Ms. Magazine,*[114] proudly telling people I was a feminist. I knew I wanted to be a writer. But I also expected to be a mother. From the time I was a toddler, my parents had trained me to follow my stay-at-home mother's example. Yes, writing and music were fine, as long as they didn't interfere with a woman's primary job: taking care of her home, husband and children. *We're glad you're getting good grades in school, and it's nice that you got your poem published, but can you bake a cake? Can you hem a skirt? Can you diaper a baby?* TV shows and movies from the 1950s and 60s formed me in the Doris Day mold. Whatever else I might want to do, I would get married and have children.

It didn't turn out that way.

How about you? I know I'm older than many of my readers, so maybe your experiences were different. Were you raised to be a mom or was that just one of many options? I'd love to hear what you have to say on this.

Anonymous: I graduated high school in the early nineties. Small town society expected you to either go on to college or find full-time employment. Those who found employment were usually the ones who had been dating someone for ages and would likely marry a few years after graduation. A family would of course follow.

I was discouraged from going the college route. I wasn't great at anything, and my parents felt college would be a waste of money. I hadn't been taking any administrative assistant classes, so I really wasn't on a fast track to any "great" job. I was however dating an older guy at the time. I suppose my parents expected me to marry and move from their house to his.

My mother certainly groomed me for a life of grocery planning, how to run a cost-efficient household, and how to use Saturday mornings for housecleaning, and Saturday nights for a date with the husband.

I felt like a fish out of water. My classmates were excited about college acceptance letters and summer jobs while I was trying to decide what the heck to do. I certainly didn't have money to have the usual college experience, and no one was helping me to wrangle a student loan. I had no idea what I was good at so finding a full-time job seemed pretty daunting. I didn't even really like my boyfriend, but that didn't seem to matter to anyone either.

All I knew was that eventually my life would be preparing three meals a day, putting up with children, and polishing the wood furniture on Saturday mornings.

Community college saved me. I found I was able to afford the first semester, which was all I needed to get myself on a path. I was thrilled to find that I loved college so much more than high school. Doors were finally opening.

I spent the next 15 years doing my best but unhappily making poor choices based on what I thought I "should" do. I'm finally finding my way, based on what I "want" to do. But I'm nearing 40 and I don't have any children. My parents have mellowed and seem proud of me. Still, a little part of me feels like I let them down.

If I had better guidance, maybe I wouldn't have made so many bad decisions. Perhaps I made poor choices because of an immature need to defy my parents. Either way, if I'm lucky enough to have a child, I will do things quite differently.

SFL: Anonymous, thank you so much for sharing your story. My parents didn't encourage me to go to college either. The prevailing thought back then was that education for girls was a waste because they'd just become moms anyway. Community college was a godsend for me, and I'm so grateful I went on to get a degree because I needed to support myself.

I know my parents wished they had grandchildren, but they were still proud of me. You have to live your own life and hope they'll be happy for you no matter what you do.

Elena: I'm exactly 20 years younger than you. For my generation, it was mostly normal that I should get as good an education as I could get. And also, make a good start in a career. We looked down on girls who said, "I'll marry anyway." Our role models were our mums, starting work again after a few years of "baby time." My mum's generation certainly didn't have it easy. They were the generation to fight their way back into work after years of absence. They had to defend themselves from the suggestions that they were bad mums because they worked part-time. They tried to make their own personal biography and reach their own goals even if that meant divorce. So our role model was: Yes, sure I'll have a good education and I won't stop working just because I will have kids. Notice something? Yes. The kids are still in there.

Getting the good education and career start prolonged the time we waited for making them. Not wanting to end up in marriages which would end in divorces, we also took our time finding a partner. The pill helped us a lot to be free to make these choices (as you talked about in another post). No pressure to marry just to be able to have sex. You can even plan baby and career. Nobody told us that you can actually wait too long. Nobody told us that even if we were so clear about what, how and when we wanted, the men we found as partners hadn't given things as much thought as we had. It sure is great not to be an "old spinster" or divorcee not even able to support myself financially. But nobody told me that when the "career plus baby" plan failed, I would be left with NO plan. Because "just career" was never the plan. It's one big failure, not one part of a plan missing. I wonder if you can understand that.

SFL: Thanks for sharing this, Elena. I'm older than you, but my plan was the same: career AND babies. My mother's career was being a wife and mother, and she did it well. But I went straight from high school into college and into a journalism career, always expecting I would combine the two. Thank God I had the career when marriage and motherhood didn't work out.

IS A CHILDLESS WRITER HANDICAPPED?

Is a writer—or any artist—without children lacking an important component for her art? Can she ever portray a complete human experience without giving birth and raising children? On the other hand, can a mother ever be free to fully pursue her art?

This discussion, which never ends, came up recently after the death of best-selling Irish author Maeve Binchy.[115] Most of the news articles mentioned her childlessness. In an essay in the Daily Telegraph,[116] writer Amanda Craig argued that Binchy would have been a better writer if she had been a mother, giving her a "deeper understanding of human nature." Binchy, who struggled with infertility, had written[117] about how much she wanted children but was unable to have them. It wasn't a choice for her. But did it make her less of a writer? Many famous authors of the past, including Virginia Woolf, the Bronte sisters, and Jane Austen, were childless. In their day, it was believed you couldn't be both a successful writer and a mother. Which argument is right?

For me, I admit I have some gaps in my knowledge. At a meeting last night, things moved into talk about doing a program at the local schools. Suddenly the parents in our group had all these suggestions that obviously came from their experiences with their kids. I felt like a guy must feel in a discussion about makeup: clueless.

Although I haven't had the same experiences, I have been a child, growing up with other children. I have been a stepmother, and I have been around other people's kids and families all my life. That has to count for something. If I wanted to volunteer at the school, I could learn what those people at the meeting know. I have also raised dogs—which makes parents of humans roll their eyes—but this week, as I'm treating Annie's third ear infection this year, I feel pretty darned motherly. (It's getting much better, thank you.)

Let's look at the other side of the equation. Because I live alone with my dog, I have been able to spend my day like this: I got up when I felt like it, did a little accounting before eating a leisurely breakfast with no one else to feed, spent over an hour playing the piano and starting to write a new song before going to a doctor's appointment, decided on the spur of the moment to take myself to lunch at a wonderful restaurant overlooking the ocean, then came home and spent the next three hours finishing the song. Even without children, I have never had so much uninterrupted time. For songwriting, I need complete concentration. I need to be able to keep going over the song, smoothing out the bumps until I can sing and play it with confidence, and that takes hours.

Whether it's writing, music, art or whatever our passion, it is easier without children. Of course, when we're done, we wish we had somebody to share it with, but let's be honest. A childless woman has a lot more freedom to create. Whatever grief or loss we might feel, that is a blessing for which we should be grateful.

Your thoughts?

Anonymous: It IS possible to be a mother without giving birth, of course. As a foster parent, then as an adoptive parent, I learned far more about myself and about life than in any other context. Ten years later, I'm still learning.

Motherhood teaches you about love in a way that few other experiences can . . . or at least, few experiences have for me. I didn't become a mother until I was 38, so it could be argued that somehow I might have picked up on some of these life lessons anyway. But most of them are directly linked to motherhood. There's nothing quite like having a captive audience to put things in perspective.

Anonymous: Maeve Binchy: "Her novels, which were translated into 37 languages, sold more than 40 million copies worldwide . . . was mourned as the passing of Ireland's best-loved and most recognizable writer. Her books have outsold those of other Irish writers such as Oscar Wilde, James Joyce, Samuel Beckett, W. B. Yeats, Seamus Heaney, Edna O'Brien and Roddy Doyle. Recognized for her "total absence of malice" and generosity to other writers, she finished ahead of Jane Austen, Charles Dickens and Stephen King in a 2000 poll for World Book Day."

But never mind all that. Let the MommyBloggers/media obsess over "but didn't she have children? Did she *understand*?"

Magdalen: The experiences are bound to be different. I've had all sorts of interesting-deep-etc. experiences, emotions, spiritual happenings since becoming stepmom to an older child, and then more-new-different ones since becoming a biological mom. I've also had more-new-different experiences since my husband got a traumatic brain injury. I think mother-writers are interesting to women now because for so many years, writing was supposed to be a Guy Thing. Most of the women who broke into writing novels and such were childless.

roddma: I have wondered this same thing about women writers, but many writers write about things they haven't experienced. I think "mommy" bloggers forget writers were kids once, too.

While some may say they experience a love like never before being a mother, being childless has opened up my eyes and mind. For example, I never knew there was such a thing as childless by choice. If I had become a parent, I might not have been so open-minded. Like most women 40ish, I was raised to believe women only had one path in life. And if I was to be a parent by some miracle, I would still be respectful of other people's choices.

Becky: Great post. I can't imagine anyone reading Jane Eyre and thinking Charlotte Bronte didn't understand the full human experience, regardless of being childless. Just one more reason I admire her so much!

Jen: Childfree and childless women are stereotyped as cold, loveless, and incapable of emotion. It's like you can't feel anything unless you've had a baby. No one would place this standard upon a man.

Anonymous: Really interesting post. I went on a writing course for a day recently, and the entire class was made up of women, with only myself and one other lady there not having children. For the first half hour, the women with children discussed how many kids they had, what their children's names were, and a whole lot of other mum things. I felt totally excluded until someone had the forethought to ask a really good question: "So, what are people writing at the moment?" I wish mothers didn't feel the need to bond firstly over their children. Whilst I felt excluded, it made me realize how full my life was with so many other things unrelated to kids. That is what I bring to my writing, a totally exceptionally different point of view. As important as a parent's point of view. I would actually turn the question around and ask what amazing learning and life experiences do you miss by following the well-trodden path of having children?

GRADUATION DAY: EVERYTHING WAS POSSIBLE

On June 7, 1974, I sat with my fellow journalism graduates in the middle of the football field at San Jose State's Spartan Stadium, baking in our caps and gowns. Everything was changing that month. After 16 years of school, I would finally be free of classes, homework, finals and term papers. I could pursue my blossoming career in newspapers, and in two weeks, I was getting married.

I don't remember who spoke at the ceremony. I have vague memories of people passing marijuana cigarettes and tossing a ball around. My classes done, I was obsessing over clothes. A sewing maniac in those days, I had made the blue and white seersucker mini-dress that I wore under my robe. I was making my wedding gown, one of the bridesmaid's dresses and new outfits for the honeymoon. I was dealing with flowers, photographers, and last-minute bridal showers. I was setting up our new apartment, which I had no doubt would be only a temporary home until we bought a house. Soon I would be having babies and writing books, living the life I had always expected to live.

I was so very young, 22 going on 12. Look up "naïve" in the dictionary, and you'll find a picture of me. Webster's defines it as "deficient in worldly wisdom or informed judgment." That pretty much nails it. Raised in an extremely restrictive home, I hadn't had my first date until my first year of college. By the middle of my second year, I was engaged. I had had three actual boyfriends in those 18 months or so before I hooked up with Jim.

Hooking up didn't mean what it means now. I was a virgin until three months after I started dating Jim. And I probably would have stayed a virgin a bit longer if he hadn't pressured me so hard to have sex, and if I hadn't gotten drunk and let him because I knew he'd dump me if I didn't. Ladies, how many of us have given in simply because we were afraid to lose the guy?

Anyway, coming from this strict Catholic background with minimal knowledge of the world, I assumed that since we were having sex, we were getting married. And since he was getting pressured by his parents to find a wife, he said, *yeah, sure, we'll get married.* No ring, no down-on-his-knees proposal, and oh by the way, *let's not tell anybody yet.* Anybody hear warning bells? I heard them, too, but I thought I had made this commitment and had to stick with it.

As for having kids, I had no idea he wouldn't want them. He was great with other people's children, and I just assumed he'd be great with ours. Did we talk about it? Nope. He did escort me to the college health clinic to get birth control pills. He did have a supply of condoms on hand. After we were married, his theme song was "not yet." Turns out he wasn't big on employment, monogamy or sobriety either, but lest you think he was just a big shit, I loved the guy with all my heart. We had a wonderful time together. The sex was amazing, and we could talk for hours. I thought we'd be married forever.

I thought I'd be a mom. Our parents would be fabulous grandparents. I'd also have the career of my dreams. Like I said, naïve. As the marriage died, we agreed that we could have had a fantastic affair but should never have gotten married.

If I had just said no to sex with Jim or enjoyed the sex but realized I didn't have to marry him, my life might have been completely different. He would have dumped me, and I might have married someone with a good job, someone who wanted the house and kids, maybe even someone who'd go to church with me. But no. I thought this was it.

It didn't have to be "it."

I haven't talked to Jim in over 40 years. I have heard that he got married two more times and never had any children of his own. I don't think much about him or our six-year marriage. Fred, who came later, was my real husband. I didn't have babies with him either, but the love we had was worth it. And we did talk about it.

On that sweltering day when I graduated from San Jose State, I had no idea what was coming. What would I have done if I'd known? Should a person get married two weeks after graduation? I don't recommend it. Live a bit first. And take time to make sure you have the right partner. Life is not like "The Bachelorette,"[118] where you have to make a decision in a few weeks. Be sure. And if you're not sure, don't do it.

Does this stir any thoughts or memories? I'd love to hear your comments.

Candy: This post stirred some sadness in me and made me ask myself, "What the hell were you thinking???" I was 20 years old marrying a 28-year-old man with a child and a vasectomy. Never did I imagine I wouldn't have children with him. So, Sue, you will find my picture right next to yours with the definition of naive!!!

Cheryl: When I graduated high school, I thought I would get married and have children. I married at 25, started trying at 26. Looking back, my husband never ever spoke about having a baby, never showed interest in children. I wasn't close with my sister or mother and moved away from home at 21. In hindsight, if I knew then what I know now, I would've walked away and found someone who did.

I teared up reading this post, Sue, and agree, Candy, this was not how I thought my life would be. Mine is the third picture of the definition of naive.

Tony: Sue, I've seen many people have the same experience that you have. I agree, if you're not sure about your fiancé, don't do it. I believe that you would have made a wonderful mother. I didn't think I'd have made a good father for years. I was wrong. I would have.

Laura: Had you not had that experience with Jim, you would not be giving us this safe and familiar forum for us to share in our united childless story. So perhaps you did not have that life you had expected. Many of us haven't. But your life all the same had lessons, meaning and purpose. I for one am thankful that I have a forum where my childless angst can be understood.

Erica: I can really relate to this for sure. I think the best day of my life was my first night at college. Everything was still possible, and I hadn't messed anything up yet. At that point, I wanted to be a doctor. I also assumed that I would get married and have children at some point.

As time went on, I compromised more and more of myself. I got good grades, but they weren't straight A's, so I decided not to keep working towards applying for med school. I now know there were people who managed to get in, although sometimes out of the country or a DO [osteopath] school with my grades or even lower and I should have kept at it. I met my current husband during my first year in college, and then compromised just about everything else. I had thought of getting a PhD in psychology instead, but when he wouldn't move near the schools I could get into, I dropped it. I married him knowing he didn't want children, naively thinking that maybe that would change, because all married people end up having kids magically somehow, right? Obviously he didn't, so eventually I compromised that final dream also. I think by graduation, I already kind of knew I was on the road to ruin but hoped maybe things would turn around without me having to do anything. I wish I had realized that I was so young and still could have changed everything, but somehow at 21, I already felt old.

IF EGG AND SPERM HAD COME TOGETHER

The night I lost my virginity to the man who would become my first husband was probably the only time we had unprotected sex. If my math is correct, I was ripe for conception, my young eggs eager to hook up with his sperm. If I had conceived that night, almost two years before we got married . . .

We were near Los Angeles, visiting friends of his whom I barely knew. We had spent the day at Disneyland, where he kept bugging me to have sex. We were drunk. Our friends had gone to bed, and he invited me to join him on the floor in the two sleeping bags he had zipped together. One thing led to another . . .

He hustled me off to get birth control as soon as we got home from that trip. I remember I had told my mother, "We're not going to do anything down there that we wouldn't do here." Ha. What if I had come home pregnant? My parents would have lost their minds. It was 1972. Out-of-wedlock babies were still a scandal. My reputation would have been trashed forever—or not, if we got married quickly enough to make it look like it happened on the honeymoon. But there is no quick marriage for Catholics, not with the six-month prep.

However it worked out, I would have had a child.

We probably would have gotten married sooner. I don't think he would have left me. His parents wouldn't let him, and he did everything they said. As it was, we got married two weeks after I graduated from college. If I had had a baby, would I have graduated at all?

Would we still have lived in that two-bedroom apartment by the freeway? We would have had to use my "office" for the baby. Where would I have done my writing? The sound of the typewriter annoyed my husband. Maybe we would have lived elsewhere. Or moved in with his parents, God forbid.

We would have missed some fabulous trips. Or maybe not. Maybe I would have been out in the desert or the mountains with my baby bump. Maybe we'd still be making love on the tailgate of the Jeep or on a rock by a river. Maybe our child would be a backpack baby.

I have a feeling he would have started cheating sooner. Maybe he would have been drunk even more often. The marriage would have ended anyway. We were just not compatible. But I would have that child, and maybe I'd be a grandmother now.

It would have been hard to do my newspaper work, with all those late meetings and deadlines and all that running around doing interviews and taking pictures—not that I could get a newspaper job without a degree.

My parents weren't the kind who would step up and babysit. My in-laws were still working. My ex clearly wasn't up for childcare. He didn't even take care of our dog and cat.

But I would have this child. When I met Fred, I would be a single parent. My child, around 11 years old, would be older than his youngest, who turned 7 shortly after we met. Fred would have welcomed him or her. He liked older kids, just didn't want to deal with a baby. Maybe this child would have helped me through Fred's illness and my widowhood. I might have had a son-in-law or daughter-in-law, too. I could live near them and do holidays with "the kids" like my friends do.

Maybe I would write about kids and motherhood instead of dogs and dying husbands. Maybe I'd write children's books . . . .

At church Sunday, a young couple with a baby a few months old sat in the pew right beside the piano. I watched that baby the whole time. So cute. So magical with that perfectly clear skin, those tiny fingers, and those blue eyes observing everything. His parents clearly adored him. Mid-Mass, the mom nursed him under a blanket, and then he fell asleep. Oh, I melted. I started to think about how I never got to care for a baby like that. The pain started. I chased it away. Not here, not now. I had music to play. But . . . shit. You know.

I mourn the child I might have had, but at the same time, I know I was lucky. If I had had a baby with husband number one, I would have been tied to him and his family forever, even after I married Fred. That would have been complicated, to put it mildly. My career would have been trashed. I guess I should be grateful.

So that one time, I did not get pregnant. God knows, lots of people do get pregnant after one passionate night. In the movies, it happens all the time. One night together, and bam, the pregnancy test comes out positive. In the novel I finished reading recently, the couple didn't have sex very often, but every time they did, the woman conceived. For a lot of people, it's not that easy. Not even close.

Have there been times when you might have had an oops baby? What if you had? Does it kill you to remember what might have been?

Anon S: What if's.

There was the time the condom broke. I was newly divorced, enjoying some "freedom" and "fun." Behaving NOT like myself. Had we gotten pregnant then—it would have been incredibly awful and embarrassing in our highly religious families. We were just starting to see each other, and so soon after the divorce? No! That would not do.

I wasn't pregnant, and sometimes I do wonder. Would my husband have grown up a lot quicker and stopped his drinking? Maybe. But probably not. Likely our marriage would have imploded in other ways (rather than the way it actually did). And probably sooner. With a child in the mix, I don't think we'd have been able to fix anything. I think it would have gotten worse—way worse. I'd probably have become one of those women who end up staying married, raising the child with little help from him, finding pieces of happiness and hoping he died first so I could have a little shot at joy before I died.

So no baby for us. But a different drama. And a great deal of time to fix the broken parts of us. I'm very happy with my husband and my life now. Things happened the way they were supposed to happen.

Another time in our marriage, I really did think I was pregnant. At that time, we had been married a couple of years, and it would have been "okay" to have been pregnant. Sure, we still had our issues, but it seemed hopeful then. At that time I believe a baby could have helped our marriage. We had a cute little house, he was doing a good job at staying sober. I think at that point he would have thrown himself into fatherhood, and it would have been "okay."

Lately I've been daydreaming about adoption. Adopting a kid (not a baby). One whom we could rescue and change his or her life. I know without a doubt that my husband would shine and we'd work well together. We've put a lot of garbage behind us, and we'd appreciate a child. I know I'd be doing the heavy lifting and he'd be the "fun one," but I wouldn't care. If we adopted an older child, we (I assume) could continue on with the careers we've built. We wouldn't be building a life. We've already done that. We would simply be sharing our life with a child and making a difference.

I'm on the threshold of a handful of exciting things right now. I'm a bundle of nerves, but it's exciting good stuff. Fingers crossed that it will all work out. Just give it time. Life is good in a way I never dreamed possible. Even without a child, that counts for something. It's been more than "okay," and I'll take it.

Drans: What if . . . my high school sweetheart had not passed away at 31? We broke up six months before but probably would have gotten back together and had that baby and marriage. We purposely did not want to be the young Latino couple having babies all over the place. The day he died was the worst my heart could have ever broken. I'm 36 now, still hurting, but I have found someone. He is not Latino and doesn't care for babies or marriage. This breaks my heart again.

My grandma passed in hospice, and nearing the end, she told me not to be like some of my aunts and to make sure I have babies. My only sibling had cancer, and although she is healthy again, there is only a small chance that fertility was unaffected.

All of these things, plus feeling responsible for not giving my parents grandchildren (since they are sweet and cuddly), and being a Latina with these cultural standards to live up to is putting a lot of pressure on my mind and heart.

I'm still young enough to have them but not willing to give up this great guy I found. He is not perfect but is willing to work on himself for me. He is not as loving as I am. He is more rigid and less emotional than some other men. He is still a good man from a good family and with minimal vices. I have made him mine and don't want to give him up. We were going to break up tonight because we saw a different future. We decided to stay. Part of this decision means me giving up the idea of kids and marriage.

It seems silly to give him up for a little shit that does not even exist yet. And for what? To find a man who wants kids and marriage but is a cheater or addict?

I'm hurting during this transition. It breaks my heart to make this choice. It hurts to cut the bloodline here for my family. It hurts to tell my grandma that I didn't do as she asked. It hurts to tell God that I reject the gift he gave me as a woman. It hurts to want it because I know I would be good at it but chose not to.

This is a hard transition for me, and my heart will be broken for a little while. I will talk to my aunt about how she dealt with it. In all honesty, she is doing very well, even retired early because she could. My mind tells me it's okay; I can take my career to the next level. Just that my feeliest of feels doesn't like it. I'm in the middle of my *what if*. What if I don't have a baby? Then I can travel. Then I can have a great career. Then I can really take care of my parents as they get older. Then I can be a good role model for someone who doesn't have a mom. Then I can make sure my pup is happy in her old age. What if I don't have a baby and I am still happy with my choice? What if?

Thank you for the blog, I needed to put this out there.

Anon S: Drans, my heart is with you. You've been through a lot. However, I wonder if you are settling too soon. If you truly want a family someday, you owe it to yourself to step back from the relationship and consider that another man could better suit you. You seem like a really caring person. You deserve someone who is equally as caring.

Daniel: Hey Drans, I am a father, and I love it. I have had many friends over the years express the desire not to have children, ever. They all have one thing in common. Each of them is extremely selfish and self-absorbed. Now, I love these friends, don't get me wrong, but I am glad I don't spend every day with them. It would be a waste of my time.

That said, if you are in a relationship with a guy that will only stay with you if you agree not to have children, you are just playing into his extreme selfishness. What will happen if you do something else that cramps his style? If you think that his selfishness will not affect your relationship in the future, you are out of your mind. Get rid of him before he takes the best years of your life and later discards you.

God has someone better for you. Don't let yourself be robbed just so someone else can be selfish.

CROCHETED BABY SNEAKERS SET ME OFF

I was looking through Facebook the other day when I saw pictures of little crocheted sneakers for babies. Friends showered the post with likes and loves, as if they had never seen such things before. But I had.

The pictures took me back to the 70s when I was a newlywed crocheting baby booties shaped like sneakers. I had all kinds of fun patterns for baby shoes, and also for stuffed animals. I had graduated from college with a degree in journalism two weeks before we got married, but then I couldn't get a newspaper job. We were in the middle of a recession, and nobody was hiring. My husband was still in school.

I wound up working part-time stocking shelves in the housewares department at JC Penney. That left a lot of spare time. I spent it watching TV, starting with the early afternoon soap operas, continuing into the talk shows, and then into Star Trek (the original one). Every day. It wasn't much different from my mother's life. Between lunch and dinner, she did needlework and watched TV, too. In my mind, that's what moms did, and I was going to be a mom. Of course. Love, marriage, baby carriage.

I made a ton of baby booties, along with little squirrels and bears, rattles, and tiny hats, which I stashed away for the babies I was sure were coming. No one had ever told me otherwise.

My TV-and-crochet afternoons ended when the people who had loaned us their television took it back. We couldn't buy our own. We were really poor, so poor Chevron took our one credit card away for non-payment and some days we lived on zucchini and Christmas cheese boxes. Eventually I got a newspaper job. It didn't pay much, but it got me off the couch.

Decades later, I still have some of those crocheted booties and stuffed animals in the closet. They're too cute to throw away. For a while, I thought I'd sell them at boutiques, but I didn't have enough, and since I wasn't having any babies, I didn't feel like making any more.

Silly little things like crocheted baby sneakers can bring all the feelings back. How many of you have made or collected things for future babies? Did you have any doubt at the time that you'd be using them? What do you do with them now?

I never envisioned that I'd be collecting my senior discount at the grocery store as I buy my dog food and dinners for one, nothing for a husband or for kids who might drop in, but that's where I was yesterday, and those baby sneakers are still in the closet.

I had no idea I wouldn't live a version of my mother's life, that the marriage wouldn't last or that my ex would not want to have children. If I'd known, would I have married him? I hope not. I never thought to ask him, "Hey do you want to have kids?" Or even, "How many kids do you want to have?" Sure, he hustled me into the student health center for birth control pills, but that would end once we got married, wouldn't it? We'd have lovely brown-eyed, brown-haired babies.

I hope most young women are not as dumb as I was. My advice now to anyone getting serious about a relationship is to ask the questions: *Do you want to have kids? How many? How soon? Is there any reason why you might not be able to?* You also need to ask about birth control—what is he/she using?—and STDs, maybe not in the same conversation. Ask in a joking way if you need to, but find out. How do you bring it up without risking your relationship? I'm not sure. Choose your moment, but you have to take that chance. If they run away, maybe that will save you a lot of grief.

Most readers here have already gotten into situations where they're being prevented from having children. Now they need to know whether they should leave or stay. They're forced to choose between their partner and the children they might, maybe, possibly have with someone else. It's so hard. If only we had asked sooner.

If only we hadn't crocheted all those little red squirrels, brown bears, and itty-bitty sneakers.

Phoenix: Oh yes, I saved a lot of things because I wanted to show them to my children. And as a former elementary school teacher, I bought a lot of kids' books, assuming my children would read them one day. I've given away most of the "stuff," but I still have all of the kids' books.

But the onesies. I still have about five onesies that I bought before I knew I was infertile. I haven't wanted to give them away. I may make them into a quilt one day or I may just keep them forever. Whatever I choose to do will be okay.

I really love your crocheted critters.

singlechildlessover40: And sometimes you do all the right things, ask all the right questions at precisely the right time (with every new relationship), holding your breath that the answers line up . . . and the relationships still don't work out. Or they lied and you find out in the worst possible way. Or the answers don't line up and you give up the chance to have children for the chance to be in a relationship (and not be alone), and he still leaves. Then you find yourself never married, no children, with 20 years spent trying to get someone to love you feeling like a massive waste of time. A walking cautionary tale for every woman younger than you—and everyone seems to pick up on that.

I never dared to gather and collect baby supplies as I thought it might jinx me, or that I didn't deserve it, or that it might scare off fate and I'd come across as desperate. I wanted it so badly, and I feared that indulging myself would guarantee that it wouldn't happen. Well, I didn't indulge myself, and it still didn't happen.

Amanda: It's similar to the hope chest in the past when it was hope you would get married. In some cases, they may have made quilts and such in anticipation. I could imagine the disappointment if you were say, pushing 30 with no hope. It's a shame that so many things likely never got used after the women spent so much time making them.

I did crochet/knit baby things when my husband and I first married and kept saying I was going to give them away whenever someone had a child. But looking back, it seemed like lying to myself when I knew the real reason for making them was hoping for a baby myself, which never happened. I stopped making baby things. As with the hope chest, it's a toss of the dice either way, though I'd never buy baby things these days in anticipation.

SFL: Thanks for sharing this. I had a hope chest, too. Luckily I did get married. Now it's more of a memory chest. There's nothing wrong with planning for our dreams, even if they don't come true.

16

OLD AGE WITHOUT CHILDREN

I JUST FINISHED READING A BOOK called *Widow to Widow*[119] by the late Genevieve Davis Ginsburg, M.S.,[120] who traded in her therapy practice to lead Widow to Widow, a Tucson support group for widows. Overall, it's an easy read, often comforting and informative, but this book was published in 1995, and times have changed. As a widow in the 21st century, my situation is different.

Ginsburg portrays most of us new widows as helpless housewives. So not true. She also assumes that we have children. She goes on and on about dealing with the kids' attempts to help "Mom," effectively communicating your needs, and easing each other through your shared grief.

She does note in one brief passage that not everyone has children. She writes, "Too often women are made to feel that widowhood would be less painful had they had children. One of the first questions widows ask each other on first meeting is, 'Do you have children?' Then 'How many?' and 'Where do they live?'—as though their blessings can be counted by those answers." In the next paragraph, she tells how parents often go on to complain about the things their children do or don't do. And finally, she says, children can be an important link in a widow's transition to singleness but not the only one. Ultimately she has to find her own way.

If we have stepchildren, as I do, there's no guarantee they'll be around. So far, now that the services are over, they're not. Would adult biological children of my own be calling every day to check on me, or would they be buried in their own grief and the demands of their own lives? I'll never know.

If Fred and I had kids together, they might still be teenagers living at home. That would change the picture completely because I'd have to behave like a mom at a time when I might not feel like it. So many unknowns. Does it matter? What is, is. I share my house with my dog Annie, and neither one of us is helpless. We're sad sometimes but perfectly capable of figuring out the rest of our lives without a husband and without children.

Side note to young women considering marrying men who don't want children, especially if they are significantly older than you are: Think about what it might be like years from now if he dies and you find yourself back where you started, only older. Is he worth it? Can you live with it? Something to consider.

Lynn: Firstly, I am sorry for the loss of your beloved. Secondly, I thank you so much for writing on this topic as I am finding it to be a very difficult road, a road that I'm not sure I can handle. My fiancé is 13 years older, with three adult kids (29, 25, 23) from two different wives. I am 37 and childless, was promised a child with him, but that has been revoked. I am so absolutely torn and feel the torture of possibly making the wrong decision to stay . . . every day! I simply loved my partner completely and was willing to try to make it work with his kids so that I could see if I could be satisfied with that.

The "kids," namely the daughters, have skillfully been manipulating their guilt-ridden father to do their best to break us apart. I initially thought he was worth it, but every argument about his kids or NOT having kids has deteriorated our connection. I'm four years in, and it is not getting better. Instead, the resentment is building. Your candid posts moved me, as I didn't think that anyone could possibly understand this heart-wrenching dilemma. I do not love his kids and frankly don't think I ever could. I always wanted to have kids BECAUSE I had found the man I wanted to create them with. Now the clock is hammering, and I'm deathly afraid of what the future may hold if I choose to stay and try to fit into his family. I have the opportunity to share a remarkable life with my fiancé, but that also entails having to always be linked to his kids. My obvious apathy is hard to miss, but I am always respectful and wish them well . . . but FAR away from us. Thank you for sharing. It really makes me reconsider what I have taken on. I pray for your heart to be soothed and soul to be comforted during this difficult time and until you and Fred meet again.

Bmoreliketrese: I am in a similar situation, and it is comforting to hear words from someone feeling my confusion and pain. I am 24 years old, and my fiancé is 29. He has a 7-year-old daughter who lives with her mother, and I love her. From the moment we decided to take our relationship seriously, I knew that I wanted kids and he didn't. I guess we both thought the other person would come around. Surprise, I am five weeks pregnant, and he doesn't want the baby.

I know that I can't make him be a father, and I don't want to force him into the situation. I just don't know if I could go the rest of my life kidless. I want a baby but only in a healthy situation. I feel that I should leave. But I can't manage to do so because I love him and his daughter. I just needed to vent. So thank you for creating a place where I can.

SavvasKoulla: I am a 31-year-old widow. In my lifeless house, only me and my dog Annie (same as you). Nineteen months without him. Every tomorrow is worse than yesterday. If only I had a child, our child. Oh God, how much I miss him.

SFL: Dear SavvasKoulla, I'm so sorry. It hurts like crazy, but you will go on, and you're still young. Anything could happen.

WHO CAN YOU COUNT ON TO CARE FOR YOU?

Tomorrow would have been my mother's 85th birthday. Unfortunately, she never got to be that old. She died of cancer six days after her 75th birthday.

The year Mom died was a hellacious one. That year, we lost 13 people we loved, including my mother, my mother-in-law, and my ex-husband's mother. Everyone I had ever called "Mom" was gone.

People who don't worry about old age without children—because they have children—are always telling me that even if you have kids you can't count on them to be there when you're old and sick. I know that's true in some cases, perhaps many, but that's not how it works in my family.

When Fred's father's health started to fail, he and his mother moved from Las Vegas to Newport, Oregon to be close to us. Fred's mom didn't ask, "Would you like to take care of us?" She just decided they were moving to our town. Fred's dad, who appeared to be in the early stages of dementia and had been diagnosed with congestive heart failure, died suddenly of a massive stroke two months after they arrived. We drove Fred's mother to the hospital in Portland, stayed with her through it all and took care of her for the next four years until she died of lung cancer.

A few months later, my mother was diagnosed with colon cancer. In those months when she went through chemo and repeated hospitalizations, I spent so much time in San Jose I never unpacked my bags. When she died, Fred and I were there with my dad and my aunt. I was working and halfway through my master's degree, but when your mother is sick, you drop everything and take care of her. You don't say, "Well, I'm busy."

When I hear people say you can't count on your kids, I say, "Nonsense. You should be able to, and if you can't, something's wrong."

But that doesn't mean no one will help if you don't have children. For example:

Yesterday turned out to be an odd Fourth of July. My friends Carol and Jerry were coming up from California and stopping to see me on their way to Portland. We agreed to meet at the farmer's market in Waldport. When I got there, I saw an ambulance in the parking lot and wondered who it was there for. I had no idea until I got a message from Jerry on my cell phone that Carol was inside. She had complained of feeling strange and nearly collapsed when she got out of the car. So they called 911.

Well, I had plans for the rest of the day, meeting other friends to see a local parade and have lunch after, but as I waited for the paramedics to check Carol out, I realized I had only one choice now. I would accompany my friends to the hospital and stay with them as long as necessary. After all, this was my town, they had never been here before, and they were my friends.

Carol was suffering from low blood sugar. After treatment with glucose and food, she was soon her chatty self and able to laugh about reuniting under these crazy circumstances on Fourth of July. I missed the parade, but we had a good visit anyway, and I thank God my friend is all right.

Like me, Carol and Jerry are childless. Both wanted to have children, both were married before in situations where it didn't happen, and now that it's too late, they share life with three dogs, six cats, and Carol's elderly mother.

As we talked about my *Childless by Marriage book*, Carol admitted that she sees what she's doing for her mother and wonders who will do that for her if her husband isn't around anymore. Don't we all?

I pray that when the need arises for her and for me, someone will be there. I believe a friend, a sibling, a cousin, someone will step up, but don't tell me it doesn't make any difference whether or not you have children.

What do you think about this?

Anonymous: I've heard of people who have kids and even grandkids and can't count on them, but yes it's discouraging that I won't have any descendants once I reach old age. At least I will have nieces and nephews, though it's not the same thing. I'm hoping that I can also make a new long-term close friendship that will carry me into my old age . . . .

Anonymous: I have mixed feelings about this. Do people have kids because they want someone to care for them in their old age? Is this a reason to procreate? My grandmother stubbornly refused to live with any of her offspring when she could no longer care for herself. She did not want to be a burden to her children or to their families. We visited her in the nursing home, and of course took her home with us for visits, which must have had some impact on her well-being. My step-grandfather (other side of the family), was somewhat the same way. He had actually outlived his only biological child and all of his siblings, but he also had plenty of friends and other family who visited him in his last days. Anyway, I don't think this is why I miss having children. Maybe I will if I live that long, but for now, it isn't!

SFL: My mother-in-law also refused to move in with us or her other son. She had both her mother and her mother-in-law live with her in old age and swore she'd never do that to her own kids. But I'm sure she was glad we were nearby. In the end, I don't think anyone wants to depend on other people, children or not.

Laura: I, too, have worried about this. I'd hate to be an additional burden to my nieces and nephews. That said, the Japanese are making quite the headway in designing robots to take care of their aging population. (Seriously!)[121]

Anonymous: I've lost many hours of sleep thinking about this. Sometimes I talk to God and ask him to take me before I'm too old where I can't take care of myself.

Childless Chicken: I've been asking myself the same questions you bring up. I've never been married and it doesn't look like that's in the future for me, so I've started reading a lot of books on retiring single and researching communities for retirement that are single-friendly. I will need a community, and I want to be there for others, too. I've done my will, I have a dear friend who is a nurse also as my medical POA, and I'm putting every single penny I can into debt reduction, savings and retirement. I will need it! I hope I'm financially secure in my future. It worries me a lot. I have a brother, and he has kids. My nieces and nephews will be financially okay already. Our parents and my sister-in-law's parents will provide for them, so I've been researching what to do with any excess money that may remain. I'm going to see about setting up a college scholarship for single, childless older women. We all know that being single and childless does not always mean that there are extra resources for things.

SilverShil0h: I do think of this subject often, and have for over 10 years now. My steps can't even take care of themselves; how can they take care of me, and why would they take care of me? I have a nephew whom I don't get to see as often as I did in years past, so my relationship with him has really suffered over the years, although I'm excited for him to have a gorgeous, healthy, active family. I read an article awhile back that with one in five women (random statistic I pulled off a tweet last week) not having children in the U.S. (this trend has been steadily growing since the 80s), there is a surge in adults with no adult kids to care for them. Many are buying long-term care insurance now to prepare for the day you describe. The article described that some are moving to active senior living communities in Panama, which is far more "childless friendly" than the U.S.

My plan until something happens to change it is to find a few friends with no adult kids/grandkids and live together, support and encourage one another, keep an eye out, help each other as needed and so on to the point that when/ if the day arrives that I do need a nursing home/care facility it will be a short stay before I pass on. It sounds lovely and logical, and we all know that life is far from logical, even on a good day. No amount of planning can plan for every possible scenario. So I do the best I can, and because I have a strong faith, I trust God to take care of the rest. That is what faith is about, right? At any rate, losing sleep over this situation so far into the future won't help; in fact, it will hurt me. One day at a time.

Here's an article that crossed my path on this very subject. I guess co-housing is my first choice. http://www.nextavenue.org/childfree-older-americans-tak-ing-the-future-into-your-own-hands[122]

CHILDLESS OR NOT, YOU'RE ON YOUR OWN

Lately I've been living a double life. On March 25, my 95-year-old father broke his upper leg, the same leg with the artificial hip from when he broke it in 2014. He wasn't doing anything special, just washing dishes, when the bone gave way and he fell on the floor, banging his head so hard on the wall he left a layer of hair behind. He was alone, just like he was with the hip. Luckily, he had his cell phone in his pocket.

Since then, I have been traveling back and forth between Oregon and California, trying to do as much as I can to help. I was there when Dad moved from the hospital to a skilled nursing facility, when he left there for a nursing home, and when he went back to his own house last week.

But I'm not there now. A paid caregiver ($27 an hour) is there for three hours in the morning and three hours around suppertime. Sometimes people visit. My brother Mike drives six hours every weekend to help him, but mostly Dad is alone. My father has two children in their 60s, two grandchildren in their 30s, and three great-grandchildren under the age of 4. Plus nine nieces and nephews. None of us are there. We live far away. We have jobs to do and lives to lead. And Dad wants it that way. Back then, when I suggested that maybe my dog and I should just move in, he said no.

Those of us without children worry about being alone in old age. I'm alone most of the time. It's scary. But the truth is that for most families, even when there are children, there's no guarantee they will be on call 24/7 to help. I do know people who devote their lives to caring for their elderly parents, but for most of us it's a juggling act. If you have children of your own, you need to take care of them, too. Even you don't have kids, you have other responsibilities.

You can't be everywhere at once. Last week when I was moving Dad back to his house, my brother was in the middle of a wildfire disaster at his home near Yosemite. With fire all around them, his family was ordered to evacuate. From Merced, they watched the news and prayed their home and their town would still be standing when they went back. They were among the lucky ones. Their house and their town survived, and they were allowed to return after nearly a week. But during that time, Mike was not about to run to San Jose to help Dad.

People are always telling me how having children does not assure that you won't wind up alone. It's true. Granted, my brother and I have done a lot for our father. We have paid his bills, mowed his lawn, and interacted with doctors, social workers, and nursing home staff. We arranged his transitions from one institution to another, and I sat with him at each of his appointments with the orthopedic surgeon. But we're not there now. If there's another crisis, we'll get there as soon as we can.

I have no children. What will I do when it's my turn? What will you do? So far, friends have helped me when I needed surgery or was stuck on crutches with a sprained ankle. I already have my legal paperwork in order in case someone else needs to make decisions for me. But I know I need to make more formal arrangements for the future. If I don't acquire a new husband or a housemate, I hope to move into some kind of group living situation so there will be people around to help. I don't want to live alone forever.

If I had children, would I want them to give up their lives to take care of me? No.

Ultimately we are all on our own. So let's figure it out. Who will you call if you get hurt? Who will handle your bills if you can't do it? Who will make phone calls and talk to the doctors? If you do end up having children, that's a bonus. They'll be glad you got yourself organized.

What do you think about aging without kids? Have you made any plans?

Mali: This is something we talk about a lot, as we are the ones left to care for my parents-in-law. We haven't made specific plans yet, as we're tossing up where we might live when we retire. We have no family in this city, but it is where we've had our life, and where our friends live. What we are aware of, though, is the need to make decisions, and to make them early! I often write about this too.

mrsp: I'm just trying to make sure I have a decent pension, so that I can pay for care.

I have just stopped working fulltime—I've cut my hours to four days a week, in an attempt to cope with working and caring for my husband. Of course, he's annoyed that I haven't stopped working completely, and thinks that I'm "greedy" for worrying about my pension.

I have no siblings, and there's zero chance I'd get any help from his kids if I needed it. I had to cope by myself when he had his bypass (open-heart) and, later, his stroke.

SFL: You need to take care of yourself. Don't let him make you feel guilty.

Samantha: I have two elderly grandmothers, and they both reside in nursing facilities. Their children are nearby but not equipped to handle their medical needs. It is such a common misconception that children will take care of you in old age. There are so many factors that could impede this from happening. I will be getting long-term-care insurance and continue to contribute to my IRAs. Not having to pay over 200K to raise a child does have advantages—more income.

Mia: This was my plan, too, until both my in-laws ended up partly disabled in their 80s, and living in an assisted living facility.

There is so much to do that isn't covered by the paid aides: We get my in-laws new clothes in stripes because they love stripes, the correct shoes for their orthopedic needs, lotion in their favorite scents, and apply it to their dry skin, etc.

Who will do any of this for us? I worry about this *daily*. The in-laws are three decades older than us, so it's ridiculous to worry about it now, but it's the one part of our childless status that I cannot emotionally resolve and let go. I would appreciate any suggestions anyone has.

Anonymous: This is the hardest part for me of being childless. I'm terrified that my husband will die and leave me alone without family, as I was before I met and married him. Coming from an abusive family, I don't have family of my own. I have a sister out there, but she quite literally beat me up last time I saw her (as did my father. Who needs that? Better to be alone). My husband has family, but—no surprise, given that we both come from abusive families, one of our bonding areas—we are currently estranged from his sister, and she would disappear out of my life if he died. Having no family has been the biggest burden of my life. I have spent so many Christmases alone. You might think that friends or whoever could step in, and that is true at Thanksgiving, but Christmas is a time people spend with their families. It has felt terrible to me, and I dread the possibility. It feels like a sick joke from the universe that in addition to not having contact with my birth family, now I can't create my own family with my husband.

Mary: It's nice to know I'm not alone in being terrified of being alone. I know some older ladies who are actually alone; their husbands passed and they don't have children. There is a gaggle of older ladies at church who care for them (and each other) like sisters. Maybe we can't have the life we want, but we can work towards the life we need, maybe by contributing to a church community, maybe by creating a blog. I'm glad your Dad is still alive, still puttering around his house by himself in his 90s. That's amazing! You do have a long, healthy life to look forward to, Sue, if his genes are any indication.

YOU CAN COUNT ON YOUR FRIENDS

I'm writing this in a dentist's waiting room while my friend Pat has dental surgery. The nurse has gone over a daunting list of post-op instructions. Medications, meals, bleeding, pain. She'll be loopy for a while, so I can't let her drive or make important decisions. I have her purse and her medications here next to me. Shades of taking care of my dad and my husband through their various medical procedures.

Before I left home this morning, Pat sent me a text: Emergency: bring TP. So I did. That's what friends are for.

You might think Pat is childless and alone like me, but no. She has a wonderful husband who happens to be recovering from back surgery at a rehab facility right now. She has two grown children and a stepson, plus seven grandchildren who all love her very much, but none of them live nearby. When it comes to this sort of situation, I'm her person, and she is mine. She has seen me through colonoscopies, endoscopies and two cataract surgeries and will be there for whatever comes next. And frankly, I'd rather have Pat around than most of my family.

For those readers who are worrying about who will take care of you in your old age, the answer is: friends. If you wind up without spouse or children, if you don't happen to live with or near other family members, you will look to your friends. The people you see most often will take care of you, and you will take care of them. They won't mind you asking for help. They'll be miffed if you DON'T ask.

I'm terrible at asking for help. I was raised to take care of things by myself, but there are some things you just can't do alone—like driving home after surgery. If you have a good friend, she will be there. And it will have nothing to do with having children because they'll be off living their lives and expecting their parents to live theirs.

If you don't have any friends, you need to work on that. Strike up a conversation, ask someone to lunch, go for a walk together, friend them on Facebook. If I can do it, so can you.

I'm not saintly, for anyone thinking that. I am so grateful it's not my mouth they're working on right now. I'm feeling a little righteous about my healthy teeth. I hate the way this place smells of chemicals and disinfectant and the way the women at the desk keep whispering to each other. I am not fond of the sound of the drill and the suction hose. I'll be glad to get out of here. But this is what you do. You help your friends.

Bottom line: Don't worry. If you never have children, you won't be alone.

Mitch: Yes! Thanks, Sue. So much in common with you. I'm making a list of all the reasons I didn't have/didn't want/refused to have children; so far I'm up to 481 and still gathering. It's endless. I'm 2,127 miles away from my BIG family so my friends are my family in most circumstances, especially healthcare. I'm in a lifestyle where my family has become my friends, and my friends are my family (hmmm . . . note to self; must work that concept into a song). Must also get and read your book. Thanks again.

Kathryn: I would love to see that list of reasons!!

Candy: You are right! Friends are a blessing!!!! I needed one badly this past Saturday, and she was there for me, willing to drop everything to help me. Rick and I were in a car accident, and our truck was totaled. By the grace of God (literally), we had only minor injuries. My friend was there for us every step of the way. Now if we had only Rick's son to rely on . . . we couldn't have. He is too busy taking drugs to think of anyone but himself. So in the real world, children aren't always the answer.

17

WHAT WILL BE OUR LEGACY?

I HAD BUCK TEETH. My top front teeth stuck out, and I may have been called Bucky Beaver a few times. My parents, kind souls that they were, took me to an orthodontist and got the teeth moved into a more pleasing configuration. The doc straightened out the jumbled bottom teeth, too. When I was 19, they paid for oral surgery to fix a problem with my lower lip.

None of this was fun. Methods were more primitive back in the 1960s. I had wires attached to metal bands around each tooth, tightened every few weeks. I wore a headgear at night, rubber bands that squeaked when I opened my mouth, and a retainer which kept the embarrassment going after the bands were removed. My teeth ache just thinking about it. My braces were expensive. Mom spent countless afternoons driving me to the orthodontist, and I went through a lot of pain, but it was worth it. Over the years, people have often complimented me on my smile. I know how lucky I am. Not every family can afford any kind of dental care.

Lately, my lower teeth have started jumbling up again. I think I'm stuck with it. Braces are pretty low on my priority list now. Mom isn't around to take care of it.

But here's the thing. I was not the first one in my family to wear braces. It's very likely that if I had children, they would have inherited my crooked teeth. My mother wore braces. In old photos, it looks like my paternal grandmother, who died before I got a chance to know her, had buck teeth, too. She also wore glasses and was probably nearsighted like me. My other grandmother gave me the Roman nose with the bump shared by most of her siblings.

Heredity. Whether it's crooked teeth, a bumpy nose, mental illness or a fatal disease, people pass their traits down through the generations. Of course, some genetic traits are wonderful things. I got my brown eyes and lively mind from my mom, too. I have to credit both parents for my good health. I'm proud to carry on the Avina and Fagalde family lines.

But I'm not carrying them very far. As the end of my branch of the family tree, I won't pass on either the brown eyes or the buck teeth. My cousins with their many children and my brother with his one biological child are passing on their share, but no one will inherit my exact combination of traits.

Our guest speaker at our writer's group Sunday shared a piece she wrote about being adopted. She will never know how she came to be the way she is. That seems like such a loss. She and her husband have cats, no kids. Will she wind up being just a "one-off," no one behind, no one ahead?

Depending on how you look at it, having no one to inherit our genetic traits is either very sad or a relief. My brother's teeth came out straight. His daughter's teeth are good. With luck, the buck teeth stop with me.

Do you think about what you are not passing on if you don't have children?

Candy: My first niece was born blind in one eye. It is a nerve issue, and nothing will fix it, so she will forever be blind in one eye. My second niece was born with Torticollis[123] and spent the first two years of her life in physical therapy trying to reshape her skull. When she finally was discharged, her head was close to being a normal shape; however her one ear was substantially lower than the other and they both stuck out like an elf. She never wore a ponytail as a little girl, as other kids would question or make fun of her. She ended up having surgery to correct the ears. Her parents' insurance would not pay a penny of the surgery because they viewed it as cosmetic, so they went into debt. My third niece was diagnosed with Type 1 diabetes at age 6, and that family's lives have never been the same. So for me to think if I did have a child that it would turn out perfect and healthy is a pretty big stretch, and that's not including all the drunks and drug addicts on both sides of our family. As much as I regret never having children, I can't help but think that it's true when people say, "God won't give you more than you can handle."

aplentifullife: It's interesting because I often think that my path to not having children may have been a blessing in disguise. A few years after it became clear that my husband and I were not going to have a child together, I learned that I have a condition called Cavernous Angiomas. In short, it is a condition in my brain where I can have bleeding on the brain or even worse, a stroke. It is a rare disorder, and I am still not sure whether it is genetic or not. I have heard two important things. One is that it could cause a problem for me during delivery of a child. The second and even more important is that it could be passed down genetically. I would have felt beyond horrible if I had passed this condition down to our child. I have three angiomas and have thankfully been lucky, having only mild symptoms, but it does not mean that our never-to-have-been-born child could have been as lucky. So many people believe that when they have children, they will be born perfect and healthy. Most are, but there are many that are not.

Jenny: Yes, I think this. It helps me rationalize childlessness, to some extent. My mum is bipolar. It was first triggered when she was post-natal after having me. Physically, mentally and emotionally, I am more like my dad, but I do wonder if it could have been triggered in me if I'd had a child. Or if a child of mine might have had it.

I can also relate to what your speaker who was adopted said. My parents and cousins are my closest blood relatives. We live 100 miles from them, seeing them every two months or so. I spend most of my life surrounded by my husband's family, who all look similar to one another. I am often in a room with their wider family and find myself thinking I am the only person in this room with no blood tie to anybody else. I feel like an oddity amongst them.

CHILDLESS COUPLE GIVE IT ALL TO CHARITY

"Childless adults make huge impact with charitable donations"[124] is the title of a recent article in *The Toronto Star*. Writer Marsha Barber talks about how a childless couple, Margaret and Charles Juravinski, are creating an endowment fund of $100 million to support health research.

One of Barber's friends, also childless, willed her house and land to the Indigenous community in her area.

Barber goes on to discuss how childless people give far more to charity than those without children. Parents are focused on providing for their families, both during their lives and after they die.

My first reaction to this was, ha, childless or not, I don't have a fortune to donate to anyone. But wait. I give regularly to my church, the Alzheimer's Association, and agencies that feed the poor. I have enough to spare a bit every month. Maybe if I had children, I'd be using every penny of my income for them. Whatever I could save might go for their education. Isn't that what parents do?

Most of us leave a lot more than money. I am the keeper of the family heirlooms. I have my maternal grandmother's silver tea set, handwritten recipes from her notebooks, and her diamond engagement ring, my step-grandmother's poetry, both grandmothers' china cups and saucers, and craft supplies and clothing from my mother and my mother-in-law. In fact, I'm wearing my mom's blue knit shirt right now.

Many mornings I sit in Grandma Avina's wooden rocker softened with the pillows I crocheted for it and rock as I write in my journal. I wonder what will happen to the many volumes of my journal after I die. Should I burn them to hide my secrets? Or should I keep them for future biographers, in case I became famous?

Seriously, who will sort and disperse my stuff? Who will care? Will it all end up in a dumpster? I need to do whatever I can now to make sure that doesn't happen.

In my will, I leave most of my "estate" to my stepchildren and my niece and nephew. I also specify that my instruments and music supplies go to needy music students and my books to the local libraries. I have left instructions for what to do about the published and unpublished work I have written.

If I had a fortune, I'd love to give it to a charity that can really help people in need. I won't have children who are counting on an inheritance.

I talk about this in my *Childless by Marriage* book, noting some of the crazy things childless people do with their money. For example, playwright George Bernard Shaw is said to have bequeathed millions to anyone who could devise a new alphabet that made more sense than the one we have. It should have 40 letters, he specified. Luis da Camara, a Portuguese man with no family, picked strangers out of the Lisbon phone book to receive his wealth. Ruth Lilly, a poet, left $100 million to a poetry magazine that had repeatedly rejected her work. She also gave millions to various charities.

Without children, *if* we are lucky enough to make some money and keep it—no natural disasters, health crises, or investments gone awry—we can do whatever we want with it, including giving it away.

Or we could not worry about making any money because we don't have any children to support. Investments? What for? Life insurance? Why?

How about you? Does not having children enable you to give freely to charity now or when you die? What do you say when people state that childless people are selfish? If you could give money to anyone, who would it be?

Mali: I love love love this post! Especially the ideas to leave books to libraries and instruments/music to needy music students. I'm going to look into those for my own will. Some years ago, my husband and I updated our wills. We chatted about it with friends who are also childless, noting that it gets complicated. They were astounded, because they'd never thought of leaving their worldly goods to anyone but family. But we want to make some sort of mark, and so have stipulated a large proportion goes to medical research. Unfortunately, we don't have $100 million to really make an impact!

Don't get me started on what I say when people say childish people are selfish! I've ranted about it several times on my blog. [125] It infuriates me.

BENEFICIARIES? NO EASY ANSWER

I'm filling out forms to receive payments from one of my late father's investments. The man had money in many pockets. I wish he had spent some of it on himself and my mother. It's too late now, and I know I am blessed to have it. The monthly payments will make up for the job I no longer have (insane boss, had to move on). BUT the forms want to know who my beneficiaries are in case I die before the money runs out. What to put in these blanks is obvious for people who have spouses and children. It was easy for my father, but I'm stumped. Can I leave it to my dog?

These are the sorts of things in life that frazzle the childless widow. That and questions like "Why are you saving all this stuff?" and "How many grandchildren do *you* have?"

It's the same thing when I have to fill out medical forms listing who to call in case of an emergency. My brother lives too far away to be any immediate help. I list friends who I hope are in town and in good health when I get in trouble. So far, that has worked out.

How I wish I had children whose names and contact information I would know as well as my own to plug into those blank spaces on the forms.

I'm reading a novel that takes place in a Native American community where all of the older women are "aunties," no matter whether they gave birth or not. I think that is my role, too, at this point. I am going to list my niece and nephew as my beneficiaries. After all, they are my father's grandchildren as well as my closest younger relatives.

How about you? Are there situations in which your lack of children sends you into a brick wall that parents sail right over?

Lynne: Sue, I struggle with some of those same questions as a fellow childless widow. Even to know who my executor should be when I die. Now, those roles are filled with friends who are my age or older. I know I will someday need to replace them with a younger generation. But it won't be MY younger generation. I have designated charities to get a portion of my estate so that might actually be an option for you. And who can forget Leona Helmsley leaving millions to her dog!?

Anonymous: I care about what happens to my stuff and the stuff I will inherit from my parents. I want someone to find it meaningful just as I find it meaningful. I want someone to treasure these things because they have a long history. I realize that without having the daughter I thought I would, I don't have an automatic chain of inheritance but there weren't any guarantees of that anyway. Perhaps there will be a niece or a nephew. Or some non-related young person will come into my life and become the link. I do think about it so thank you for writing about this issue.

mdoe37: I recently went away for a couple of weeks and hired a cat sitter as my 83-year-old mom can't manage it anymore. She was very thorough, asking questions. Which vet, how sick, what if it's bad? Then she asked . . . if something happened to me, who would take the cats?

Good grief. Now I need to name a guardian for the cats.

I think I'm heading in the direction of a trust. I'll start an endowment or do a charitable donation. There are professional executors. It doesn't matter at that point, I guess. I know at some point I will need to figure out who will collect and bury me. There are no close family members at all.

SFL: I had to name a guardian for my dog when I hired a new pet sitter. I volunteered my neighbors, then checked later to make sure it was okay. It was fine. They love Annie. Of course, if we had grown children, they might not want our pets, so we'd still need someone else.

Anon S: I just spoke to a person yesterday who told me that their elderly neighbors were like second grandparents to their children. They mourned when the older couple passed. When the property sold, my friend looked on in horror as the children of their former neighbors came to "clean house." Most of the deceased's belongings ended up in a dumpster parked next to the home. Even family photos! My friend and her children went "dumpster diving" and rescued a few treasured mementos that they couldn't bear to see trashed. Later they did pass on the family photos to people who cared. Here is proof that having children doesn't mean anything in terms of legacy and even material possessions.

This is why I intend to constantly be making friends and authentic connections. I want to be missed. I want the things I own to be loved and valued. It makes me sick to think that something as silly as my beautiful prom dress could end up in a dumpster instead of bringing joy to someone, somewhere.

SilverShil0h: Sue, my husband had a hard time with me naming friends as beneficiaries in my will, but he called an older and wiser friend who explained to him this is perfectly normal in my situation. I've named friends, friends' kids, cousins' kids and non-profit organizations in my will. As far as the pets go, I listed which friend's kid gets each. It took a long time to sort it out, and I'll probably change it along the journey every now and then. I empathize completely—this is an awkward and poignant reminder of my childlessness (as if I needed one).

Jenny: Can I add a thought? I am childless, but have a husband. I am also lucky enough to have a reasonable amount of money I inherited from an elderly uncle.

I am an only child, so no nieces and nephews, but there are some on my husband's side. We live in the same community as them, but rarely ever see them (Christmas and their birthday, when they call in briefly to collect their presents).

Hubby says we should leave any money we have and our house to them. I think, why should we? We have no relationship with them. We have argued about this in the past, and consequently, have not made a will.

So, you widows, it's not all rosy having a husband. They can be a bloomin' nuisance!

18

CHILDLESSNESS DIDN'T STOP THEM

HAVE YOU EVER HEARD OF MAY SARTON? Sarton, who lived from 1912 to 1995, was a poet, novelist and memoirist in an era when most women stayed home and had babies. She published more than 50 books. Her book *Journal of a Solitude*,[126] published in 1973, describes a year she lived alone in a small town in New Hampshire. Although she battled loneliness and depression, she was convinced that solitude was essential to her career as a writer. She did not see how she could have succeeded if she were married and had children. The demands of motherhood did not allow the necessary time, energy or focus. Although many friends visited, and she often went out for public appearances or to spend time with a mystery lover she called X, she was always anxious to be alone again.

A wonderful list of Sarton quotes at Goodreads.com[127] includes this one: "It is harder for women, perhaps, to be 'one-pointed,' much harder for them to clear space around whatever it is they want to do beyond household chores and family life. Their lives are fragmented . . . the cry not so much for 'a room of one's own' as time of one's own."

I found myself having a lot in common with Sarton, except that I still believe it is possible to write and raise children. The early years might be difficult, but once the kids start school, you have guaranteed hours when someone else is taking care of them. It worked for me those years when Fred's youngest son lived with us. He was just turning 12 when he moved in, and he was a self-sufficient kind of boy, so I was able to write all day. I could have become more involved in Michael's life, volunteering at school, baking cookies, or whatever, but my work was always a high priority. I often think God planned for me to be childless, so I could be a writer. Too often, I burn dinner while I'm engrossed in my work. How would I care for a baby?

Of course, many moms these days need a job outside the home. That makes it hard to do anything else. Sarton was wealthy. She had a maid, gardeners and a handyman taking care of things around the house while she spent hours perfecting a line of poetry.

Then there's Elizabeth Gilbert,[128] famous for *Eat Pray Love*[129] and several other books. Readers of her work know she chose to be childless. In an interview, she said she struggled with her decision. Motherhood seemed to be the natural path, but it didn't feel right for her. She finally decided, "Okay, this is my path. I'll take it with its risks and with its liberation because it's mine." Her decision, which left her free to travel, write and explore, feels more right every year, she said.

Women have more choices these days in lifestyles, careers, and reproductive decisions. Perhaps if they switched eras, Sarton and Gilbert would have made different choices.

A CHILDLESS LIFE WELL-LIVED

One of the women I interviewed for my *Childless by Marriage* book passed away last week. Jill Baker had been suffering from heart problems for years. She was married once in her youth, divorced, and never remarried. She never had children. But none of that defines who Jill was. Full of life, even when her body was failing, a large presence even though she was a small woman, Jill stood out wherever she went. She was funny, opinionated, and loaded with talent.

I first met Jill in the Central Coast Chorale, a singing group that I joined shortly after I moved to Oregon. Jill was the one always raising her hand with suggestions or laughing loudly from the alto section. We were both chosen to sing in a smaller ensemble called Octet Plus. You could count on Jill to hold down the low notes while the rest of us warbled up above. She was also a talented flute player. After I moved on to other musical endeavors, Jill rose to assistant director of the chorale.

Jill taught music—piano, flute, voice, and more. She sang in small groups and professional choruses. She had also worked in bookkeeping, accounting and computer software because it's hard to make a living with a music degree, but she was finally able to focus on music after she moved to the Oregon coast.

Back in the 1960s, she was engaged to be married when she discovered she was pregnant. Her fiancé took off as soon as she told him. She had an abortion in a motel room.

"She was some kind of a nurse and did illegal abortions, and it was awful," Jill said. "I hemorrhaged for six months, during my final six months of college."

Once the baby wasn't an issue, her fiancé came back, and they got married. He refused to even discuss having children. Eventually the marriage ended. She said she never found another man she felt strongly enough about to marry.

Before our interview, Jill had never told anyone about the abortion, but she had reached a point where she was willing to share her story and happy to have me use her real name.

Jill never knew for sure whether that abortion affected her ability to have children. Suffering from fibroid tumors, she had a hysterectomy in her 40s. "I guess it wasn't meant to be," she said.

When I asked how she felt about never having children, she said, "I felt lucky in that I didn't have that massive craving to have a child. I would have liked to have kids, but only if I was in a marriage where the husband could be a father. I never wanted to have kids just to have kids."

Instead of having her own children, she dove into the role of aunt to her siblings' children and dog mom to her precious canine companions. Jill was the one holding her sheet music with one hand and petting her dog with the other in the chapter of my book about dog moms. Asked if she felt left out when her friends talked about their children, she laughed. "No. I get 'em back; I talk about my dog. I get irritated when people feel sorry for me. I really detest that because I think I've had a good life. I don't believe you have to have a husband or kids to be happy."

As for old age, she was determined to live on her own as long as she could, moving into a retirement home if necessary. She never had to. As she left this life, her hospital room was full of friends who loved her like family.

Rest in peace, Jill.

THESE CHILDLESS SISTERS LIVED FULL LIVES

Virginia Silveira died last week. She was 101. Virginia was my great-aunt Edna's half-sister, one of those people who are not technically family, but they really are.

I'm sad about her loss, although I rarely saw her in recent years. When my dad gave me the news, I wished there was someone to whom I could send a sympathy card. But there's no one. She never married or had children. She outlived her sister and her friends.

Virginia was an odd duck. Tall and gawky, perpetually argumentative, she was not exactly warm and fuzzy. Everyone loved Edna, who, although married to my Uncle Tony Sousa, never had children either. Attractive, gregarious and cheerful, she was fun to be around. But Virginia, not so much.

Edna was my mother's favorite aunt and often served as a substitute mother, more upbeat and worldly than her own mother. My mother's death of cancer caused Edna great pain. I still remember how she held me and we cried together. "Oh, Susan," she sobbed. The memory still makes me cry.

But Virginia was her own person. She didn't let anyone get too close.

The two sisters lived on Monroe Street in San Jose, each in a large house that would sell for over a million dollars now in San Jose's overpriced market. After Edna's husband died of cancer, the sisters continued to live separately, each tending her own rose garden. They went to St. Martin's church together every Sunday, always sitting in the front row on the right. When I went to church with my father, he insisted on sitting in the back, but I would go up to say hello to the sisters, Virginia so tall, Edna's hair so white and fluffy. Both dressed to the nines, they would smile and clutch my hands in their frail old hands.

In an age when most women became housewives, Edna and Virginia worked, Edna in the office at Pratt-Lowe Cannery, Virginia as Accounting Officer at San Jose State University. I'd see her there sometimes when I was a student trying to work through the endless fees and paperwork of college life. She was always friendly at the college, much more herself than among the family, I think. Sometimes our families are the ones who know the least about who we really are.

In their retirement years, a long time considering Edna lived to 100 and Virginia to 101, the sisters traveled together, visiting 49 different countries by plane, train and boat. Virginia planned the trips, researching their destinations, learning a bit of the language. The sisters grew up with Portuguese-speaking parents, so they were good with the Latin languages and made several trips to the old country.

I interviewed them together for my book *Stories Grandma Never Told: Portuguese Women in California*.[130] We met in Edna's kitchen, me with my green steno pad and tape recorder. They were among the first people I interviewed, and they gave me a lot of wonderful information. Every time Edna got started on a subject, Virginia would interrupt. She was opinionated and quotable. There's a lot of her in my book. I think she was pleased with it. I hope she was.

Virginia did not want to be pigeonholed as Portuguese. "They'd have to tar and feather me before I'd speak the language outside the house," she said. Edna, on the other hand, had no problem bouncing between the two languages.

Edna moved from her home to a senior residence after she had a stroke. She had some difficulties but continued to thrive. For her 100th birthday, a crowd jammed Harry's Hofbrau's banquet room. Virginia's 100th was a much quieter affair.

Virginia had serious health problems in her later years, including breaking her neck in a fall and needing to be tube fed for about a year. But she was tough. She recovered. She always made it back to her house and her independent life.

I feel bad and a little frightened when I realize Virginia has no immediate family to celebrate her life. What if this happens to me? What if no one is left when I die?

Her wake is tonight, her funeral is scheduled for tomorrow at St. Martin's, followed by entombment at the Santa Clara Mission Cemetery where Edna is buried. I suspect Virginia figured all that out a long time ago, and so will I.

My last memory of Virginia is at a dinner at a younger aunt's house. The guests were my father, elderly cousin Francis, Virginia, and I. We ate split pea soup, I remember. Virginia was wearing a neck brace. She complained about all the foods she could not eat. She seemed to contradict or interrupt everything my father said. Her head shook. But her mind was sharp and her memories clear.

One might argue that Virginia failed at life by not having a husband and children. But no, Virginia lived Virginia's life. We all have to live our own lives, whether they follow the usual paths or not.

Virginia's obituary[131] offers a few surprises for me. I didn't know she had two degrees from SJSU or that her colleagues established a scholarship in her honor for undergraduates at the SJSU School of Business. I didn't know she was a cancer survivor. Instead of listing children and grandchildren, her obituary notes that she leaves many cousins and friends throughout the world. That's not a bad legacy.

I sent Virginia a Christmas card every year. She'd send one back, thanking me for thinking of her. I prayed for her every morning. This morning I got to where I usually insert her name and sighed. I changed my prayer. God, please take good care of Virginia now that she's with you. If she tries to tell you how to run heaven, be patient. She means well.

Virginia and Edna are taking the most exciting trip of all.

EVELYN R'S CHILDLESS STORY

Although Evelyn had always loved children and wanted to have her own so badly she hoped she would get pregnant on her honeymoon, somehow it didn't happen.

By the time she got married at age 24, she had a job she loved. Her husband, Leonard, had just gotten out of the military and was struggling to find himself. The time wasn't right and they didn't even discuss having children.

As the years went by, she still liked her job, her nice home and their unfettered lifestyle and wondered if she wanted to give it all up to be a mother. They had been married 10 years when she decided to stop using birth control and see what happened. Nothing happened. She never went to a doctor to find out why they didn't conceive, nor did she urge her husband to get himself checked. That way neither one of them could blame the other for their failure to have children, she said.

Once, in the days before people could buy home pregnancy tests, she thought she might be pregnant. At first she felt annoyed, she said. "Then I got kind of happy about it." She was shopping for maternity clothes when she felt a pain in her abdomen and discovered that her period had started. "So that was that."

Free from the burden of parenthood, they traveled, socialized, bought new cars regularly, and lived in expensive houses, enjoying the fruits of their earnings. Most of their friends were also childless. The only time she felt out of place, Evelyn said, was when they moved into a housing tract full of young couples just starting their families. They had nothing in common. "We couldn't even hold a conversation."

During her 42-year career with a Bay Area school district, Evelyn was surrounded by children. When she started as a principal's secretary in 1941, the year after she graduated from Heald Business College, she wasn't much older than the students she met. She soon became secretary to the district superintendent and spent the rest of her career in that position. She met co-workers and students who became lifelong companions. Friends half her age visited and watched over her. She planned to leave her possessions to them when she died.

When we talked, years ago, Evelyn was 77 years old. She said she was too busy to even have a dog or a cat. She went to water aerobics classes four times a week and loved to golf, bowl, shop and visit friends. "I have more real close girlfriends than anyone I know," she said. She also had several young gay friends she considered her best friends. She was going to a friend's house in the wine country for Thanksgiving and was planning a winter trip to Cabo San Lucas. "I'm having a hell of a time," she said.

What did she say when people asked if she had children? "I say, 'No, I don't. I don't have any children, and I'm an only child, but I've got a lot of friends.' If you say, 'Gee, I wish I had children,' you're dead."

At age 88, Evelyn was honored as the grand marshal of the city of Fremont's annual Fourth of July parade. Interviewed in the local paper, she talked about how she met former students every day, and they're all her "kids." She didn't say a word about the biological children she never had.

Those of us who mope about our childless state and worry about old age might follow Evelyn's example. Grieve if you need to, but don't let the lack of children ruin the rest of your life.

ACKNOWLEDGMENTS

Love or Children is a discussion, not a monologue. I said my piece in the original *Childless by Marriage* book. My posts would fall flat without the constant support and lively comments of the readers of the Childless by Marriage blog. These women and men have shared things with me that they have never told anyone else, and they don't hesitate to jump in with sympathy and advice for others in their situation. When I get it wrong, they let me know, and when I'm feeling down, they boost me up. When asked if I could use their comments in this book, they were quick to say yes.

I don't have a string of publishing industry professionals to credit for this book, although I am grateful to every editor who has published my work during my career, which began so long ago at the Milpitas Post, a weekly newspaper in California.

I'm grateful for the support of the wonderful community of Oregon writers. I'm thankful for my parents, Elaine and Ed Fagalde, both gone now, who never said a negative word about my not having children, although God knows they would have loved to have a few more grandchildren. They never understood this writing business, but they never stopped me from doing it either.

Finally, thanks to my dog Annie, the closest I'll ever come to having a baby.

ABOUT THE AUTHOR

SUE FAGALDE LICK is the author of the book *Childless by Marriage* and the related blog at https://www.childlessbymarriage.com. She also blogs at https://unleashedinoregon.com. After a long career in journalism, she earned her MFA in creative writing at Antioch University Los Angeles and launched a second career teaching and writing books. Her works include three books about Portuguese Americans, two novels, and two poetry chapbooks.

When not writing, Lick leads an alternate life as a musician. She sings and plays piano, guitar, and mandolin wherever anyone will let her.

Like her readers, she is childless by way of marrying men who couldn't/wouldn't have children with her.

A native of San Jose, California, she lives with her dog Annie in South Beach, Oregon.

Visit https://www.suelick.com for more information.

NOTES

1   "Lick, Sue Fagalde. "Will You Regret Not Having Children?" Childless by Marriage blog post, Nov. 11, 2015. https://childlessbymarriageblog.com/2015/11/11/will-you-regret-not-having-children.

2   Hax, Carolyn. "She's Having Second Thoughts on Going Childless." *Providence Journal*, July 20, 2015. https://www.providencejournal.com/article/20150720/ENTERTAINMENTLIFE/150729977

3   Vasectomy reversal success rates. http://www.vasectomy.com/vasectomy-reversal/faq/vasectomy-reversal-success-rates-will-it-work

4   "How Can You Reverse a Vasectomy?" http://www.webmd.com/infertility-and-reproduction/vasectomy-reversal-vasovasostomy

5   Vasectomy reversal. https://www.vasectomy.com/vasectomy/faq/is-a-vasectomy-reversible

6   "The Bachelor." https://abc.com/shows/the-bachelor

7   U.S. Centers for Disease Control fertility statistics. https://www.cdc.gov/nchs/fastats/infertility.htm

8   VasClip. https://vasweb.com/vasclip.html

9   Brady Bunch sitcom, 1969-74. https://www.imdb.com/title/tt0063878/

10 Auerbach, Klara. "The Rise of the Only Child," *Washington Post*, June 19, 2019. https://www.washingtonpost.com/lifestyle/on-parenting/the-rise-of-the-only-child-how-america-is-coming-around-to-the-idea-of-just-one/2019/06/19/b4f75480-8eb9-11e9-8f69-a2795fca3343_story.html

11 Saner, Emine. "The Truth About Only Children," *The Guardian*, May 31, 2018. https://www.theguardian.com/lifeandstyle/2018/may/31/truth-about-only-children-insular-confident-worry

12 Gerhrman, Elizabeth. "The Case Against Having Only One Child," *Boston Globe*, May 4, 2017. https://www.bostonglobe.com/magazine/2017/05/04/the-case-against-having-only-one-child/uNEYrxSMpgSEMqOTaYZkYJ/story.html

13 "Thirteen Things Everyone Should Know About Only Children," https://greatist.com/live/things-everyone-should-know-about-only-children#1

14 The Waltons TV show, https://www.imdb.com/title/tt0068149/?ref_=fn_al_tt_1

15 "Childfree Life: Kids Really Do Ruin Marriages, StudyFinds." *Huffington Post*. https://www.huffingtonpost.ca/2014/01/13/childfree-life_n_4590503.html

16 Faircloth, Kelly. "Sorry, parents: Childless Couples Say They're Happier Together," *Jezebel*, Jan. 13, 2014. https://jezebel.com/sorry-parents-childless-couples-say-theyre-happier-t-1500251220

17 "Happier Relationships for Couples without Children," *The Telegraph*, Jan. 12, 2014. https://www.telegraph.co.uk/lifestyle/wellbeing/10567260/Happier-relationships-for-couples-without-children.html

18 Haag, Pamela. *Marriage Confidential: The Post-Romantic Age*. (New York: Harper, 2011). https://amzn.to/3hGyepu

2. STAY OR GO? WHAT SHOULD I DO?

19 Banschick, Mark. "The High Failure Rate of Second and Third Marriages," *Psychology Today*, Feb. 6, 2012. https://www.psychologytoday.com/us/blog/the-intelligent-divorce/201202/the-high-failure-rate-second-and-third-marriages

20 Rodman, Abby. "8 Tough Truths to Consider When Your Partner Doesn't Want Kids," *Huffington Post*, March 24, 2015. https://www.huffpost.com/entry/8-tough-truths-to-consider-when-your-partner-doesnt-want-kids_b_6931134

21 Bentham, Rebekah. "I left the husband I loved because he refused to have children (and had IVF twins alone)" *Daily Mail*, May 30, 2012. https://www.dailymail.co.uk/femail/article-2152318/I-left-husband-I-loved-refused-children-IVF-twins-alone.html

3. PARENTHOOD DELAYED

22 Sachs, Wendy. "The 'Big Lie' in Putting Off Pregnancy," cnn.com, Jan. 22, 2014. https://www.cnn.com/2014/01/22/living/pregnancy-big-lie-tanya-selvaratnam-books/

23 "Leave It to Beaver" 1950-60s sitcom, https://www.metv.com/shows/leave-it-to-beaver

24 Lebowitz, Shana. "Nine Ways Millennials are Approaching Marriage Differently from their Parents," *Business Insider*, Nov. 19, 2017. https://www.businessinsider.com/how-millennials-gen-x-and-baby-boomers-approach-marriage-2017-11#millennials-are-more-accepting-of-premarital-sex--1

25 Steverman, Ben. "Young Americans are Killing Marriage," *Bloomberg*, April 4, 2017. https://www.bloomberg.com/news/articles/2017-04-04/young-americans-are-killing-marriage

26 Great Depression. https://www.history.com/topics/great-depression

27 Great Recession birthrates. https://www.prb.org/usrecessionandbirthrate/

28 Davies, Madeleine, "With Environmental Disasters Looming, Many are Choos-

ing Childless Futures." *Jezebel*, Feb. 5, 2018. https://jezebel.com/with-environ-
mental-disasters-looming-many-are-choosing-1822730080

4. BABY LUST

29   "Jane the Virgin" TV show. https://www.imdb.com/title/tt3566726/
30   Fake a Baby. https://www.fakeababy.com
31   "Empty Cradle," 1993 TV movie. https://en.wikipedia.org/wiki/Empty_Cradle
32   "One Hundred Years of Maternity Fashion." https://www.whattoexpect.com/
     tools/photolist/100-years-of-maternity-fashion
33   Saltz, Dr. Gail. "Fake Babies Ease Women's Anxiety, Sadness," *Today*, Oct. 1,
     2008. https://www.today.com/health/fake-babies-ease-womens-anxiety-sadness-
     wbna26974105
34   "My Fake Baby: New Life with Reborn Dolls," 2007 documentary film. https://
     documentarylovers.com/film/my-fake-baby/

5. HOW DO YOU HEAL FROM CHILDLESS GRIEF?

35   Axelrod, Julie. "The Five Stages of Grief," PsychCentral, July 8, 2020. https://
     psychcentral.com/lib/the-5-stages-of-loss-and-grief
36   Ferlic, K. "Leaving and Grieving Ceremony/Ritual," Releasing Your Unlimited
     Creativity, 2009. http://ryuc.info/common/honoring_ig/leaving_grieving_rit-
     ual.htm
37   Fisher Therese. "Grieving Ceremony," 2009. http://www.reikiweaver.com/art-
     Projects/Greiving_Ceremony.pdf
38   p. 115, 128, 133 Ankylosing spondylitis: https://spondylitis.org/about-spondy-
     litis/types-of-spondylitis/ankylosing-spondylitis/: Ankylosing spondylitis (pro-
     nounced ank-kih-low-sing spon-dill-eye-tiss), or AS, is a form of arthritis
     that primarily affects the spine, although other joints can become involved.
     It causes inflammation of the spinal joints (vertebrae) that can lead to severe,
     chronic pain and discomfort.
39   Savvy Auntie. http://savvyauntie.com/defaulthome.aspx
40   Notkin, Melanie. "My Childless Grief: Over 35, Single and Childless," *Psychol-
     ogy Today*, Jan. 18, 2012. https://www.psychologytoday.com/us/blog/savvy-aun-
     tie/201201/my-secret-grief-over-35-single-and-childless
41   "Finding a Therapist Who Can Help You Heal" https://www.helpguide.org/arti-
     cles/mental-health/finding-a-therapist-who-can-help-you-heal.htm
42   "Symptoms of Depression," WebMD https://www.webmd.com/depression/
     guide/detecting-depression#1
43   English, Jane. *Childlessness Transformed* (Earth Heart, 1989). https://amzn.to/3d-
     JVeAC

6. LEARNING TO ACCEPT CHILDLESSNESS

44   Serenity Prayer. https://www.beliefnet.com/prayers/protestant/addiction/serenity-prayer.aspx

45   Miller, Kenneth. "Jessica Lange Can Finally Relax," *AARP the Magazine*, July 18, 2017. https://www.aarp.org/entertainment/television/info-2017/jessica-lange-news-interview.html

46   "Orange is the New Black," Netflix TV show. https://www.netflix.com/title/70242311

47   Tonkin, Lois. *Motherhood Missed* (London: Jessica Kingsley Publishers, 2018). https://amzn.to/2XO9tzy

7. CHILDLESS VS. CHILDFREE

48   Jonathan Kay. https://en.wikipedia.org/wiki/Jonathan_Kay

49   Wikipedia definition of "breeder." https://en.wikipedia.org/wiki/Breeder

50   Urban Dictionary definition of "breeder." https://www.urbandictionary.com/define.php?term=Breeder

51   Popescu, Adam. "The Octomom has Proved Us All Wrong," *New York Times*, Dec. 12, 2018. https://www.nytimes.com/2018/12/15/style/octomom-kids-2018.html

52   Cannold, Leslie. *What? No Baby?* (Fremantle, Australia: Fremantle Press, 2005) https://amzn.to/2YqsuqQ

53   Cain, Madalyn. *The Childless Revolution* (Cambridge, MA: Perseus Publishing, 2001) https://amzn.to/30w4fdp

54   Crispin, Jessa. review of *The Childless Revolution* on Bookslut, Dec. 2002. http://www.bookslut.com/nonfiction/2002_12_000429.php

55   Fisher, Janet. A Place of Her Own (Amazon kdp, 2014) https://amzn.to/37keLWT

56   Quiverfull. https://www.patheos.com/blogs/nolongerquivering/what-is-quiverfull/

57   The Duggar Family. http://www.duggarfamily.com/about

8. LOCKED OUT OF THE MOM CLUB

58   The Children's Place, retail store specializing in clothing for babies and children. https://www.childrensplace.com/us/home

59   Meriam Webster definition of "family." https://www.merriam-webster.com/dictionary/family

60   "We are Family." https://www.youtube.com/watch?v=uyGY2NfYpeE

61   "The Birdcage." https://www.imdb.com/title/tt0115685/

62   Urban Dictionary definition of family. https://www.urbandictionary.com/define.php?term=family

63   Adetayo, Ayoola. "On whether a married couple without kids should be consid-

ered family or not," *Nigerian Pulse Opinion*, June 7, 2019. https://www.pulse.ng/lifestyle/relationships-weddings/is-a-married-couple-without-kids-still-considered-a-family/z3xs4j5

9. THE MALE POINT OF VIEW

64   Downs, Michael. Him+17. http://himplus17.blogspot.com/

65   Gillespie, Bruch and Lynn Van Luven, *Nobody's Father* (Victoria, BC: Touchwood Editions, 2009) https://amzn.to/2YFOpdJ

66   Kluger, Jeffrey, "Too Old to Be a Dad? *Time*, April 11, 2013. https://healthland.time.com/2013/04/11/too-old-to-be-a-dad/

67   Manni, Robert. "What My Son has Taught Me in the First 100 Days," *Huffington Post,* Oct. 28, 2013. https://www.huffpost.com/entry/what-my-son-has-taught-me-in-the-first-100-days_b_4080184

68   Lick, Sue Fagalde. "Another Man Drops the No-Kids Bomb," Childless by Marriage, Aug. 16, 2017. https://childlessbymarriageblog.com/2017/08/16/another-man-drops-the-no-kids-bomb/

69   "Bachelor in Paradise," ABC television show. https://abc.com/shows/bachelor-in-paradise

70   Lytle, Brandi Not So Mommy blog. https://www.notsomommy.com

10. I CAN'T BELIEVE THEY SAID THAT

71   Notkin, Melanie. "4 Unfair Assumptions About Childless Women" *Today's Parent*, March 13, 2014. https://www.todaysparent.com/family/parenting/4-unfair-assumptions-about-childless-women/

72   Sunderland, Ruth. "Childless is Not a Synonym for Weird." *The Guardian*, May 24, 2009. https://www.theguardian.com/commentisfree/2009/may/24/women-feminism-childless-ruth-sunderland

73   Big Brothers Big Sisters. https://www.bbbs.org/

74   Loribeth. "The A Word: Why We Didn't Adopt" The Road Less Traveled, March 15, 2015. https://theroadlesstravelledlb.blogspot.com/2015/03/the-word-why-we-didnt-adopt.html

75   National Adoption Center. http://www.adopt.org/

76   Adoption Fact Sheet. http://archive.pov.org/offandrunning/fact-sheet/

77   Statistics About Adoption. https://www.americanadoptions.com/pregnant/adoption_stats

78   Freer, Bridget. "What Does It Take to Adopt a Child in Britain?" *The Telegraph*, Nov. 5, 2012. https://www.telegraph.co.uk/lifestyle/9646811/What-does-it-take-to-adopt-a-child-in-Britain.html

79   "About Adoption from Foster Care." https://www.adoptuskids.org/adoption-and-foster-care/overview/adoption-from-foster-care

80   Davis, Emma. "Curious About Adopting from Foster Care? Here's What It's Really Like?" *Today*. Aug. 5, 2015. https://www.today.com/parents/family-all-my-own-why-adopting-foster-care-easier-it-t34871

81   "Adopting from Foster Care." https://www.adoptivefamilies.com/how-to-adopt/foster-care-adoption/adopting-from-foster-care/

82   Dave Thomas Foundation for Adoption. "5 Reasons Why You Won't Adopt from Foster Care, and Why They're Wrong." https://www.davethomasfoundation.org/5-reasons-you-wont-adopt-from-foster-care-and-why-

83   Thomas, Abigail. *A Three Dog Life* (Boston: Mariner Books, 2007) https://amzn.to/3fgLJKe

84   Terrill, Ceiridwyn. *Part Wild* (New York: Scribner, 2011) https://amzn.to/3cRGkrG

85   LaBastille, Anne. *Woodswoman: Living Alone in the Adirondack Wilderness* (New York: Penguin Books, 1991) https://amzn.to/2UQLhLh

86   Anderson, Allen and Linda. *Dogs and the Women Who Love Them* (Novato, CA: New World Library, 2010) https://amzn.to/3fixuEG

11. DO THE CHILDLESS GET RIPPED OFF AT WORK?

87   Jody Day, Gateway Women. https://www.gateway-women.com

88   NotMom Summit, Cleveland, OH, 2017. https://www.thenotmom.com/

89   Walker, Ellen. "Discrimination Against Childfree Adults," *Psychology Today*, May 2, 2011. https://www.psychologytoday.com/us/blog/complete-with-out-kids/201105/discrimination-against-childfree-adults

90   Marcotte, Amanda. "Family-Friendly Workplaces are Great, Unless You Don't Have Kids," *Slate,* June 21, 2013.

91   Guerrero, Aaron. "Do Childless Employees Get the Shaft at Work?" *U.S. News & World Report*, July 17, 2013. https://money.usnews.com/money/careers/articles/2013/07/17/do-childless-employees-get-the-shaft-at-work

92   Theresa May, former UK prime minister. https://www.tmay.co.uk/

93   Angela Merkel, Chancellor of Germany. https://en.wikipedia.org/wiki/Angela_Merkel

94   Gladys Berejiklian, Premier of New South Wales. https://en.wikipedia.org/wiki/Gladys_Berejiklian

95   Julia Gillard, former prime minister of Australia. https://en.wikipedia.org/wiki/Julia_Gillard

96   Lara Giddings, former premier of Tasmania. https://en.wikipedia.org/wiki/Lara_Giddings

97   Overington, Caroline. "Berejiklian, Gillard, May, Merkel: Power to Childless Women? The Australian, Jan. 27, 2017. https://www.theaustralian.com.au/commentary/opinion/berejiklian-gillard-may-merkel-power-to-childless-women/news-story/004e9d8eaf2940ba43ce39d3bd86fc3b

98 Caroline Overington, Australian journalist. https://www.carolineoverington.com/

99 Sarah Palin, former governor of Alaska and 2008 Republican candidate for U.S. vice president. https://www.biography.com/political-figure/sarah-palin

12. IF YOU DON'T HAVE CHILDREN, YOU WILL NEVER . . .

100 Crow, Sarah McCraw. "6 Surprising Benefits of Pregnancy." Parents.com http://www.parents.com/pregnancy/my-body/changing/benefits-of-pregnancy/

13. WHERE DOES GOD FIT IN?

101 Carroll, Laura. *The Baby Matrix* (LiveTrue Books, 2012) https://www.lauracarroll.com/book-review/the-baby-matrix/

102 Carroll, Laura. *Families of Two* (Xlibris, 2000) https://www.lauracarroll.com/book-review/ebook-families-of-two-interviews-with-happily-married-couples-without-children-by-choice/

103 Centers for Disease Control and Prevention statistics on births to unmarried mothers. https://www.cdc.gov/nchs/fastats/unmarried-childbearing.htm

104 Detailed history of birth control, Planned Parenthood, 2015. https://www.plannedparenthood.org/files/1514/3518/7100/Pill_History_FactSheet.pdf

105 Fertility Awareness Method. https://www.foryourmarriage.org/family-planning

106 Catholic views on sex and birth control, United States Conference of Catholic Bishops. https://www.usccb.org/respectlife.

107 National Abortion Federation fact sheet. https://prochoice.org/education-and-advocacy/about-abortion/abortion-facts/

108 Smietana, Bob. "Fetuses Not People, Catholic Hospital Says in Court," *USA Today*, Jan. 24, 2013. https://www.usatoday.com/story/news/nation/2013/01/24/fetuses-not-people-catholic-hospital-says-in-court-case/1863013/

109 Britt, Kara and Roger Short. "The Plight of Nuns: Hazards of Nulliparity." *The Lancet*, Dec. 8, 2011. https://www.thelancet.com/journals/lancet/article/PIIS0140-6736(11)61746-7/fulltext

110 Mirena Coil, hormone-releasing intrauterine device. https://www.mirena-us.com/about-mirena/

14. THE JOYS OF STEPPARENTING

111 Yvette, Patricia. *Being Fruitful without Multiplying* (Seattle: Coffeetown Press, 2012) https://amzn.to/2zDTaMA

112 Manterfield, Lisa. *Life without Baby* (Redondo Beach, CA: Steel Rose Press, 2016) https://www.lifewithoutbaby.com/blog/

113 Martin, Wednesday Ph.D. *Stepmonster: A New Look at Why Real Stepmothers*

Think, Feel, and Act the Way We Do (Amazon CreateSpace, 2015) https://amzn.
to/314uqbE

15. NOT THE LIFE I EXPECTED

114 *Ms. Magazine.* https://www.msmagazine.com
115 Maeve Binchy http://maevebinchy.com/
116 Craig, Amanda. "If Maeve Binchy had been a Mother" *The Telegraph*, Aug. 3, 2012. https://www.telegraph.co.uk/culture/books/9446816/If-Maeve-Binchy-had-been-a-mother-....html
117 "This Life: Maeve Binchy on Being Unable to Have Children," *Daily Mail*, Sept. 27, 2008. https://www.dailymail.co.uk/home/you/article-1059797/This-Life-How-Maeve-Binchy-childless.html
118 "The Bachelorette." https://abc.com/shows/the-bachelorette

16. OLD AGE WITHOUT KIDS?

119 Ginsberg, Genevieve Davis, *Widow to Widow.* (New York: Da Capo Lifelong Books, 2007) https://amzn.to/3hBTahh
120 Genevieve Davis Ginsberg bio. https://plaza.sbs.arizona.edu/376
121 Lee, Don. "Desperate for Workers, Aging Japan Turns to Robots for Healthcare," *LA Times*, July 25, 2019. https://www.latimes.com/world-nation/story/2019-07-25/desperate-for-workers-aging-japan-turns-to-robots-for-healthcare
122 Dixon, Laura. "What It Means to Be a Childfree Older Adult," *Next Avenue*, April 24, 2017. http://www.nextavenue.org/childfree-older-americans-taking-the-future-into-your-own-hands/

17. WHAT WILL BE OUR LEGACY?

123 Torticollis is a problem involving the muscles of the neck that causes the head to tilt down. https://www.webmd.com/parenting/baby/what-is-torticollis#1
124 Barber, Marsha, "Childless Adults Make Huge Impact with Charitable Donations," *The Star*, June 16, 2019 https://www.thestar.com/opinion/contributors/2019/06/16/childless-adults-make-huge-impact-with-charitable-donations.html
125 "Mali's" No Kidding in New Zealand blog. https://nokiddinginnz.blogspot.com/

18. CHILDLESSNESS DIDN'T STOP THEM

126 Sarton, May. *Journal of a Solitude.* (New York: WW Norton, 1992) https://amzn.to/2Cc6CYP
127 May Sarton quotes. https://www.goodreads.com/author/quotes/13166.May_Sarton

128 Elizabeth Gilbert web page. https://www.elizabethgilbert.com/

129 Gilbert, Elizabeth. *Eat Pray Love* (New York: Riverhead Books, 2007) https://amzn.to/2NmBBE9

130 Lick, Sue Fagalde. *Stories Grandma Never Told* (Blue Hydrangea Productions, 2007) https://amzn.to/30UsulL

131 Virginia Silveira's obituary. https://www.legacy.com/obituaries/name/virginia-silveira-obituary?pid=187177671

Made in the USA
Columbia, SC
21 July 2021